Stadler, Quandra
Prettyman, comp.

Out of our lives

DATE			

Out of Our Lives

OUT OF OUR LIVES

A Selection of Contemporary Black Fiction

EDITED BY

Quandra Prettyman Stadler

HOWARD UNIVERSITY PRESS • WASHINGTON, D. C. • 1975

Printed in the United States of America.

Library of Congress Cataloging in Publication Data

Stadler, Quandra Prettyman, comp.
    Out of Our Lives; a Selection of Contemporary
    Black Fiction.

    1. American fiction—Negro authors. I. Title.
PZ1.S77540u   [PS647.N35]   813′.01   74-7092
ISBN 0-88258-027-2

Any anthologist's gratitude should go totally to the writers who have made the book. I would, however, also like to thank some of my students for their kind and willing assistance: Nancy Dorsinville, Dana Daych Faulkner, Joan Lewis, and Julianne Perry; Patricia Ballou and Natalie Sonevetsky of the Barnard College Library who, often without even knowing, have helped me with the nitty-gritty aspects of getting an anthology together; my friends Susan Schrader and Barbara Walker, whose professional skills I have borrowed quite beyond anything friendship should ask; my editor Roberta Palm for both her patience and her confidence when all about us had lost both; and, of course, my husband John and our daughter Johanna, who have coped.

Grateful acknowledgment is also made to the following:

The Antioch Review for permission to reprint "Daddy Was a Number Runner" by Louise Meriwether. Copyright © 1967 by The Antioch Review, Inc. First published in *The Antioch Review*, Vol. 27, No. 3; reprinted by permission of the editors.

James Brown Associates, Inc., and Albert Murray for permission to reprint "Stonewall Jackson's Waterloo" by Albert Murray from *Harper's Magazine*, February 1969. Copyright © 1969 by Albert Murray.

Pearl Crayton for permission to reprint "The Gold Fish Monster" by Pearl Crayton from *The Texas Quarterly*, Summer 1967, Vol. 10, No. 2.

The Dial Press for permission to reprint, "Three Men" from *Bloodline* by Ernest J. Gaines. Copyright © 1963, 1964, 1968 by Ernest J. Gaines.

Junius Edwards and his agent, Robert P. Mills, Ltd., for permission to reprint "Mother Dear and Daddy" by Junius Edwards, from *The Angry Black*, edited by John A. Williams. Copyright © 1962 by John A. Williams.

Darrell Gray for permission to reprint "A Harsh Greeting." Copyright © 1970 by Darrell Gray. From *A Galaxy of Black Writing* by R. Baird Shuman, Moore Publishing Company, 1970.

Grove Press, Inc., for permission to reprint "The Screamers" from *Tales* by LeRoi Jones. Copyright © 1967 by LeRoi Jones.

Martin J. Hamer for permission to reprint "Sarah" by Martin J. Hamer from *Atlantic Monthly*, January 1964. Copyright © 1964 by *Atlantic Monthly*.

Harcourt Brace Jovanovich, Inc., for permission to reprint "To Hell With Dying" by Alice Walker from her volume *In Love and Trouble*. Copyright © 1967 by Alice Walker.

Houghton Mifflin Company for permission to reprint "The New Mirror" from *Miss Muriel and Other Stories* by Ann Petry. Copyright © 1971. This story originally appeared in *The New Yorker*, May 29, 1965.

The Massachusetts Review for permission to reprint "Bright An' Mownin' Star" by Mike Thelwell from *The Massachusetts Review*, Vol. VII, No. 4. Copyright ©1966, The Massachusetts Review, Inc.; and for permission to reprint "Tell Martha Not to Moan" by S. A. Williams from *The Massachusetts Review*, Vol. IX. Copyright © 1968, The Massachusetts Review, Inc.

R. J. Meaddough for permission to reprint "Poppa's Story" by R. J. Meaddough from *The Liberator*, Vol. 9, No. 3, March 1969.

Harold Ober Associates, Inc. for permission to reprint "A Friend for a Season" by Deloris Harrison. Copyright © 1969 by the Redbook Publishing Company. Vol. 133, No. 4, August 1969.

Phylon for permission to reprint "The Funeral" by Ann Allen Shockley from *Phylon*, Spring 1967.

Random House for permission to reprint "Aunt Sue's Stories" by Langston Hughes. Copyright © 1926 by Alfred A. Knopf, Inc., and renewed 1954 by Langston Hughes. Reprinted from *Selected Poems* by Langston Hughes, by permission of the publisher; and for permission to reprint "Gorilla, My Love" from *Gorilla, My Love* by Toni Cade Bambara. Copyright © 1971 by Toni Cade Bambara.

University of Iowa Press for permission to reprint "Black for Dinner" from *The Beach Umbrella* by Cyrus Colter. Copyright © 1970 by Cyrus Colter.

For Mother and Daddy
who *"not without misgivings"*
have made my freedom possible

Foreword

When Charles Chesnutt, the earliest Black American writer to achieve a significant reputation for his short stories, appeared, he found an audience by temporarily concealing his race. "A literary work," he wrote, "by an American of acknowledged color was a doubtful experiment, both for the writer and for the publisher, entirely apart from its intrinsic merit." There was a paucity of Black magazines; those that existed had more immediate and pressing concerns. The leading American literary magazines of the nineteenth century were racist. White America was ever afraid of hearing Black versions of the Black experience.

Chesnutt was followed by a poet whose short stories are generally felt to be more reflective of the dominant plantation tradition than revealing of the Black experience, or more accurately put, his own Black experience. That poet, Paul Laurence Dunbar, was ensnared by the "catch-22" which awaits the Black American writer; writers do re-create from reading as well as from life. Chesnutt was enmeshed in the acceptable tragic vein, Dunbar in the comic vein. Both were sensitive to their dilemmas and disturbed by the restrictions placed upon their development. Chesnutt abandoned writing; Dunbar abandoned life.

During the heyday of the Harlem Movement, Black writers had greater difficulty in placing their short stories than in having their novels published. Thus, during the twenties and early thirties, novelists emerged in numbers, but few short stories were published. The always exceptional Langston Hughes was the exception. With his collection of short stories, *The Ways of White Folks*, published in 1934, he became the third Black writer in the history of American literature to have a commercial edition of his stories published.

Chester Himes began to publish short stories in *Esquire* in the thirties. Richard Wright arrived in time for the Marxist interest in Negroes and the more open pages of their publications. But although the Communist magazines welcomed more stories of racial oppression and hardship, few non-political Black writers found their way into these pages. Ralph Ellison benefited from an apprenticeship similar in some ways to Wright's and cracked ajar some of the American literary (as distinct from political) magazines. James Baldwin, through the medium of the essay rather than the short story, opened these pages a bit wider.

The short story requires the magazine, or perhaps the magazine's need calls forth the short story. In any event, the two came into literary history hand in hand, and may be exiting the same way. As white magazines opened up a bit, finished, extraordinary talents emerged, among them Toni Cade Bambara, James McPherson, Ernest Gaines, Cyrus Colter, Martin Hamer. Still, in compiling this list, one becomes aware of a disquieting sense of each magazine having one Black apiece—an echo of the days when the *Atlantic* had Chesnutt, *Esquire* had Himes.

It might be said that LeRoi Jones walked in through the door left ajar by James Baldwin and walked out

Imamu Baraka. The sixties and seventies have seen the emergence of a number of Black magazines, making it possible for Black writers to serve apprenticeships and develop their talents. Most writers are made, not born, but Black American writers have had little opportunity to go from bad to good to great, from amateur to professional.

Black writers have always found Black publications a place to grow. In *The Quality of Hurt*, Chester Himes recalls:

My first short stories were published in weekly news-papers and in magazines published by blacks: the Atlanta World, *the* Pittsburgh Courier, *the* Afro-American, *the* Bronzeman, Abbott's Monthly, *and other similar publications.*

Louise Meriwether's earliest stories appeared in Black magazines. But the number of these magazines has been few, and because their orientation has been social and political rather than literary, they have published little creative writing. In worse financial condition than their poor white counterparts, these magazines historically have been unable to provide more than the most meager payment to the writers. They deserve saluting, and more important, studying, for the services they have performed in keeping alive the possibility of publication, in spite of inadequate payment.

Writers of African descent who live in America now stand atop Hughes's "racial mountain":

We younger Negro artists who create now intend to

express our individual dark-skinned selves without fear or shame. If white people are pleased we are glad. If they are not, it doesn't matter. We know we are beautiful. And ugly too. The tom-tom cries and the tom-tom laughs. If colored people are pleased we are glad. If they are not, their displeasure doesn't matter either. We build our temples for tomorrow, strong as we know how, and we stand on top of the mountain, free within ourselves.

Coming as these writers do from many places, many experiences, and many walks of American life, their stories reflect this diversity in the variety of themes treated and the variety of styles used. All have, of course, suffered prejudice and oppression as Blacks in their experience with the white community, and this encounter has provided a major theme. Superficial students of Black literature tend to experience that body of writings as a literature of protest and pleading, but these free writers have chosen to develop their stories around the richness of life in the contemporary Black community. "The tom-tom cries and the tom-tom laughs."

Quandra Prettyman Stadler
JANUARY 1974

Contents

Aunt sue's stories

Aunt Sue has a head full of stories.
Aunt Sue has a whole heart full of stories.
Summer nights on the front porch
Aunt Sue cuddles a brown-faced child to her bosom
And tells him stories.

Black slaves
Working in the hot sun,
And black slaves
Walking in the dewy night,
And black slaves
Singing sorrow songs on the banks of a mighty river
Mingle themselves softly
In the flow of old Aunt Sue's voice,
Mingle themselves softly
In the dark shadows that cross and recross
Aunt Sue's stories.

And the dark-faced child, listening,
Knows that Aunt Sue's stories are real stories.
He knows that Aunt Sue
Never got her stories out of any book at all,
But that they came
Right out of her own life.

And the dark-faced child is quiet
Of a summer night
Listening to Aunt Sue's stories.

Langston Hughes

Out of Our Lives

Darrell Gray

A harsh greeting

To be born Black in America has a special significance long before the Black child perceives it. He begins with a shorter life-expectancy than had he been born white. At birth, his chances of graduating from college will be less —and his chances of being arrested will be greater—than they would be if his skin were white. At birth, his chances for earning the median American income will be less—and his chances for being on welfare will be greater— than they would be if he had not arrived Black. The child will not arrive knowing this; but sometime before he departs childhood, he will learn. Before he has mastered the three R's, he will grapple with what it means to be Black in America.

Darrell Gray was born in Baltimore, Maryland, and was graduated from Johns Hopkins University, where he is now a medical student. In "A Harsh Greeting," he portrays a particular and unique experience, so specific in this story, so universal for Black children.

During my years of lollipops and wading pools, an incident occurred that will never escape my memory. Probably as with all six-year-olds, I was filled with many fantasies and puerile perceptions about the outside world: Good triumphs over Evil, heroes over villains, right over wrong, love over hate. My bubbles of fantasy were to burst on a brisk but mild Saturday morning in autumn.

The normal shopping day was Saturday, since I was a child of working parents. This particular Saturday morning was no exception.

"How would you like to get a new pair shoes today?" my mother asked.

"Oh, boy!" was my instant reply. "Can I get a pair of desert boots this time, Mom?"

"I was thinking in terms of dress shoes, but we'll see about that," she replied.

My family owned one car at the time, and since my father was scheduled to work over-time on this particular Saturday, he drove to the Social Security Building. My mother and I were left with two alternatives: the taxicab or the bus. We decided to stand on the bus-stop corner and catch whatever came first, be it cab or bus. Soon, we were traveling south; the bus, speeding as if it were challenging the wind to a race, nearly tipped over as it rounded corners.

I enjoyed viewing the activity inside the buses in those days. Mothers often scolded their children, old men babbled to themselves, and bus drivers whistled tunes signifying happy days for them.

We eventually reached our destination. Running ahead of my mother, I reached the shop and gazed at all the different styles and colors of shoes.

"I like these, Mother, and these are nice, too!" I rattled

anxiously. Mother, paying little attention to my childish banter, proceeded to lead me through the door and into the main area of the store, which was not particularly crowded. The five or six salesmen were busily bringing pairs of shoes from the storeroom to waiting customers.

We took seats and waited our turn. We had been waiting a long while before I noticed that some people who had come into the store after us were being waited on while we sat and quietly waited for service that was overdue.

"Mother," I asked, completely puzzled, "why are people being served before us?" She smiled weakly and said that we would discuss it later. Although my mouth was closed then, my mind was just beginning to open up. It seemed that this was not the first time we had been forced to wait an unusual length of time for service. There had been other instances, but I had been too young to understand what was happening. No, my mother would not have to discuss it later. The facts were as obvious and clear as if I had been told them. As far as the salesmen were concerned, my mother and I could have sat in that store all day without service. They were white, and we were black, and that fact alone made all the difference between good service and no service.

A terrible expression that I had once heard on a playground now rang incessantly in my mind.

"If you are white, you're right. If you're black, stay back."

After finally receiving service, we picked out two pairs of shoes. Finally, a salesman came to us. Hurriedly, we completed the rest of our day's shopping. This day marked an end to fantasy and the beginning of reality in my life.

Later, at the dinner table as I poked listlessly at my food, my mother turned to me and said, "Young man, welcome to the world."

Toni Cade Bambara

Gorilla, my love

A signature found in a sketchbook in her great-grandmother's trunk gave Toni Cade Bambara the surname she has chosen to connect her with her past community. Finding the name affirmed her long-held sense of the continuity and the specialness of the Black community which she has so well expressed by exploring the resources of its language. Her talents as a dancer (she was a student of the dance) and as a linguist (she was also a student of linguistics) are combined in the graceful movement and realistic expression of "Gorilla, My Love," in which a young girl moves toward that maturity that comes when children see that the adult world is not exactly what adults have said it is.

That was the year Hunca Bubba changed his name. Not a change up, but a change back, since Jefferson Winston Vale was the name in the first place. Which was news to me cause he'd been my Hunca Bubba my whole life-time, since I couldn't manage Uncle to save my life. So far as I was concerned it was a change completely to somethin soundin very geographical weatherlike to me, like somethin you'd find in a almanac. Or somethin you'd run across when you sittin in the navigator seat

5

with a wet thumb on the map crinkly in your lap, watchin the roads and signs so when Granddaddy Vale say "Which way, Scout," you got sense enough to say take the next exit or take a left or whatever it is. Not that Scout's my name. Just the name Granddaddy call whoever sittin in the navigator seat. Which is usually me cause I don't feature sittin in the back with the pecans. Now, you figure pecans all right to be sittin with. If you thinks so, that's your business. But they dusty sometime and make you cough. And they got a way of slidin around and dippin down sudden, like maybe a rat in the buckets. So if you scary like me, you sleep with the lights on and blame it on Baby Jason and, so as not to waste good electric, you study the maps. And that's how come I'm in the navigator seat most times and get to be called Scout.

So Hunca Bubba in the back with the pecans and Baby Jason, and he in love. And we got to hear all this stuff about this woman he in love with and all. Which really ain't enough to keep the mind alive, though Baby Jason got no better sense than to give his undivided attention and keep grabbin at the photograph which is just a picture of some skinny woman in a countrified dress with her hand shot up to her face like she shame fore cameras. But there's a movie house in the background which I ax about. Cause I am a movie freak from way back, even though it do get me in trouble sometime.

Like when me and Big Brood and Baby Jason was on our own last Easter and couldn't go to the Dorset cause we'd seen all the Three Stooges they was. And the RKO Hamilton was closed readying up for the Easter Pageant that night. And the West End, the Regun and the Sunset was too far, less we had grownups with us which we didn't. So we walk up Amsterdam Avenue to the Washington and *Gorilla, My Love* playin, they say, which suit me just fine, though the "my love" part kinda drag Big Brood some. As for Baby Jason, shoot, like Granddaddy say, he'd follow me into the fiery furnace if I say come on. So we go in and get three bags of Havmore potato chips which not only are the best potato chips but the best bags for blowin up and bustin real loud so the matron come trottin down the aisle with her chunky self, flashin that flashlight dead in your eye so you can give her some lip, and if she answer back and you already finish seein the show anyway, why then you just turn the place out. Which I love to do, no lie. With Baby Jason kickin at the seat in front, egging me on, and Big Brood mumblin bout what fiercesome things we goin do. Which means me. Like when the big boys come up on us talkin bout Lemme a nickel. It's me that hide the money. Or when the bad boys in the park take Big Brood's Spaudeen way from him. It's me that jump on they back and fight awhile. And it's me that turns out the show if the matron get too salty.

So the movie come on and right away it's this churchy music and clearly not about no gorilla. Bout Jesus. And I am ready to kill, not cause I got anything gainst Jesus. Just that when you fixed to watch a gorilla picture you don't wanna get messed around with Sunday School stuff. So I am mad. Besides, we see this raggedy old brown film *King of Kings* every year and enough's enough. Grownups figure they can treat you just anyhow. Which burns me up. There I am, my feet up and my Havmore potato chips really salty and crispy and two jaw-

breakers in my lap and the money safe in my shoe from
the big boys, and here comes this Jesus stuff. So we all
go wild. Yellin, booin, stompin and carryin on. Really to
wake the man in the booth up there who musta went to
sleep and put on the wrong reels. But no, cause he holler
down to shut up and then he turn the sound up so we
really gotta holler like crazy to even hear ourselves good.
And the matron ropes off the children section and flashes
her light all over the place and we yell some more and
some kids slip under the rope and run up and down the
aisle just to show it take more than some dusty ole velvet rope to tie us down. And I'm flingin the kid in front of
me's popcorn. And Baby Jason kickin seats. And it's
really somethin. Then here come the big and bad matron,
the one they let out in case of emergency. And she totin
that flashlight like she gonna use it on somebody. This
here the colored matron Brandy and her friends call
Thunderbuns. She do not play. She do not smile. So we
shut up and watch the simple ass picture.

Which is not so simple as it is stupid. Cause I realize
that just about anybody in my family is better than this
god they always talkin about. My daddy wouldn't stand
for nobody treatin any of us that way. My mama specially. And I can just see it now, Big Brood up there on
the cross talkin bout Forgive them Daddy cause they
don't know what they doin. And my Mama say Get on
down from there you big fool, whatcha think this is, play-
time? And my Daddy yellin to Granddaddy to get him a
ladder cause Big Brood actin the fool, his mother side of
the family showin up. And my mama and her sister
Daisy jumpin on them Romans beatin them with they
pocketbooks. And Hunca Bubba tellin them folks on they

knees they better get out the way and go get some help
or they goin to get trampled on. And Granddaddy Vale
sayin Leave the boy alone, if that's what he wants to
do with his life we ain't got nothin to say about it. Then
Aunt Daisy givin him a taste of that pocketbook, fussin
bout what a damn fool old man Granddaddy is. Then
everybody jumpin in his chest like the time Uncle Clay-
ton went in the army and come back with only one leg
and Granddaddy say somethin stupid about that's life.
And by this time Big Brood off the cross and in the park
playin handball or skully or somethin. And the family in
the kitchen throwin dishes at each other, screamin bout
if you hadn't done this I wouldn't had to do that. And me
in the parlor trying to do my arithmetic yellin Shut it off.

Which is what I was yellin all by myself which make
me a sittin target for Thunderbuns. But when I yell We
want our money back, that gets everybody in chorus.
And the movie windin up with this heavenly cloud music
and the smart-ass up there in his hole in the wall turns
up the sound again to drown us out. Then there comes
Bugs Bunny which we already seen so we know we been
had. No gorilla my nuthin. And Big Brood say Awwww
sheeet, we goin to see the manager and get our money
back. And I know from this we business. So I brush the
potato chips out of my hair which is where Baby Jason
like to put em, and I march myself up the aisle to deal
with the manager who is a crook in the first place for
lyin out there sayin *Gorilla, My Love* playin. And I never
did like the man cause he oily and pasty at the same time
like the bad guy in the serial, the one that got a hideout
behind a push-button bookcase and play "Moonlight
Sonata" with gloves on. I knock on the door and I am

furious. And I am alone, too. Cause Big Brood suddenly got to go so bad even though my mama told us bout goin in them nasty bathrooms. And I hear him sigh like he disgusted when he get to the door and see only a little kid there. And now I'm really furious cause I get so tired grownups messin over kids just cause they little and can't take em to court. What is it, he say to me like I lost my mittens or wet on myself or am somebody's retarded child. When in reality I am the smartest kid P.S. 186 ever had in its whole lifetime and you can ax anybody. Even them teachers that don't like me cause I won't sing them Southern songs or back off when they tell me my questions are out of order. And cause my Mama come up there in a minute when them teachers start playin the dozens behind colored folks. She stalk in with her hat pulled down bad and that Persian lamb coat draped back over one hip on account of she got her fist planted there so she can talk that talk which gets us all hypnotized, and teacher be comin undone cause she know this could be her job and her behind cause Mama got pull with the Board and bad by her own self anyhow.

So I kick the door open wider and just walk right by him and sit down and tell the man about himself and that I want my money back and that goes for Baby Jason and Big Brood too. And he still trying to shuffle me out the door even though I'm sittin which shows him for the fool he is. Just like them teachers do fore they realize Mama like a stone on that spot and ain't backin up. So he ain't gettin up off the money. So I was forced to leave, takin the matches from under his ashtray, and set a fire under the candy stand, which closed the raggedy ole Washington down for a week. My Daddy had the suspect it was me cause Big Brood got a big mouth. But I explained right quick what the whole thing was about and I figured it was even-steven. Cause if you say Gorilla, My Love, you suppose to mean it. Just like when you say you goin to give me a party on my birthday, you gotta mean it. And if you say me and Baby Jason can go South pecan haulin with Granddaddy Vale, you better not be comin up with no stuff about the weather look uncertain or did you mop the bathroom or any other trickified business. I mean even gangsters in the movies say My word is my bond. So don't nobody get away with nothin far as I'm concerned. So Daddy put his belt back on. Cause that's the way I was raised. Like my Mama say in one of them situations when I won't back down, Okay Badbird, you right. Your point is well-taken. Not that Badbird my name, just what she say when she tired arguin and know I'm right. And Aunt Jo, who is the hardest head in the family and worse even than Aunt Daisy, she say, You absolutely right Miss Muffin, which also ain't my real name but the name she gave me one time when I got some medicine shot in my behind and wouldn't get up off her pillows for nothin. And even Granddaddy Vale— who got no memory to speak of, so sometime you can just plain lie to him, if you want to be like that—he say, Well if that's what I said, then that's it. But this name business was different they said. It wasn't like Hunca Bubba had gone back on his word or anything. Just that he was thinkin bout gettin married and was usin his real name now. Which ain't the way I saw it at all.

So there I am in the navigator seat. And I turn to him and just plain ole ax him. I mean I come right on out with it. No sense goin all around that barn the old folks talk

about. And like my mama say, Hazel—which is my real
name and what she remembers to call me when she bein
serious—when you got somethin on your mind, speak up
and let the chips fall where they may. And if anybody
don't like it, tell em to come see your mama. And Daddy
look up from the paper and say, You hear your mama
good, Hazel. And tell em to come see me first. Like that.
That's how I was raised.

So I turn clear round in the navigator seat and say,
"Look here, Hunca Bubba or Jefferson Windsong Vale
or whatever your name is, you gonna marry this girl?"

"Sure am," he say, all grins.

And I say, "Member that time you was baby-sittin me
when we lived at four-o-nine and there was this big snow
and Mama and Daddy got held up in the country so you
had to stay for two days?"

And he say, "Sure do."

"Well. You remember how you told me I was the cutest
thing that ever walked the earth?"

"Oh, you were real cute when you were little," he say,
which is suppose to be funny. I am not laughin.

"Well. You remember what you said?"

And Granddaddy Vale squintin over the wheel and
axin Which way, Scout. But Scout is busy and don't care
if we all get lost for days.

"Watcha mean, Peaches?"

"My name is Hazel. And what I mean is you said you
were going to marry *me* when I grew up. You were going
to wait. That's what I mean, my dear Uncle Jefferson."
And he don't say nuthin. Just look at me real strange like
he never saw me before in life. Like he lost in some weird
town in the middle of night and lookin for directions and

there's no one to ask. Like it was me that messed up the maps and turned the road posts round. "Well, you said it, didn't you?" And Baby Jason lookin back and forth like we playin ping-pong. Only I ain't playin. I'm hurtin and I can hear that I am screamin. And Granddaddy Vale mumblin how we never gonna get to where we goin if I don't turn around and take my navigator job serious.

"Well, for cryin out loud, Hazel, you just a little girl. And I was just teasin."

" 'And I was just teasin,' " I say back just how he said it so he can hear what a terrible thing it is. Then I don't say nuthin. And he don't say nuthin. And Baby Jason don't say nuthin nohow. Then Granddaddy Vale speak up. "Look here, Precious, it was Hunca Bubba what told you them things. This here, Jefferson Winston Vale." And Hunca Bubba say, "That's right. That was somebody else. I'm a new somebody."

"You a lyin dawg," I say, when I meant to say treacherous dog, but just couldn't get hold of the word. It slipped away from me. And I'm crying and crumplin down in the seat and just don't care. And Granddaddy say to hush and steps on the gas. And I'm losin my bearins and don't even know where to look on the map cause I can't see for cryin. And Baby Jason cryin too. Cause he is my blood brother and understands that we must stick together or be forever lost, what with grownups playin change-up and turnin you round every which way so bad. And don't even say they sorry.

Albert Murray

Stonewall jackson's waterloo

The thrust of Albert Murray's writings, his
fiction and his essays, has always been an
affirmation of the strengths of the Black community. He knows, and his writing shows,
that Black has always been proud, even before
one dared to make this statement aloud. His
writing does not conceal the pain of the Black
experience in America, but its power comes
from revealing the experience's continuity
and vigor.

Murray, who now lives in New York City, was
born in Nokomis, Alabama, and spent his childhood in Mobile. He is the author of *The Omni-
Americans, South to a Very Old Place, The Hero
and the Blues,* and *Train Whistle Guitar.*

Sometimes a thin gray, ghost-whispering midwinter
drizzle would begin while you were still at school and
not only would it settle in for the rest of the afternoon but
it would still be falling after dark as if it would continue
throughout the night. That, as Miss Lexine Metcalf for
one never failed to remind you, was always the coziest
time to get your homework done, even when it was
arithmetic. But as nobody ever needed to tell me or any-

body else I knew, it was also one of the very best of all good times to be where grown folks were talking, especially when there were people visiting because somebody was there from out of town and you could stay up beyond your usual time to be in bed. Not even the barbershop was better than that.

Their chairs always formed the same family-style semicircle before the huge open hearth, and from my place in the chimney corner you could see the play of the firelight against their faces and watch the shadows spreading up the newspaper wallpaper walls to the ceiling. They would be talking and, aware of the roof-sanding night weather outside, I would be listening, and above them on the mantelpiece was the old-fashioned pendulum clock, which was Papa's heirloom from that old Manor of antebellum columns and calico kitchens in which his mulatto grandmother had herself been an inherited slave until Sherman's March to the Sea.

Sometimes it was obvious enough that they were only telling the most outrageous lies they could either fabricate or remember, and sometimes you could be every bit as certain that their only purpose was to spell out as precisely as possible the incontestable facts. Uncle Jerome would always be there, clearing his throat even when he was not going to say anything, squinting his eyes and making a face and clearing and swallowing because he was a preacher. Because although he had been a longshoreman for the last twenty-five years and a farmer for thirty years before that, he was also supposed to have The Call, although he had never been called by any congregation to pastor any church.

Sometimes Mister Dock (for dockhand) Donahue would be there too, but they wouldn't be drinking wine if he were there; because stevedore that he was, he said that wine was for women, children, and Christmas morning; and he would get up and get the longshoreman's knapsack he always carried and bring out a jug of corn whiskey, and Papa Whit would look at Mama and get just about tickled to death. They would be passing it around, pouring against the light of the fire, and there would be that smell then, which also went with cigar ashes and freshly opened Prince Albert tobacco cans.

I always said Papoo to Papa Whit (*who was not really my flesh-and-blood father, whom I have never seen, just as Mama was not my flesh-and-blood mother*), who used to call me his little gingerbrown Papoose-boy, which may have been why I called him Papoo, who himself was as white as any out-and-out white man I have ever seen in my life. Who not only was said to be more than half white but was also said quite accurately to be acknowledged by most of his white relatives much more readily than he himself was ever willing to acknowledge any of them. I myself once overheard Mama telling Aunt Cat Callahan that the main reason they moved down into Mobile County when the war boom came was to get away from Papa's white kinfolks in the country; and another time I heard her telling Miss Sadie Womack about how red Papa's ears used to get when the white people back in the country used to see him driving her into town in the buckboard and pretend that they thought she was one of his black field hands.

Papa himself never talked about white people as such. But sometimes when they were talking about hard times, somebody would get him to tell about how he used to go off somewhere and pass for white to get a job; and that was something to hear about too; and one time when I was telling Little Buddy about it, he said, "Everybody say don't care how much of his skin and his keen nose and his flat ass Mister Whit might have got from the white folks, he got his mother wit from the getting place. That's why you don't never hear nobody calling him no shit-colored half-peckerwood, even behind his back."

There was also that time downtown by the marine store, on Government Street, and that was a white man. He and Papa knew each other and they were laughing and talking and I was having a good time looking in store windows, and I went looking all the way up to the sporting-goods store and when I came back they were talking about a job; and the man said something about something both of them had been doing somewhere, and that brought up something else *and I heard the man say that Papa was a fool for being a durned ole niggie when he could be a wyat man, and Papa just shook his head and said, you don't understand, Pete.*

Soldier Boy Crawford was the one who would always

take over when they started talking about the war, because he was an old foot trooper and sometimes he still wore his Army coat, and sometimes in the winter he would wear his wrap-around leggings too, and he also had a steel helmet that looked like a wash-basin, and he had a German Luger and some hand grenades and a bayonet and a knapsack and a gas mask too (because he said that he for one was never going to let them catch him with his pants down if he could help it). He had been to France to help them stop old Kaiser Bill. He would tell about the ocean and the torpedoes and the submarines and then about the French places he had been to, and sometimes he would mix in a lot of French words with what he was saying. He would tell all about the kind of farming country they had over there, especially the wine-making country. He would also tell about the mountain country and the churches and then he would tell all about Paris, which he said was the best town in the world, and he used to always say a man is a man over there, and somebody else would say a man ain't nothing but a man nowheres.

Old Soldier Boy Crawford was also the one who used to tell me and old Little Buddy about some of the things old Luzana Cholly used to do during the war, because old Luzana himself never did talk about that, not even when you asked him about it. Sometimes he would say he was going to save it and tell us about it when we were old enough to understand it, and sometimes he would answer one or two questions about something like how far Big Bertha could shoot, and how the Chau-Chau automatic rifle worked and things like that. But he never did sit down and tell about the actual fighting like old Sol-

dier Boy Crawford did. They used to always say that
once old Soldier Boy Crawford got worked up you
couldn't stop him from fighting the whole war all over
again.

The rain that was falling then would be crackling
down on the shingles of the gabled roof of that house,
and the fire in the hearth would sparkle as Papa poked it,
and I would be in my same chair in my same place in
the corner, and sometimes they would be telling about
some of the same old notorious rounders and roustabouts
that the guitar players and the piano players made up
songs about. Especially if Mr. Dock Donahue was there,
because he was the one who could always remember
something else about old John Henry, who went with
blue steel sparks, and old John Hardy, who went with
greased lightning. He held the floor all night one night
just describing how old Stagolee shot and killed Billy
Lyons, and they gave it to him again the next night and
he told about what happened at that famous trial.

He was also the one who used to tell about how old
Robert Charles declared war on the city of New Orleans
and fought the whole police force all by himself with his
own special homemade bullets. But the best of all the old
so-called outlaws he used to tell about was always the
one from Alabama named Railroad Bill, who was so
mean when somebody crossed him, and so tricky, that
most people believed that there was something super-
natural about him. He was the one that no jail could hold
overnight and no bloodhounds could track beyond a certain point. Because he worked a mojo on them that nobody ever heard of before or since. And the last time he
broke jail, they had the best bloodhounds in the whole

state there to track him. But the next morning they found them all tied together in a fence corner near the edge of the swamp, not even barking anymore, just whining; and when they got them untangled they were ruined forever, couldn't scent a polecat and wouldn't even run a rabbit. And nobody ever saw or came near hide nor hair of old Railroad Bill from that time on.

But naturally the white folks claimed they caught him and lynched him. But Negroes knew better than that. The white folks were always claiming something like that. They claimed that they had caught old Pancho Villa and hung him for what he had done out in New Mexico; and they claimed that they had hemmed up old Robert Charles in a steeple and burned him alive; and they also claimed that Jess Willard had salivated old Jack Johnson down in Havana that time! Well, they could go around bragging about how the great white hope had put the big black menace back in his place and proved white supremacy all they wanted to, but everybody knew that Jack Johnson, who was married to a white woman, had to trade his world championship in for his American citizenship, and thirty thousand dollars, to get back in the U.S.A. and there was a picture in every barbershop which showed him letting himself be counted out, lying shading his eyes from the Cuban sun, lying with his legs propped like somebody lying on the front porch; and as for Jess Willard, everybody knew he couldn't even stand up to Jack Dempsey, who was the same Jack Dempsey who brought back old John L. Sullivan's color line because he didn't ever intend to get caught in the same ring with the likes of Jack Johnson, Sam Langford, or even the likes of old cream-colored Harry Wills, not even with a submachine gun. Everybody knew that.

The white folks claimed that they had finally caught up with old Railroad Bill at some crossroads store somewhere and had slipped up on him while he was sitting in the middle of the floor sopping molasses with his gun lying off to one side, and they swore that they had blown the back of his head off with a double-barrel charge of Triple-O buckshot. But in the first place Railroad Bill didn't eat molasses, and in the second place he didn't have to break into any store to get something to eat. Because folks kept him in plenty of rations everywhere he went by putting out buckets of it in certain special places for him mostly along the Railroad, which was what his name was all about; and in the third place he must have broken into more than fifty stores by that time and he just plain didn't rob a store in the broad daylight, not and then sit down in the middle of the floor and eat right there—and in the fourth place there were at least a dozen other mobs in at least a dozen other places all claiming that they had been the ones who laid him low, each one of them telling a completely different tale about how and when and where it all happened. Some claimed that they had hung him upside down on the drawbridge and then riddled him and left what was left of him there for the buzzards. But they never settled on one bridge.

I didn't know very much then, but I knew enough to realize that when something happened it was always a part of something that had been going on before, and I wasn't surprised at all that time looking at Uncle Walt sitting by the fire in Papa's clothes telling about finding a way through Tombigbee Swamp, not afraid but careful, talking about how he was going to make it on across the Mason-Dixie, and I didn't really know anything at all about whatever it was he had done or hadn't done, and I still don't know what it was: but I knew that whatever it was it was trouble, and I said, *It's like once upon a time back then.* Because Mama had said it, who knew it from her grandfather, who was Uncle Walt's grandfather too, who knew it from his father when there was no hope of foot rest this side of Canada, which was also called Canaan, which was the Promised Land, and I also knew that all of that was about something called the Underground Railroad, which ran from the house of bondage to the land of Jubilo.

They were always talking about freedom and citizenship. And that was something else that Uncle Jerome used to start preaching about. He had all kinds of sermons ready for times like that. Sometimes he would be talking about the Children of Israel, and sometimes it would be the walls of Jericho, and sometimes it would be the Big Handwriting on the wall which was also the BIG HAND writing on the wall which was also the Big Hand writing on the WAR. That was when he used to say that the color of freedom was blue. The Union Army came dressed in blue. The big hand that signed the freedom papers signed them in blue ink which was also blood. The very sky itself was blue, limitless *(and gentlemen sir, before I'd be a slave, I'll be buried in my grave. And I said my name is Jack the Rabbit and my home is in the briarpatch).*

Sometimes he would also say that the freedom road was a road through the wilderness and sometimes it wasn't any road at all because there never was any royal road to freedom for anybody *(so don't you let nobody turn you around, and don't you let nobody know too much about your business either, and I said call me Jack the Bear on my way somewhere)*.

Then it would be Education again. They didn't ever get tired of talking about that, the old folks telling about how they learned to spell and write back in the old days when they used to use slate tablets and the old Blue Back Webster. The old days when they used to have to hold school whenever and wherever they could. Whenever they could spare the time from working the crops and wherever the teacher could find a place to shelter them. Whenever there was a teacher.

Then later on I was the one they meant when they said the young generation was the hope and glory. Because I had come that far in school then. And sometimes it was Geography and sometimes it was History, and sometimes I had to tell about it, and sometimes I had to get the book and read it to them. Especially when it was about the Revolutionary War. Sometimes I had to read about Columbus too, and sometimes it would also be the explorers and the early settlers. But most of the time what they wanted to hear about was how the original thirteen colonies became the first thirteen states and who said what and who did what during that time and how the Constitution was made and who the first Presidents were and what they did.

That was also when I used to love to recite the Declaration of Independence, and the Gettysburg Address

for them; and I could also recite the Preamble to the Constitution and part of the Emancipation Proclamation;
and I could also quote from the famous speeches of
Patrick Henry and James Otis and Citizen Tom Paine;
and I knew all kinds of sayings from *Poor Richard's Almanac.*

"That boy can just about preach that thing right now,"
Mister Jeff Jefferson said one night after I had recited
the William Lloyd Garrison and Frederick Douglass parts
from the National Negro History Week pageant.

"That boy can talk straight out of the dictionary when
he want to," Mister Big Martin said looking at me but
talking to everybody.

"It just do you good to hear that kind of talk."

"White folks need to hear some talk like that."

"The white folks the very one said all that, Jeff."

"What kind of white folks talking like that?"

"Histry book white folks."

"What kind of histry book white folks?"

"White folks in that same book that child reading."

"I ain't never heard no white folks believing nothing
like that, in all of my born days."

"White folks printed that book, didn't they?"

"I don't care who printed that book, that's freedom
talk."

"Well, the histry book white folks got up the Constitution, didn't they?"

"Yeah, and there was some histry book black folks in
there somewhere too, you can just about bet on that.
There was a jet black roustabout right in there with old
Christopher Columbus, and the very first one to try to
climb that Bunker Hill was a mean black son of a gun

from Boston. Ain't nothing never happened and wasn't some kind of a black hand mixed up in it somewhere. You just look at it close enough. The very first ones to come up with iron was them royal black Ethiopians."

"You right about that," Mister Big Martin said. "Ain't nobody going to dispute you about that."

"I know I'm right," Mister Jeff said, "and I still say these white folks need to hear some of that kind of gospel. These ain't no histry book white folks around here and this ain't no histry. This ain't nothing but just a plain old everyday mess!"

"Trying to keep the black man down."

"All white folks ain't like that, Phil."

"Yeah, but them that is."

"And some of us too Jesus," Minnie Stovall said. "Lord the truth is the light, and some of us just ain't ready yet."

"Amen," Mister Big Martin said.

"Amen?" Mister Phil Motley said. "What you mean Amen?"

"That's what I want to know," Mister Jeff Jefferson said.

"I mean the truth is the light just like Minnie say."

"Well, ain't none of these peckerwoods around here ready for nothing neither, but just look at them. That's some truth for the light too."

"Yeah but I still say some of us still ain't learned how to stick together yet."

"Now Big'un, you know good and well that can get to be a horse of another color," Mister Dock Donahue said. "I for one don't never intend to be sticking with any and every body coming along because he say he one of us. You know better than that."

"That why I say some of us Jesus," Miss Minnie
Stovall said.

"That's all right about all that," Mister Big Martin
said. "I'm talking about when you talking about going up
against that stone wall. I want us to be ready. I'm talking about Stonewall Jackson. I'm talking about Jericho."

"Well, we talking about the same thing then," Mister Phil Motley said.

"That's all right about your Stonewall Jackson too,"
Mister Jeff Jefferson said, "and your Vardaman and your
Pitchfork Ben and all the rest of them. This child right
here is getting old Stonewall Jackson's water ready."

They were all laughing then. Because everybody in Gaso-
line Point knew how Shorty Hollingsworth had met his
Waterloo and got the name Hot Water Shorty. His wife
had come up behind him and dashed a pot of scald-
ing lye water down the seat of his pants while he was
sitting on the front steps cleaning his shotgun and bragging about what he was going to do if she didn't have his
supper on the table in the next five minutes. He had
yelled, dropped his shotgun, and lit out across the barb-
wire fence and hadn't stopped until he was chin-deep in
Three Mile Creek. He had a new name from then on,
and he also had a new reputation: he could outrun a
striped-assed ape.

Uncle Jerome said I was learning about verbs and ad-
verbs and proverbs; and he preached his sermon on the
dictionary that time, and he had his own special introduction to the principles of grammar: "A noun is someone or something; a pronoun is anything or anybody; a
verb is tells and does and is; an adverb is anyhow, any-

where, anytime; an adjective is number and nature; a preposition is relationship; and conjunction is membership; and interjection is the spirit of energy."

Another time when Aunt Sue was visiting us from Atmore, old Mayfield Turner was there, old Sawmill Turner, the log-carriage expert. Mama said he had been trying to marry Aunt Sue for more than seventeen years, which meant that he had started before she married her first husband (she was visiting us because she had just separated from her fourth husband). Old Sawmill was wearing his blue pinstripe, tailormade suit and his Edwin Clapp shoes and smelling like the barbershop and sitting cross-legged like Henry Ford; and every time he took a puff on his White Owl, he flashed his diamond ring like E. Berry Wall. Sometimes when they were talking about him behind his back they used to give him names like John D. Rockefeller Turner and J. P. Morgan Turner and Jay Gould Turner because he also sported pearl-gray kidskin gloves, and he was always talking about stocks and bonds and worrying about the National Debt.

I was reading about Valley Forge that night, and I knew he was there just as I knew that Mister Lige and Miss Emma Tolliver and Bro Mark Simpkins and his wife, Miss Willeen, were all there, because they were always the first ones to come by to see Aunt Sue when she was in town. But at first the only ones that I was really conscious of were Miss Lula Crayton and Miss Ida Jefferson, because every time I paused Miss Lula Crayton kept saying, Tribulation tribulation trials and tribulation, and Miss Ida Jefferson would respond one time as if she were hearing some new gossip, and the next time as if I were reading the Bible itself. Saying, "Honey don't tell me." Saying, "Lord have mercy Jesus."

Then I happened to glance up and see old Sawmill again, and he had stopped puffing on his cigar. He was leaning forward with his hand under his chin, his eyes closed, his lips moving, repeating everything I was reading, word for word. He had forgotten all about Aunt Sue, for the time being at least. I was reading about how the Redcoats were wining and dining and dancing warm in Philadelphia while the ragtag bobtail Continental Army was starving and freezing in makeshift huts and hovels, and about how General George Washington himself had to get out and personally whip slackers and stragglers and would-be deserters back into the ranks with the flat of his sword. All of which was what Give me liberty or give me death really meant, which was why whenever you talked about following in the footsteps of our great American forefathers you were also talking about the bloody tracks the half-barefooted troops left in the snow that fateful winter.

Every time I glanced up I could see old Sawmill Turner still leaning forward toward me, his lips still moving, the tip of his cigar gone to ash. Then when I came to the end of the chapter and closed the book, he stood up and stepped out into the center of the semicircle as Uncle Jerome always did. "I'm a histry scholar myself," he said. "I been a histry scholar ever since I first saw the Post Office when I was a little boy back in Lowdness County." Then he ran his hand down into his pocket and pulled out a fat roll of brand-new greenbacks, which he held against his chest like a deck of gambling cards. He peeled off a crisp one-dollar bill and held it up and said,

"Old George Washington is number one because he was first in war and first in peace and first in the hearts of his countrymen. He got it started."

"And old Tom Jefferson." (Off came a two-dollar bill.) "He was a educated man and he knowed exactly what to do with his book learning. And old Abe Lincoln . . ." (he held up a five-dollar bill) "came along later on and had to save the Union. Old Alexander Hamilton didn't get to be the President, but he was in there amongst them when they started talking about how they were going to handle the money, and here he is." (He pulled off a ten-dollar bill.) "And here's old razor-back Andy Jackson." (Off came a twenty-dollar bill.) "He was against the red man but when he was up there making things better for all them old poor butt hillbillies he was laying the landmark for the black man without even knowing it. And then you come on up to old Ulysses S. Grant." (He held up a fifty-dollar bill without even pausing.) "He was the one old Abe Lincoln himself had to send for when the going got tight, and later on they made him the eighteenth President."

He held up the fifty-dollar bill long enough for everybody to see that it really was a fifty-dollar bill and then he held up a hundred-dollar bill and said, "Old Ben Franklin didn't ever even want to be the President. But old Ben Franklin left just as big a mark in histry as any of them. They didn't put him up there on no one-hundred-dollar bill for nothing. Old Ben Franklin was one of the smartest men they had back in them days, and everybody gave him his due respect. Old Ben Franklin gave them a lot of good points about how to put them clauses in the Constitution. He was just about the first one they

thought about when they had to send somebody across
the water to do some official business for the government with them fast-talking Frenchmen. And talking
about being cunning, old Ben Franklin was the one that
took a kite and Cocola bottle and stole naked lightning."

He came and stood in front of my chair then. "This boy
is worth more than one hundred shares of gilt-edged
preferred, and the good part about it is we all going to be
drawing down interest on him." Then he handed me a
five-dollar bill as crisp as the one he had held up before,
and told me to buy myself a fountain pen; and he told
Mama he was going to be the one to stake me to all
the ink and paper I needed as long as I stayed in school.
All I had to do was just show him my report card every
term.

All I could do was say thank you, and I promised I
would always do my best. And Miss Lula Crayton said
Amen. And Miss Ida Jefferson said, "God bless the
Lamb and God bless you Mayfield Turner." Then before
anybody else could say anything he excused himself,
and Aunt Sue walked him to the door and he put on his
alpaca topcoat, his black Homburg hat and his Wall
Street gloves and was gone.

All Mama could do was wipe her eyes, and all Papa
could do was look at the floor and shake his head and
smile. But Uncle Jerome was on his feet again, saying
he was talking about the word made manifest for manifest destiny; and I knew he was going to take over
where Sawmill Turner had left off and preach a whole
sermon with me in it that night. And so did everybody
else, and they were looking at me as if I really had become the Lamb or something. So I looked at the man-

tlepiece, and I heard the Mother Goose clock and outside there was the Valley Forge bitter wind in the turret-tall chinaberry tree.

I was still sitting by the reading lamp, and he came and put his hand on my shoulder. Then I had to stand up and go to the hearth and when he said, "Say not I am a child, gentlemen sir, as I am a witness," and they said amen to him, they were also saying amen to me, and amen to the Declaration of Independence, and amen to the Gettysburg Address and the Emancipation Proclamation and amen to the Constitution of the United States of America.

Louise Meriwether

Daddy was a number runner

In 1965, a piece of America went up in flames.
If a phoenix can be said to have arisen from
those flames, it rose, pen in hand, in the persons who surfaced through the Watts Workshop.
Several Black writers of promise found in that
workshop what a writer needs most: a chance
to write, and a chance to be heard. Among
them was Louise Meriwether, who, although
born in New York, had moved to California.
Ms. Meriwether had done all her professional
homework and apprenticeship; nonetheless
she had remained submerged.

Ever since I read "Daddy Was A Number
Runner" in a Watts Workshop edition of the
Antioch Review, I have been fond of it for its
exploration of the Black girl's world and for its
revelation of the caring and the love in that
world, upon which that girl's survival and development as a person have so long depended.

"I dreamed about fish last night, Francie," Mrs. Mackey
said when she opened the door to admit me. "What number does Madame Zora's dream book give for fish?"

Lord, I thought, don't let Mrs. Mackey stand here with

her big, black self telling me about her dreams. If I was late getting back to school from lunch again, Miss Oliver would keep me in.

"I dreamed about fish last night too," I said. "I dreamed a big catfish jumped off the plate and bit me. Madame Zora gives five-fourteen for fish."

Mrs. Mackey chuckled, her eyes disappearing into slits, her broad cheeks puffed out as if she were chewing bubble gum.

"That's a good hunch, child, us both dreaming about fish. Wait a minute and let me add that number to my slip."

"Mrs. Mackey, I gotta eat my lunch and be back to school by one o'clock. My father asks would you please have your numbers ready by the time I get here."

"Okay, lil' darlin', they's ready."

She handed me a number slip and a dollar bill which I slipped into my middy blouse pocket. I ran down the stairs holding my breath. Lord, but this hallway was funky, unwashed and funky. Garbage rotting in the dumbwaiter mingled with the smell of vomited wine, and a foulness oozing up from the basement meant a dead rat was down there somewhere.

Outside it wasn't much better. It was a hot humid,

day, the first of June, 1934, and the sudden heat had tumbled the tenement dwellers out of their stifling rooms and into the streets. Knots of men sat on the stoops or stood wide-legged in front of the store fronts, their black ribs shining through shirts limp with sweat. "Get yore black ass out of that street 'fore a car knocks it off," one of them yelled at three kids playing ball in the gutter.

I turned the corner at Lenox Avenue and ran down forbidden Hundred Eighteenth Street. Daddy had warned me to stay out of that street, upon pain of a whipping, because of the prostitutes, but I knew all about them anyway. Sukie had told me and she ought to know. Her sister, Little Fannie, whored right in that block.

Five or six boys, acting the fool, were pretending they were razor fighting in front of the drugstore, their knickers hanging loose beneath their knees to look like long pants. I tried to squeak past them but they saw me.

"Hey, skinny mama," one of them yelled. "When you put a little pork chops on those spare ribs I'm gonna make love to you."

The other boys folded up laughing and I scooted past, ignoring them. I always hated to pass a crowd of boys because they felt called upon to make some remark, usually nasty, especially now that I was almost twelve. I was skinny and black and bad looking with my short hair and long neck and all that naked space in between. I looked just like a plucked chicken.

I ran around the corner of Fifth Avenue, but ducked back when I saw Sukie playing hopscotch by herself in front of my house. That Sukie. She was going on thirteen, a year older than me, but much bigger. I waited until her back was towards me, then I ran towards my stoop. When she saw me her mooney face turned pinker and she took out after me like a red witch. I was galloping around the first landing when I heard her below me in the vestibule.

"Ya gotta come downstairs sometime, ya bastard, and the first time I catch ya I'm gonna beat the shit out of ya."

That Sukie. We were best friends but she picked a fight with me whenever she felt evil, which was often, and if she said she was going to beat the shit out of me that's just what she would do.

I kept on running to the top floor and collapsed on our door. The lock sprang open. Daddy was always promising to fix that lock but he never did.

Our apartment was a railroad flat, each small room set flush in front of the other. The door opened into the dining room, so junky with heavy furniture that the room seemed tinier than it was. The big buffet and matching round table, carved with ugly dragons and scratched with scars, was a gift from the Jewish plumber downstairs and was one year older than God.

"Mother," I yelled. "I'm home."

"Stop screaming, Frances," Mother said from the kitchen, "and put the numbers up."

I took the drawer out of the buffet, and reaching to the ledge on the side, pulled out an envelope filled with number slips. I put in Mrs. Mackey's numbers and the dollar and replaced the envelope on the ledge and slid the drawer back on its runners. It stuck. I took it out again and shoved the envelope farther to the side. Now the drawer closed smoothly.

"Did you push that envelope way back so the drawer closes good?" Mother asked as I went into the kitchen.

"Yes, Mother."

I sat down at the porcelain table in the kitchen which tilted crazily on its uneven legs, and absent-mindedly knocked a scurrying roach off the table top to the floor and crunched it under my sneaker.

"If you don't stop racing up those stairs like that, one of these days you gonna drop dead."

"Yes, Mother."

I wanted to tell her that Sukie had promised to beat me up again, but Mother would only repeat that Sukie would stop bullying me when I stopped running away from her.

Mother was short and wide, her long breasts and broad hips all sort of running together. She was light brown with short, thin hair, and yellow, rotting teeth. She had more empty spaces in her mouth than she had teeth and she seldom smiled. Daddy shouted and cursed when he was mad and hugged you when he was feeling good, but you just couldn't tell how Mother was feeling. She didn't curse you, but she didn't kiss you either.

She placed a sandwich before me, potted meat stretched from here to yonder with mayonnaise, which I eyed with suspicion.

"I don't like potted meat."

"You don't like nothing. That's why you're so skinny. If you don't want it, don't eat it. There ain't nothing else."

She gave me a weak cup of tea.

"We got any cream?"

"No. Put some sugar in it and be thankful you got that."

I sighed and dropped a spoonful of sugar in my tea. Seemed like we were getting poorer every day. I sipped the tea, looking at the greasy kitchen walls lumpy with layers of paint over cracked plaster. Daddy called its color vomit green.

The outside door slammed and I could tell from the heavy tread that it was Daddy. I bounced up and ran into the dining room, hurling myself against him. He laughed and caught me up in his arms, swinging me off the floor. Mother was always telling me that men were handsome, not beautiful, but she just didn't understand. Handsome meant one thing and beautiful something else, and I knew for sure what Daddy was. Beautiful. In the first place he was so big, not just tall, but thick and hard all over. He was dark, black really, with thick crinkly hair and a wide, laughing mouth. I loved Daddy's mouth. It looked as if it had been chiseled from black marble.

He sat down at the dining room table and began pulling number slips and money from his pocket.

"Get the envelope for me, Sugar."

I removed the drawer and handed him the envelope, smiling. "I dreamed a big catfish jumped off the plate and bit me, Daddy. Madame Zora gives five-fourteen for fish."

Daddy laughed. "That's a good dream, Sugar. I'll put a dollar on it."

Daddy said that of all the family my dreams hit the most.

"Jessie," Daddy called. "Where are the boys?"

Mother came to the kitchen door. "They ain't come home yet."

Daddy's fist hit the table with a bang. "If those boys

have stayed out of school again it's gonna be me and their behinds. They're hanging around with those damned Ebony Dukes, that's what's got into them lately." He turned to Mother, shaking his fist. "I'm warning you. Nobody in this family has ever been to jail and if those boys get into any trouble I'm gonna let their butts rot in jail. You hear me?"

Mother nodded. She knew as I did that Daddy would be the first one downtown if anything happened to his sons. James Junior, fifteen, and Claude, fourteen, were suddenly making a career out of playing hookey and staying out late at night, and it was true, they were messing around with the Ebony Dukes.

The Dukes were the toughest gang this side of Mt. Morris Park. When they weren't fighting their rivals the Black Raiders with knives, they were jumping the Jew boys who attended the synagogue on Hundred Sixteenth Street, or mugging any white man caught alone in Harlem after the sun went down. I had been nervous enough before about my brothers—always afraid they might fall off the roof (all the boys had to jump from one rooftop to another to prove they weren't chicken) or get run over by a car—and now I also had to contend with them getting knifed or killed in a gang fight.

Daddy started adding up the amounts on his number slips and counting the money. Mother sat down beside him and said nervously she heard that Slim Jim had been arrested.

"Slim Jim is a fool," Daddy said. "The banker he works for thinks he can buck the syndicate and Big Dutch. But Big Dutch pays off the police each and every week and all he had to do was give the cops the nod and they busted Slim Jim and his banker."

"Maybe you'd better find another job," Mother began timidly.

"There ain't no jobs for the ofays so what in the hell you expect me to do?" Daddy asked. "And how many times I gotta tell you I'm in no danger as long as the syndicate is paying off the cops?"

Mother played the numbers like everyone else in Harlem but she was uneasy about Daddy collecting them. Daddy went to work for Frenchy on commission three months ago when he lost his house-painting job which hadn't been none too steady. Frenchy was a brown-skinned Creole from Haiti with curly black hair and sleek looks. Now Frenchy was handsome, but he wasn't beautiful. He operated a candy store on Fifth Avenue as a front for his number business and was Big Dutch's right-hand man.

Daddy said the racketeers ran Harlem. They controlled the pimps who brought the white men to the prostitutes and they banked the numbers while the police looked the other way. If the police really wanted to clean up this shit, Daddy said once, they would stop picking on the poor niggers trying to hit the number for a dime, but would snatch the bankers downtown who were banking the action and making the real money.

Now he repeated to Mother that as long as Big Dutch paid off the police he was safe. Mother nodded slowly as if trying to convince herself. Then she noticed I was still there and yelled at me to get on back to school.

I went to P.S. 81 near St. Nicholas Avenue, which was

second only to P.S. 136 as being the baddest girls' school in the world. Sister gangs to the Ebony Dukes also fought with knives and scared us younger students and the teachers plenty. It's a wonder any of us learned anything.

After school I sneaked home again, avoiding Sukie, and sat on the fire escape watching her jump rope downstairs with the other kids she also beat on when she wasn't picking on me.

That Sukie. I wondered what made her so mean? She was too pretty to be so evil—all red and yellow like a plump peach with long red-brown hair that I envied. When we were best friends Sukie shared everything with me. She stole money from her mother's purse every morning and we stuffed ourselves with candy on the way to school. Once, in order to keep up, I took a dime from Mother's pocketbook, but Mother had spent a half hour on her knees looking under the couch for that lousy dime and I never stole from her again. I saved the change from milk bottles and when I got a nickel I would tell Sukie I had picked Daddy's pocket and that seemed to make her happy.

Sukie didn't like anybody, not even her mother and father. It was true that Papa Maceo was a drunk, but he was good natured and happy and being a drunk was no reason for Sukie to call him a sonofabitch. Her own father. Sukie cursed all the time as if there was a pot boiling inside her. Daddy didn't even want me to say darn. It's darn today and damn tomorrow and goddamn the next day, he was always telling me, and I was going to grow up to be a lady and ladies didn't curse. But I had to curse some to keep up with Sukie. I wouldn't play the dozens, though—that mother stuff—or take the Lord's name in vain.

Sukie cursed out everybody except her mother who would have knocked her into the middle of tomorrow if she did. Mrs. Maceo was a little yellow woman, always grumbling that her drunken husband and her no-good children didn't appreciate how hard she had to work in that laundry on the late shift. Sukie sure didn't seem to care, glad to be able to stay out late at nights, and her sister, Little Fanny, was too busy prostituting around the corner to even speak to her mother.

It was on account of Little Fannie that Sukie beat me up the last time. I had simply asked her why her sister hustled so close to home, and Sukie hauled off and punched me right in the nose. After she got through bloodying me up, she took me around the corner and we watched Little Fanny hustling the men in off the street. That Sukie. You never could tell what would set that inner pot of hers to boiling. This time she got mad at me on sight one day last week and asked if I was ready to fight. Naturally I wasn't ready and I had been dodging her ever since. I wondered what made her so mean? What I should do is go on downstairs and get my whipping over with so we could be best friends again.

I was fighting the bedbugs on the couch in the living room where I slept, and I was losing. Mother and I had pulled the couch away from the wall into the middle of the floor. Mother thought that if the couch was in the center of the room the bugs wouldn't get me. Her theory was they were in the walls. Every Saturday she scalded all of the bedsprings with boiling water and Flit but she couldn't do anything with the walls. But those bugs didn't buy Mother's theory. Every night they marched right down that wall and across the floor and got me just the same.

My brothers were in their room behind the kitchen. When they came home hours after dinner Daddy had yelled at them but he didn't beat their butts as he had promised, thank God. Now, Mother and Daddy were arguing in their bedroom right next to me and I could hear every word they were saying. Mother was asking Daddy again if she could go up in the Bronx and get some day's work.

"Why don't you stop nagging me, woman?" Daddy said. "You know I don't want you doing housework."

"It's not what we want any more," Mother said. "It's what we need. The children need shoes and winter coats. We're all practically in rags."

"They also need you to be home when they get out from school. Ain't I having enough troubles now, for Christ sakes? What you want to start that shit all over again for? We ain't starving yet."

"We ain't far from it."

Daddy didn't answer.

After a slight pause Mother said: "The relief people are giving out canned beef and butter. Mrs. Maceo is trying to get on. I don't know when is the last time we've had any butter."

"And we may never have any again if I've got to let those damned social workers inside my house to get it. Bastards act like it's their money they're handing out. For

Christ sakes, baby, there's a depression on all over the country. We're not the only family that's up tight."

"So what we gonna do?" Mother asked.

After a slight pause, Daddy's voice was gentle. "It's going to be all right, baby. I'm gonna play the piano for three rent and whist parties this weekend. I oughta make ten bucks for each one. That will help. You stop worrying now and trust me. You hear?"

I trusted Daddy. I wondered how come Mother couldn't.

On Friday night we helped Daddy practice for his parties. The boys came home early and Junior, leaning against the battered piano in the living room—another gift from the Jewish plumber downstairs—sang all the new songs he had heard on the radio, while Daddy picked out the melody and then added his swinging bass. Daddy could play any piece after hearing it only once. He played by ear. Claude was writing down the names of the songs as Daddy memorized them, his dark thin face tight and secretive as usual.

I was surprised that Claude was hanging out with the Ebony Dukes because he used to say boys who ran around with gangs were morons. Claude was smart. He had already passed Junior in school, and before he started that hookey playing he used to spend his spare time studying and shining shoes on Forty-Second Street. I don't think Junior knew the way downtown. He used to taunt Claude that he was a sucker to work so hard with that shoeshine box for so little.

Claude had a disposition like Sukie's. He didn't like anybody and he seldom smiled. Junior was just the opposite, with a sunny personality and handsome like Daddy. He had never been bright in school and had dropped so far behind that now he just didn't care. I didn't believe, though, that Junior was mean enough to be an Ebony Duke. How could he ever mug anybody? He was too gentle.

Mother sat on the couch, sewing, and patting her feet. After Daddy learned all the new songs that Junior and I knew (Claude couldn't sing) Daddy bellowed out his favorite blues: "Trouble in mind, I'm blue, but I won't be blue always. The sun's gonna shine in my back door some day," and then he left to play for the parties. We used to have fun like that every evening after dinner, but now those good times came very seldom.

Daddy brought home only nine dollars from the three parties. For tips he had been offered whiskey instead of money, and since he was not a drinking man, he had switched the drinks to food, eating Hoppin' John and chittlins all weekend long.

Mother had a fit. She raved it was either relief or housework for her. Daddy wasn't earning enough off the numbers to feed us and God alone knew when he was going to hit that big one he was always talking about. She kept it up until finally Daddy hollered that a man couldn't have any peace in his own home and yes, goddammit, go on up in the Bronx and find some work if she wanted to.

On Monday morning, Mother took the subway to Grand Concourse and waited on the sidewalk with the other colored women. When a white lady drove up and asked how much she charged by the hour, Mother said twenty-five cents and was hired for three days a week by a Mrs. Schwartz.

I spent most of my free time reading fairy tales from the library on the fire escape, trying to avoid Sukie. Then, hallelu, five-fourteen played. Daddy's dollar had dwindled to a quarter, but Mother also caught it for ten cents straight and thirty cents combination. Together they collected two hundred and fifteen dollars. A fortune.

"Where else can a poor man get such odds?" Daddy asked. "Six hundred dollars for a buck. If only I hadn't cut that number down to a quarter." But he had dreamed about his mother and had switched the dollar to nine-oh-nine which played for the dead.

That night Mother and Daddy sat at the dining room table counting that money over and over. There was something different about them, some soft way they looked at each other with their eyes and smiled. I went to bed and didn't even bother to pull the couch away from the wall, I was that happy. Let the bedbugs bite. Everybody, even those blood-sucking bugs, had to have something sometime.

We ate high off the hog for about a week. It sure was good to get away from the callie ham which you had to soak all night to kill the salt and then save the juice and skin to flavor beans and greens. I think the reason why I was so skinny was that I just didn't like poor mouth collards and salt pork. Daddy stuffed a turkey with his secret Geechie recipe and nobody had to beg me to eat that.

Daddy paid up the back rent and Mother bought us all winter coats and shoes. But before long we were back to fried cabbage and ham hocks and it was just as if the big hit had never been. It wasn't long before the explosion came.

That Saturday Mother was at work and Daddy had already left on his rounds. I was in the kitchen scorching the rice for dinner when the two plainclothes cops pushed past that rotten lock Daddy had never fixed and walked right in. By the time I got to the dining room they were poking around as if they had been invited in. I knew instantly they were cops. The oldest one was huge with loose purple jaws like a bulldog. The other one was younger and nervous.

"Where does your old man hide his numbers?" Bulldog asked me, pulling open the buffet drawers.

I was so scared I couldn't speak, so I just shook my head.

Bulldog pulled out the drawer and placed it on the table. The young one sorted through it, pushing aside Mother's sewing bag and the old rags she was saving to sell to the rag man. He replaced the drawer and it jammed. I almost cried out loud. Then he gave it a shove and it closed.

They went through the other drawers in the same manner, then Bulldog went into the kitchen and began banging the pots and pans around in the cupboard.

I heard Daddy coming up the stairs and I ran towards the door yelling: "Don't come in, Daddy! It's the cops!"

Bulldog hollered, "Grab her!"

The young cop swung me off my feet. I screamed and kicked, aiming for his private parts like Mother had told me to do if a man ever bothered me.

Daddy came through the door. With one long stride he was at the young cop's side. He grabbed me, at the same time pushing the cop backwards.

"You all right?" Daddy asked.

I nodded. He put me down and straightened up.

"Hold it right there," Bulldog said. He was pointing his gun at Daddy's chest.

"You all got a warrant to mess up my house like this?" Daddy asked. "And stop waving that gun around. I ain't going nowhere. You're scaring my little girl to death."

Bulldog put the gun back inside his shoulder holster. "Don't need no warrant," he said. "Now hand over your numbers and come along quietly."

"You ain't got no warrant," Daddy repeated.

"Search him," Bulldog ordered the young one, who approached Daddy with hesitation and went through his pocket. He pulled out an envelope. Lord, I thought, they're gonna put Daddy underneath the jail. The cop opened the envelope and pulled out an unpaid gas bill.

"The only house where we can't find a number slip," Bulldog said, "is a number runner's house. Nobody else is that careful." He reared back on his heels. "Tell you what I'm gonna do, though. I'm gonna run you in for assault and battery for pushing my partner like you did. Let's go."

I was crying loudly by this time. "Hush," Daddy said. "You're a big girl now and you know what to do."

I nodded. He meant that after he was gone I was to take the numbers downstairs to Frenchy and tell him Daddy had been arrested. And that's exactly what I did do after the police had driven Daddy away in an unmarked blue car, and I cried every step of the way.

Mother and I were drinking tea at the dining room table, very silent and glum, when Daddy returned home around midnight. My brothers hadn't been home since they left that morning, and that worried Daddy more than his arrest.

"Damn cops," he muttered, as he sat down heavily. They hadn't found any numbers on him because the people on the stoop had warned him that two strange men were lurking about. Everybody in Harlem was a lookout for the cops.

"I thought the syndicate paid off so good that this wasn't supposed to happen," Mother said.

"There was an argument about the payoff," Daddy explained. Frenchy told him the police wanted a bigger take and the syndicate balked, so the police made a few arrests to show who was boss. "They didn't touch the big boys though," Daddy said, "just a couple of small runners like me."

"You'd better stop taking numbers now before something worse happens," Mother said.

Daddy was gloomy. "The worse has happened. Frenchy says they'll probably throw my case out of court. But I've got a record now. Fingerprints. The works." He looked at Mother and shook his head sadly. "How can I keep those boys from running wild now that I've done gone and got a record?"

Silence was his answer. Mother finally cleared her throat and said: "I'm sorry this happened now because . . . well, I gotta tell you sometime and it might as well be now."

"What."

Mother averted her eyes. "If it was just you and me I

wouldn't mind. We could scuffle along. But I can't even scrape together enough food for the children no more. We've got no money coming in now except for those few pennies I get from Mrs. Schwartz. Lately you've been playing back all your commission on the numbers."

"So I play all the commission back. I guess you don't help, huh?"

"Yes, I do. And when I hit for two cents last week all of my money went to help repay what you owe Frenchy."

"All right. All right. I'll give you back your damn ten dollars."

"It's not that. It's having nothing coming in steady I can count on."

"All I'm trying to do is hit a big one again," Daddy said. "Nine-oh-nine almost played today and I had two dollars on it. Lord, how I prayed that last figure would be a nine and out pops a goddamned six. We almost had us twelve hundred dollars, Baby. That's all I'm trying to do. Hit us a big one."

"We can't wait until you hit a big one," Mother said, her voice cracking. Then it steadied. "I went to the relief place yesterday and put in an application. The social workers will be here Monday to talk to you."

Daddy jumped to his feet, his face twitching with rage, his lips working soundlessly.

"There's no other way," Mother said. "Your pride won't feed these children."

They stared at each other in a silence that wasn't quiet at all, as if they were arguing loudly without words.

"Goddammit," Daddy screamed, banging his fist down hard on the table, "I'm a fucking *man*. Why can't you understand that?"

"Your pride won't feed these children," Mother repeated quietly.

Suddenly Daddy collapsed back into his seat. His head fell forward on his folded arms. He was crying. I ran to him. "Daddy. Daddy." But he pushed me away roughly and I fell to my knees. I was up in a rush, blindly groping for the door. I heard Mother yelling at me to come back as I stumbled down the stairs.

I ran down the street looking for Sukie. I found her jumping rope with some kids on Hundred Seventeenth Street.

"You ready to fight now?" I demanded.

Sukie took a step backwards, confused.

"Fight, goddamn you!" I screamed.

She kept backing away, her mouth slack with surprise.

"Motherfucker!" I screamed, and that did it.

"Don't play the dozens with me," Sukie cried, and suddenly we were all tangled up together.

It was a one-sided battle. If Sukie landed a blow I didn't feel it. I pressed forward and she fell beneath my weight. I jumped on top of her, pinning her body to the ground, and, grabbing her by the hair, I banged her head against the sidewalk again and again. A crowd of adults joined the shrieking children.

A woman yelled: "My God! Somebody stop her! She's murdering that child!" It was Mrs. Mackey.

Strong, black arms lifted me up bodily. I screamed and kicked, aiming at the man's privates, but my kicks fell short.

Sukie was sobbing: "She tried to kill me." Mrs. Mackey led her away. Blood dripped from her swollen mouth down her chin, and the skin on her face was grated raw where it had scraped the pavement.

I stopped kicking and the man put me down. I felt lifeless, numb, and the crowd was hemming me in. I was suffocating. I pushed against the black, shoving mass until I was free of them. There was something evil in their sweating black faces, and that something was in me also.

"Goddamn," I whispered, waiting for the lightning to strike me dead. "Goddamn them all to hell." But I was not chastised for my blasphemy. Even the Lord didn't care.

I walked to the corner and, turning my face away from home, I made my way aimlessly down Fifth Avenue.

Deloris Harrison

A friend for a season

Deloris Harrison, born in Virginia, grew up
in Harlem; after obtaining a B.A. at St. Joseph's
College, she acquired an M.A. at New York
University. After a Fulbright-Hayes Fellowship
to the Netherlands, she returned and taught
creative writing at the City College of New
York and at Dartmouth. She is currently teach-
ing in New Hampshire.

"Genius, all over the world, stands hand in
hand," said Melville of Hawthorne, "and one
shock of recognition runs the whole circle
round." The reader of "A Friend for a Season"
experiences that "shock of recognition." The
genius comes from the writer; the shock for
the reader comes in the recognition. I know
the Phyllis of this story and the Cheryl. I have
never met Ms. Harrison, but her story made
me feel that she had been peeping at me. I
don't think I want to meet her; she already
knows too much about me. And perhaps you?
And perhaps us?

As children we had friends the way plays have runs on
Broadway. In the fall, fresh from camp—or, more likely,
a two-month hiatus in the South with grandparents—
we looked around the schoolyard and saw new faces. By

the crumbling concrete wall where the boys played handball you might see a frightened little girl just arrived from the South, innocent to the ways of New York. Or you might for the first time find value in an old face. Last year (as you called the months before summer vacation) this person had seemed too childish or not childish enough, and so you were oblivious of each other. Now you suddenly found beauty and worth in each other. You became friends for a season.

This was the girl who saw you through some climactic, devastating season in your life and became synonymous with it, although in most cases she had nothing to do with it.

If it was autumn, you roller-skated together; you watched the sun seem to move farther and farther away from the earth while you swung together in the park—both of you eager to fly high, as you once had, but growing ashamed that you still loved the swings, the monkey bars and the seesaws. You went to the library together. You walked home from school together.

By spring there was often a new friend, and you played hopscotch and jumped double-dutch. You walked farther away from the neighborhood. You would sit quietly like country children, as most likely you should have been, having been born in some green Southern land. You would look up at the sun through thin city trees and feel happy to be alive. Talk flowed easily with a bag of potato chips or a large dill pickle between you.

One day in the middle of March I met Phyllis Green in the doorway of MacFarland's Candy Store. Although Phyllis and I had gone to the same school for over a year, we had never approached each other.

"Hi, Cheryl. Haigies on your potato chips," she said, speaking as naturally as if we had been friends for a long time.

Phyllis had skinny legs and big feet, and so did I. There was usually a hole in the back of one of her socks, and the socks always rode down in her large, down-at-heel shoes. Phyllis walked in the middle of winter through the dull gray streets of Harlem with her coat flapping open and hanging lopsided. Her short hair was in braids. Usually either a braid was coming loose or a half-tied ribbon hung precariously from it. Phyllis was carefree, happy; and I—I was already like an unhappy mouse. She was my best friend for a while.

It was a bright day, the first one we had had since the long, dark winter. It was nearly one o'clock, and time to return to school after lunch.

MacFarland's Candy Store faced the schoolyard, and I could see the lines of students (boys at the two eastern doors and girls at the two western doors) beginning to move inside the building. Only a few belligerent boys still played handball, or stood just outside the gate, as if undecided whether or not to return to the battlefield of classrooms. Their brown and black faces were covered with sweat because they had been either playing hand-ball or running senselessly and insanely—running to exorcise a frustrated devil within themselves. On their faces was a sense of impending defeat. As always, they had discarded their jackets with defiant bravado, daring the temperature to drop again. At this they always lost too.

The girls' entrances were always locked first. In an effort to coax the gate hangers inside, the boys' doors were left open till last. None of the boys moved toward the sanctuary inside. Only Phyllis and I approached it, hand in hand.

Phyllis had an easy walk. She moved gracefully despite the way her coat hung and the size of her feet.

"I sure liked that movie, didn't you, Cheryl?" she asked. "It was good—I mean, the way he could jump all over the place and swing and everything. I mean, I never did see nothing like that, especially swinging around with a girl in his arms and sword-fighting at the same time. Don't you think it was great?" Her voice was alive with excitement.

"Yes. I certainly wish I could do it," I added. "I read *The Count of Monte Cristo* and he did all that stuff too, but it's different to see it."

"You read a lot, don't you?" She shivered as she spoke. The wind had blown her lightweight coat open and pierced the thin cotton of her dress. I was aware for the first time that she was not as warmly dressed as I. Under my heavy coat I wore a long-sleeved sweater and a winter skirt; I also had on my woolen cap, knee socks and sturdy Oxfords. Despite them I still felt the chill of winter.

"I love to read. It's lots of fun," I said after several moments.

When we reached her house, we stood on the stoop,

both reluctant to leave each other. There was a lot of walking in these relationships but not too much traffic inside each other's homes. That was too private and personal. There might be brothers and sisters with different names, a strange man in stylish clothes or someone drunk upon the floor. That was too sordid. Savagely you guarded your home and with deep respect you observed the code. The stoop was all right, and even the dingy hallway was not above a visit from a friend. But best of all was the street.

"Let me walk you to your house," she said finally.

"Okay."

I didn't want to leave her that way either. We walked toward Seventh Avenue, stopping along the way to look into dimly lighted hallways, all the while noticing other children doing the same.

We had reached my stoop. I lived on Seventh Avenue in a house that once was well kept by its inhabitants. There had been a cleaner, more prosperous look about it than the buildings crammed together in the block. The tree-lined boulevard on a glorious spring day held a grandeur and elegance that once had stirred pride in people like my father and mother. They had felt apart from the Negroes who lived farther into the block. But change had come; neglect was eating away at the once-stately buildings with aristocratic names. Already the professionals had taken flight to Sugar Hill, to Queens and Brooklyn, leaving people like my parents behind with nothing but their pride to sustain them.

"Well, Cheryl, I guess I better be going," Phyllis said to me as we stood at the steps of my building. Both my parents worked, and as a result I was alone at home a great deal. Unlike the other children, I did not think I needed to guard the sanctity of my home. In fact, I thought my home and my parents were something special and singularly wonderful, and I would have liked to share them with everyone. True, there were things I didn't wish my friends to know; for example, in the last few months there had been long, terrible arguments between my parents. But especially on Saturdays, when my father was at work, I would have liked to have a visitor. Before I could ask Phyllis, although I knew she saw the question on my face, she had hurried away, as though frightened by the thought that she might have to do the same.

I stood in the cold on the stoop, looking across the wide avenue. I thought of my father and mother. I could see his handsome, caramel-colored face, his crinkly kind of black hair, which he wore a little longer than most colored men. And next to him I saw my mother's light, cream-colored skin, her large, hazel eyes and soft, wispy brown hair. She had a tendency to be plump and was continually dieting. They were dressed to go out dancing and to listen to some jazz at "Wells' " or "Small's." There was none of the strain of the past on their faces, and I felt an arrogant pride at having such attractive, intelligent parents.

And they were intelligent. My mother worked as a typist at the Municipal Building and answered the phone for a commissioner. My father did not deliver mail but sorted it. Occasionally when a man was sick, he took over a window at the main post office, where he worked. He was always full of stories of those days— how white people registered such surprise and tried to hide their hostility when they saw him. But more than their jobs, it was the fact that my mother and father talked and read a lot. That made me know we were a lot better than most Negro families. I felt above the code of the other children, and would have welcomed Phyllis gladly into my home. . . .

"Damn it, Lettie! Why do you have to say the same thing over and over again? Don't you think I want the best for Cheryl, just like you do? I'm breaking my back trying to save money so we can get the hell out of here, and you're crying the blues all the time. Don't you ever let up on a man? I'm tired of hearing about it. I've been wearing the same damn suit since I got out of the Army. That's right—ten years! I know the neighborhood is falling apart, that they're practically selling dope in the hallway and that my daughter has to wade through drunks to get to the playground. You act like I'm not scuffling like a g.d. nigger to save her for something better. I had three lousy beers. These Italian guys working off the trucks said, 'Hey, come on, man—have a couple with us!' What am I supposed to say?"

He now speaks in a whiny, Uncle Tom's voice: ' "No, I can't go, Mr. Bossman, 'cause Miss Charlie thinks three lousy beers stand between her and a house in Queens. She thinks my daughter can't go to college or something because I have three stinking beers.' And when the checks come, what then? Sneak off to the men's room like a scared rat? Hell no!" He stopped for a moment, as if gathering his strength, and then continued more violently than before:

"I gotta once and a while say, 'Listen, man, let me pay for this round,' without you pulling your nightgown tight around your body and locking me out for it."

"Jesse, all I said was we didn't save anything this check, and that's no good." My mother's voice was low and painful. "We've got to keep saving or we'll never get anywhere."

I heard it all through the thin wall that separated our bedrooms. I heard the quarrel, my mother turn over her large body, my father's heavy breathing. I stuck my arms out of the covers, testing the temperature of the room. It was cold.

There was never any heat on Saturday night, because the super devoted this time to drinking. His wife made a fire during the day, but at night the real cold of winter settled into the old building. If my mother decided to wait up for my father, she would light the oven and sit in the kitchen, or watch TV while lying wrapped in blankets on the couch.

On happy nights my father would bring some barbecued spareribs and several cans of beer and they would laugh and listen to the phonograph. He liked to listen to what he called "low-down blues," and he loved to hear "Going to Chicago." When Joe Williams sang, "There ain't nothin' a monkey woman can do for me," he would laugh his loud, sincerely happy laugh and reach out to touch my mother. I never saw him do it, but I always knew he did, because I then would hear my mother say, "Oh, Jesse, you're such a fool." It was playful, loving talk that I felt a part of, that made me feel warm all over, in spite of the cold apartment.

He would answer her by saying, "Come on and dance, babe." They would move around the tiny living room, bumping into furniture, laughing softly to themselves. Then my father would say, "Lettie, leave the dishes and let's go to bed." My mother would open the door to my room, and in the narrow crack of light I could see her plump silhouette.

"It's a wonder you didn't wake Cheryl with all the noise you was making," she whispered.

"Did I wake up my baby?" he asked softly. I never answered, even though I was awake. They would close the door and go into their bedroom and I would go to sleep happy.

But that was long ago—or at least, that's how I felt. There were endless Saturdays of arguments and angry words that blotted out those happy times. It seemed as though my father came home later and later, and all the time I became more aware that it was actually very cold in the house and not at all happy.

"Do you think I want any of that stuff you dish out? Listen, unwrap it! Hang it out on the line, for all I care. You save it all up and give it to God or the g.d. priest in church."

"Jesse, will you stop yelling? Cheryl is right in the next room, and she doesn't need to hear your filthy mouth. Nobody decent wants to have anything to do with you, smelling like a beer barrel all the time."

"So what? So I had seven or eight beers. What the hell, I knew there wasn't a damn thing to come home to."

"I told you, Cheryl is too big and she can hear everything that goes on in here."

"She's nothing but a baby, and anyway, what's wrong with her hearing us? I'm your husband, ain't I? I'm her father! How do you think I got to be her father if I didn't—"

"For God's sake, Jesse, lower your voice! Let's go to sleep. It must be three thirty."

"Lettie . . . ain't nothin' a monkey woman can do for me . . ." he half-sung.

I heard them for a half hour more, making the same sounds that they always did, but later my mother went to the bathroom. I stood in my bare feet, shivering, outside the closed door.

"Mommy, I got to pee-pee," I said.

I heard her crying and then the toilet flush and the water running. I was seized with panic.

"Are you all right, Mommy?"

"Certainly, sweetheart. Wait just a minute and Mommy will be out," she called to me.

I rushed into the bathroom, not waiting, convinced that she was ill. When I saw her special hot-water bottle with a long tube attached to it, I was convinced, and a torrent of tears rushed from my eyes. She stood over me, still holding the bag awkwardly in her hands. I pressed my face against her and burrowed my head into her stomach. We stood there like that until we heard my father's voice.

"Can't I come in?" He opened the door and stood scratching his head. "Well, this is quite a family; everybody's up and around at four o'clock in the morning like it's afternoon. How about it—can Daddy have some privacy?"

He was in a cheerful mood, and once we left the bathroom, I could hear him whistling. My mother went to the kitchen, and I knew that in a few minutes we would have something good to eat because we were all awake.

Both of us were wearing robes and my mother had on bedroom slippers, but my father wore only his underwear, the whiteness of which stood out handsomely against his brown, well-built body. He reminded me of Errol Flynn, whom I had just seen in a film. I thought my father as beautiful as he, if not more so.

"Daddy, can you sword-fight?" I asked.

My father had been in the Second World War, and although I had been a baby at the time, I was convinced that he had been a hero.

"Sure, Pumpkin! Daddy can do everything!" His eyes were smiling, and it seemed hard to believe that he had spoken so violently to my mother only a short while before. "Boy, could I go for some Sherman's Barbecue," he said. He put his large, strong hands over my eyes. I could smell the odor of his body, which was so different from that of my mother's or my own. Even when he took his hands away, I could feel the pressure and warmth they had created across my face.

"Like magic," he said as he closed the refrigerator.

"Jesse, put some clothes on," my mother said in an unkind and brittle voice. In a softer tone she added, "You'll catch your death of cold."

My mother had turned on the oven to make the kitchen comfortable. She heated the meal, taking it from paper plates and putting it on our own dishes. When it was fixed, my father returned to the room, wearing an old Army sweater and a worn pair of pants. There was something wicked about being up and eating at four o'clock. The thought that everyone was asleep and that this was our very own time made it more precious. Even my mother had got into the spirit of it. She was smiling, and her hazel eyes were not clouded as they had been earlier.

"Daddy, I got a new friend. Her name is Phyllis Green."

We had finished eating, and my parents sat back drinking beer, my father from the can, my mother from a glass.

"Oh, yeah? What ever happened to the light-skinned little girl who lives down the street—what's her name?"

"Rosalind," I said coldly, annoyed that he could not keep up with my friends any better than that. "Oh, she's a drip and I hate her."

"Cheryl, that's not right. You shouldn't hate anybody," my mother said. My father's only comment was a muffled laugh.

"Well, she's not very smart," I continued, feeling cozy and having the sudden desire to talk and talk. I wanted to talk for hours, to extend this moment beyond the confines of its time. "She has skinny legs and big feet," I continued.

"Just like my Pumpkin," my father joked.

"Oh, Cheryl's just at that age. She'll develop nicely when she's a teen-ager, and that's not so far away from now."

I was happy that my mother had so quickly come to my defense. But my father just ran his hand across my hair, which was sticking up from having lain in bed.

"She's just a baby. Always will be Daddy's baby."

It sounded like the beginning of the old argument, and struck a cold terror in me so fierce that I grasped my father's hand tightly and began to talk feverishly.

"Phyllis is my best friend. We're going to the library to listen to stories and I'm going to stay at her house and help her look after her little brother, and we go to the movies together and eat MacFarland's potato chips and everything. . . ."

My parents weren't listening to me. They stared at each other across the table.

"All right, Lettie, so we won't ever get the hell out of this place. So we can't afford to have another baby and you're gonna work the rest of your life. I make seventy-five dollars a week—that's it. Do you think they'll ever give me a permanent place at the front window? Do you seriously think that I'll ever be a supervisor over all those white guys? Not in another fifty years! Sure, the Supreme Court can say they've got to integrate schools, but that don't change things for me. It's not that easy. . . . Oh, Lettie, it's dragging me down. It's dragging me down. It'll take a lifetime to save five thousand dollars. And I get tired of not having a car, not being able to go out for a drink once in a while. Tired of saving! But you don't seem to understand. You sit there with your righteous attitude and make me pay for every inch."

Suddenly, with an almost embarrassed expression on their faces, they looked at me. Neither spoke for quite a while, and when my mother did, her voice was strained and unnatural.

"Cheryl, go to bed. It's so late. Go to bed, honey."

My father echoed her. "That's right, Pumpkin. You better hit the sack."

Before I went to bed, I walked to one end of the table into my father's arms and received his hug, then to the other end. As I did, I noticed that the paint was peeling off the table. It was old. My mother kissed me. My feet were cold against the floor, and I rushed to bed, eager to find the warmth and security I missed.

Phyllis took a handful of potato chips. Her hands, like her feet, were oversized. She looked across the Harlem River toward the Bronx. It was bright, and spring actually had come to the city. There was no escaping it, and somehow beauty could be found everywhere. Phyllis and I had decided to go down to the river. We had walked to the pier, along a street lined with factories, and tin buildings for storage. Already there were boys who had come to take a quick plunge in the water or to sit on the docks and fish with a piece of string. They never, to my knowledge, caught anything, but the time passed, the sun was gentle and kind and there was always laughter.

I had suggested that we take this walk after school so that I could muster up the courage to talk to her, more than to enjoy the glorious day. Things lay heavy inside me. Although Phyllis and I went to the movies together on Saturdays, walked through the streets together, swung in the swings and even had gone as far down-

town as 65th Street to the zoo together, a polite awk-
wardness hung between us. It didn't matter that I had
coerced her into going to the library with me or that we
had gossiped about our former friends. What was important was that we never had really talked about our
families. Neither of us had met the other's parents
or set foot in the other's house.

Easter vacation had come and gone, and for those
ten days we hadn't seen each other. When the holidays
were over we greeted each other with genuine delight, yet I had no more idea how she had passed those
days than she had of how I had spent mine.

As we stood side by side on the pier, our hands greasy
from potato chips, we appeared close. It did not seem
possible that there could be secrets between us, but
we had learned from necessity to live by the rules of
friendship. Now, however, I felt compelled to violate
them.

"Does your father live with you?" I asked after a long
time. My voice sounded strange and far off and not
credible. This startled me, as my question did Phyllis.

She answered, however, quite casually. "No. I never
seen him."

"Do you miss not having a father?" I asked. She appeared at the moment much taller and older than I. She
hesitated and then spoke.

"No, I don't miss something I never had. My brother's
father comes around sometimes, but he don't like me
'cause I'm dark."

I couldn't think of anything to say. I had not expected
her to have problems too. I had thought that because
she never spoke or cried or seemed affected by anything, there were no hurts for her, only for me.

"Phyllis. . ." I began. I moved the bag of potato chips between us. Clumsily I offered her the last handful. I felt sure that I would cry, and tried to prevent it by looking up into the sky. "My father went away. He doesn't live with us any more," I finally managed to say.

"Oh," she commented unemotionally. "Did he fight with your mama a lot?"

"No," I answered quickly. I was appalled that my father should be accused of hurting my mother.

"Then why did he go away?" she asked.

"I don't know," I replied. I thought I had told too much already. There were things I didn't understand myself. Obviously she couldn't understand what had happened in my home. There had been no drunken fights or policemen or running up and down the stairs in the middle of the night. I had come home from the movies one Saturday and my mother, with no tears in her eyes but a frightful shaking in her large body, had said simply that my father would not be coming home, that he had decided to live somewhere else but that he still loved me and always would. When he was settled he would come and see me. And on Easter Sunday he had come. They had talked in low voices in the living room and he had taken me on his lap for a little while. Then he was gone. I had an address and phone number in Brooklyn. It could have been any stranger's.

"Phyllis, let's start back," I said. It was getting dark and there was a cold breeze and the smell of garbage from the river. When we reached my stoop, Phyllis stood on the sidewalk as I proceeded up the stairs. I turned to say good-by and saw that she was ready to follow me. For the first time I had no desire for her to come into my house. The super rarely scrubbed the hallway and the light had been out for nearly a week. I could not articulate it, but now I was no better than she, and that was the greatest pain. She could never enter my house or meet my family. All I could do was offer to walk her back to her house, for the street was the only place where we were equal.

LeRoi Jones (Imamu Baraka)

The screamers

LeRoi Jones (Imamu Baraka) may only have the life span of an ordinary mortal, but he has engaged in enough careers to carry a cat through nine life spans—poet, essayist, playwright, propagandist, novelist, politician, editor, teacher, spiritual leader—and maybe more. He now resides in his native Newark after an educational sojourn through Howard University, Columbia University, and the New School for Social Research, earning a B.A. and two master's degrees.

Jones's prodigious output defies the brief bibliographer, but his most recent works have been *It's Nation Time; Jello; Kawaida Studies: The New Nationalism; Raise, Race, Rays, Raze;* and *African Congress: A Documentary of the First Modern Pan-African Congress.* A forthcoming work, *Creation of the New Ark,* will be published by the Howard University Press. He returns, in this work, as a historian and chronicler of the New Ark created fictionally in some of his earlier works.

Lynn Hope adjusts his turban under the swishing red green yellow lights. Dots. Suede heaven raining, windows yawning cool summer air, and his musicians watch him grinning, quietly, or high with wine blotches on four-dollar shirts. A yellow girl will not dance with me, nor will Teddy's people, in line to the left of the stage, readying their *Routines*. Haroldeen, the most beautiful, in her pitiful dead sweater. Make it yellow, wish it whole. Lights. Teddy, Sonny Boy, Kenney & Calvin, Scram, a few of Nat's boys jamming long washed handkerchiefs in breast pockets, pushing shirts into homemade cummerbunds, shuffling lightly for any audience.

"The Cross-Over," Deen laughing at us all. And they perform in solemn unison a social tract of love. (With no music till Lynn finishes "macking" with any big-lipped Esther screws across the stage.) White and green plaid jackets his men wear, and that twisted badge, black turban/on red string conked hair. (OPPRESSORS!) A greasy hipness, down-ness, nobody in our camp believed (having social worker mothers and postman fathers; or living squeezed in light skinned projects with adulterers and proud skinny ladies with soft voices). The theory, the spectrum, this sound baked inside their heads, and still rub sweaty against those lesser lights. Those niggers. Laundromat workers, beauticians, pregnant short haired jail bait separated all ways from "us," but in this vat we sweated gladly for each other. And rubbed. And Lynn could be a common hero, from whatever side we saw him. Knowing that energy, and its response. That drained silence we had to make with our hands, leaving actual love to Nat or Al or Scram.

He stomped his foot, and waved one hand. The other hung loosely on his horn. And their turbans wove in among those shadows. Lynn's tighter, neater, and bright gorgeous yellow stuck with a green stone. Also, those green sparkling cubes dancing off his pinkies. A-boomp bahba bahba, A-boomp bahba bahba, A-boomp bahba bahba, A-boomp bahba bahba, the turbans sway behind him. And he grins before he lifts the horn, at Deen or drunk Becky, and we search the dark for girls.

Who would I get? (Not anyone who would understand this.) Some light girl who had fallen into bad times and ill-repute for dating Bubbles. And he fixed her later with his child, now she walks Orange St. wiping chocolate from its face. A disgraced white girl who learned to calypso in vocational school. Hence, behind halting speech, a humanity as paltry as her cotton dress. (And the big hats made a line behind her, stroking their erections, hoping for photographs to take down south.) Lynn would oblige. He would make the most perverted hopes sensual and possible. Chanting at that dark crowd. Or some girl, a wino's daughter, with carefully vaselined bow legs would drape her filthy angora against the cardboard corinthian, eyeing past any greediness a white man knows, my soft tyrolean hat, pressed corduroy suit, and "B" sweater. Whatever they meant, finally to her, valuable shadows barely visible. Some stuck-up boy with "good" hair. And as a naked display of America, for I meant to her that same oppression. A stunted head of greased glass feathers, orange lips, brown pasted edge to the collar of her dying blouse. The secret perfume of poverty and ignorant desire. Arrogant too, at my disorder, which calls her smile mysterious. Turning to be eaten by the crowd. That mingled foliage of sweat and shadows: *Night Train* was what they swayed to. And smelled each other in The Grind, The Rub, The Slow Drag. From side to side, slow or jerked staccato as their wedding dictated. Big hats bent, tight skirts, and some light girls' hair swept the resin on the floor. Respectable ladies put stiff arms on your waist to keep some light between, looking nervously at an ugly friend forever at the music's edge.

I wanted girls like Erselle, whose father sang on television, but my hair was not straight enough, and my father never learned how to drink. Our house sat lonely and large on a half-Italian street, filled with important Negroes. (Though it is rumored they had a son, thin with big eyes, they killed because he was crazy.) Surrounded by the haughty daughters of depressed economic groups. They plotted in their projects for mediocrity, and the neighborhood smelled of their despair. And only the wild or the very poor thrived in Graham's or could be roused by Lynn's histories and rhythms. America had choked the rest, who could sit still for hours under popular songs, or be readied for citizenship by slightly bohemian social workers. They rivaled pure emotion with wind-up record players that pumped Jo Stafford into Home Economics rooms. And these carefully scrubbed children of my parents' friends fattened on their rhythms until they could join the Urban League or Household Finance and hound the poor for their honesty.

I was too quiet to become a murderer, and too used to extravagance for their skinny lyrics. They mentioned neither cocaine nor Bach, which was my reading, and the flaw of that society. I disappeared into the slums, and fell in love with violence, and invented for myself a mysterious economy of need. Hence, I shambled anonymously thru Lloyd's, The Nitecap, The Hi-Spot, and Graham's desiring everything I felt. In a new English overcoat and green hat, scouring that town for my peers. And they were old pinch-faced whores full of snuff and weak dope, celebrity fags with radio programs, mute bass players who loved me, and built the myth of my intelligence. You see, I left America on the first fast boat.

This was Sunday night, and the Baptists were still praying in their "faboulous" churches. Though my father sat listening to the radio, or reading pulp cowboy magazines, which I take in part to be the truest legacy of my own spirit. God never had a chance. And I would be walking slowly towards The Graham, not even knowing how to smoke. Willing for any experience, any image, any further separation from where my good grades were sure to lead. Frightened of post offices, lawyer's offices, doctor's cars, the deaths of clean politicians. Or of the imaginary fat man, advertising cemeteries to his "good colored friends." Lynn's screams erased them all, and I thought myself intrepid white commando from the West. Plunged into noise and flesh, and their form become an ethic.

Now Lynn wheeled and hunched himself for another tune. Fast dancers fanned themselves. Couples who practiced during the week talked over their steps. Deen and her dancing clubs readied avant-garde routines. Now it was *Harlem Nocturne,* which I whistled loudly one Saturday in a laundromat, and the girl who stuffed in my khakis and stiff underwear asked was I

a musician. I met her at Graham's that night and we
waved, and I suppose she knew I loved her.

Nocturne was slow and heavy and the serious dancers
loosened their ties. The slowly twisting lights made
specks of human shadows, the darkness seemed to float
around the hall. Any meat you clung to was yours those
few minutes without interruption. The length of the
music was the only form. And the idea was to press
against each other hard, to rub, to shove the hips tight,
and gasp at whatever passion. Professionals wore jocks
against embarrassment. Amateurs, like myself, after
the music stopped put our hands quickly into our pockets, and retreated into the shadows. It was as mean-
ingful as anything else we knew.

All extremes were popular with that crowd. The
singers shouted, the musicians stomped and howled.
The dancers ground each other past passion or moved
so fast it blurred intelligence. We hated the popular
song, and any freedman could tell you if you asked that
white people danced jerkily, and were slower than our
champions. One style, which developed as Italians
showed up with pegs, and our own grace moved towards
bellbottom pants to further complicate the cipher,
was the honk. The repeated rhythmic figure, a
screamed riff, pushed in its insistence past music. It
was hatred and frustration, secrecy and despair. It
spurted out of the diphthong culture, and reinforced the
black cults of emotion. There was no compromise,
no dreary sophistication, only the elegance of something
that is too ugly to be described, and is diluted only at the
agent's peril. All the saxophonists of that world were
honkers, Illinois, Gator, Big Jay, Jug, the great sounds
of our day. Ethnic historians, actors, priests of the uncon-

scious. That stance spread like fire thru the cabarets and joints of the black cities, so that the sound itself became a basis for thought, and the innovators searched for uglier modes. Illinois would leap and twist his head, scream when he wasn't playing. Gator would strut up and down the stage, dancing for emphasis, shaking his long gassed hair in his face and coolly mopping it back. Jug, the beautiful horn, would wave back and forth so high we all envied him his connection, or he'd stomp softly to the edge of the stage whispering those raucous threats. Jay first turned the mark around, opened the way further for the completely nihilistic act. McNeeley, the first Dada coon of the age, jumped and stomped and yowled and finally sensed the only other space that form allowed. He fell first on his knees, never releasing the horn, and walked that way across the stage. We hunched together drowning any sound, relying on Jay's contorted face for evidence that there was still music, though none of us needed it now. And then he fell backwards, flat on his back, with both feet stuck up high in the air, and he kicked and thrashed and the horn spat enraged sociologies.

That was the night Hip Charlie, the Baxter Terrace Romeo, got wasted right in front of the place. Snake and four friends mashed him up and left him for the ofays to identify. Also the night I had the grey bells and sat in the Chinese restaurant all night to show them off. Jay had set a social form for the poor, just as Bird and Dizzy proposed it for the middle class. On his back screaming was the Mona Lisa with the mustache, as crude and simple. Jo Stafford could not do it. Bird took the language, and we woke up one Saturday whispering Ornithology. Blank verse.

And Newark always had a bad reputation. I mean, everybody could pop their fingers. Was hip. Had walks. Knew all about The Apple. So I suppose when the word got to Lynn what Big Jay had done, he knew all the little down cats were waiting to see him in this town. He knew he had to cook. And he blasted all night, crawled and leaped, then stood at the side of the stand, and watched us while he fixed his sky, wiped his face. Watched us to see how far he'd gone, but he was tired and we weren't, which was not where it was. The girls rocked slowly against the silence of the horns, and big hats pushed each other or made plans for murder. We had not completely come. All sufficiently eaten by Jay's memory, "on his back, kicking his feet in the air, Ga-ud Dam!" So he moved cautiously to the edge of the stage, and the gritty muslims he played with gathered close. It was some mean honking blues, and he made no attempt to hide his intentions. He was breaking bad. "Okay, baby," we all thought, "Go for yourself." I was standing at the back of the hall with one arm behind my back, so the overcoat could hang over in that casual gesture of fashion. Lynn was moving, and the camel walkers were moving in the corners. The fast dancers and practicers making the whole hall dangerous. "Off my suedes, motherfucker." Lynn was trying to move us, and even I did the one step I knew, safe at the back of the hall. The hippies ran for girls. Ugly girls danced with each other. Skippy, who ran the lights, made them move faster in that circle on the ceiling, and darkness raced around the hall. Then Lynn got his riff, that rhythmic figure we knew he would repeat, the honked note that would be his personal

evaluation of the world. And he screamed it so the
veins in his face stood out like neon. "Uhh, yeh, Uhh,
yeh, Uhh, yeh," we all screamed to push him further. So
he opened his eyes for a second, and really made his
move. He looked over his shoulder at the other
turbans, then marched in time with his riff, on his
toes across the stage. They followed; he marched across
to the other side, repeated, then finally he descended,
still screaming, into the crowd, and as the sidemen
followed, we made a path for them around the hall.
They were strutting, and all their horns held very high,
and they were only playing that one scary note. They
moved near the back of the hall, chanting and swaying,
and passed right in front of me. I had a little cup full
of wine a murderer friend of mine made me drink, so
I drank it and tossed the cup in the air, then fell in line
behind the last wild horn man, strutting like the rest
of them. Bubbles and Rogie followed me, and four-eyed
Moselle Boyd. And we strutted back and forth pumping
our arms, repeating with Lynn Hope, "Yeh, Uhh, Yeh,
Uhh." Then everybody fell in behind us, yelling still.
There was confusion and stumbling, but there were no
real fights. The thing they wanted was right there and
easily accessible. No one could stop you from getting
in that line. "It's too crowded. It's too many people
on the line!" some people yelled. So Lynn thought further, and made to destroy the ghetto. We went out into
the lobby and in perfect rhythm down the marble steps.
Some musicians laughed, but Lynn and some others
kept the note, till the others fell back in. Five or six
hundred hopped up woogies tumbled out into Belmont
Avenue. Lynn marched right in the center of the street.

Sunday night traffic stopped, and honked. Big Red yelled
at a bus driver, "Hey, baby, honk that horn in time or
shut it off!" The bus driver cooled it. We screamed and
screamed at the clear image of ourselves as we should
always be. Ecstatic, completed, involved in a secret
communal expression. It would be the form of the
sweetest revolution, to hucklebuck into the fallen
capitol, and let the oppressors lindy hop out. We marched
all the way to Spruce, weaving among the stalled cars,
laughing at the dazed white men who sat behind the
wheels. Then Lynn turned and we strutted back towards the hall. The late show at the National was turning out, and all the big hats there jumped right in our
line.

Then the Nabs came, and with them, the fire
engines. What was it, a labor riot? Anarchists? A nigger
strike? The paddy wagons and cruisers pulled in from
both sides, and sticks and billies started flying, heavy
streams of water splattering the marchers up and down
the street. America's responsible immigrants were
doing her light work again. The knives came out, the
razors, all the Biggers who would not be bent counter-
attacked or came up behind the civil servants, smash-
ing at them with coke bottles and aerials. Belmont
writhed under the dead economy and splivs floated in
the gutters, disappearing under cars. But for awhile,
before the war had reached its peak, Lynn and his
musicians, a few other fools, and I, still marched,
screaming thru the maddened crowd. Onto the sidewalk, into the lobby, half-way up the stairs, then we
all broke our different ways, to save whatever it was
each of us thought we loved.

Ann Petry

The new mirror

Ann Petry's first novel, *The Street*, dealing with life in Harlem, won her a Houghton Mifflin Fellowship in 1945. That novel grew from several years during which she lived in New York working in advertising and journalism. Ms. Petry, skillful and talented writer that she is, could with great success, turn her gaze on the city in which she briefly lived, but I feel that she casts the most brilliant light on the setting where she was born and reared—the New England small town.

The South is peculiarly ours, but Black families have survived in other parts of America for generations. In "The New Mirror", Ann Petry returns to the small-town setting and the professional milieu which was her cradle. Born into a family of chemists and pharmacists, she practiced pharmacy briefly herself. She continues to live in Old Saybrook, Connecticut, where she was born.

My mother said, "Where is your father?" She was standing outside the door of the downstairs bathroom. Even if she had been farther away, I would have understood what she said, because her voice had a peculiar quality just this side of harshness, which made it carry over longer distances than other people's voices.

From inside the bathroom, I said, "He's in the back yard listening to the bees."

"Please tell him that breakfast is ready."

"Right away," I said. But I didn't tell him right away. I didn't move. We had had a late, cold spring, with snow on the ground until the end of April. Then in May the weather turned suddenly warm and the huge old cherry trees in our yard blossomed almost overnight. There were three of them, planted in a straight line down the middle of the back yard. As soon as the sun was up, it seemed as though all the honeybees in Wheeling, New York, came to the trees in swarms. Every sunny morning, my father stood under one of those bloom-filled cherry trees and listened to the hum of the bees. My mother knew this just as well as I did, but she was sending a bathroom dawdler to carry a message to a cherry-tree dawdler so that she would finally have both of us in the dining room for breakfast at the same time.

I spent the next ten minutes looking at myself in the new plate-glass mirror that had been hung over the basin just the day before. A new electrical fixture had been installed over the mirror. My mother had had these changes made so that my father could shave down-stairs. She said this would be more convenient for him, because it placed him closer to the drugstore while he shaved. Our drugstore was in the front of the building where we lived.

The bathroom walls were white, and under the bril-liant, all-revealing light cast by the new fixture I looked like all dark creatures impaled on a flat white surface: too big, too dark. My skin was a muddy brown, not the clear, dark brown I had always supposed it to be. I turned my head, and the braid of hair that reached halfway down my back looked like a thick black snake. It even undulated slightly as I moved. I grabbed the braid close to my head and looked around for a pair of scissors, thinking I would cut the braid off, because it was an absolutely revolting hair style for a fifteen-year-old girl. But there weren't any scissors, so I released my grip on the braid and took another look at myself—head on in the glittering mirror. I decided that the way I looked in that white-walled bathroom was the way our family looked in the town of Wheeling, New York. We were the only admittedly black family in an all-white community and we stood out; we looked strange, alien. There was another black family—the Granites—but they claimed to be Mohawk Indians. Whenever my father mentioned them, he laughed until tears came to his eyes, saying, "Mohawks? Ha, ha, ha. Well, five or six generations of Fanti tribesmen must have caught five or six generations of those Mohawk females named Granite under a bush somewhere. Ha, ha, ha."

He never said things like that in the drugstore. He and my mother and my aunts kept their private lives and their thoughts about people inside the family circle, deliberately separating the life of the family from the life of the drugstore. But it didn't work the other way around, for practically everything we did was decided in terms of whether it was good or bad for the drugstore. I liked the store, and I liked working in it on Saturdays and after school, but it often seemed to me a monstrous, mindless, sightless force that shaped our lives into any old pattern it chose, and it chose the patterns at random.

I turned out the light and went to tell my father that breakfast was ready. He was standing motionless under the first big cherry tree. He had his back turned, but I could tell from the way he held his head that he was listening intently. He was short, and, seen from the back like that, his torso looked as though it had been designed for a bigger man.

"Yoo-hoo!" I shouted, as though I were calling someone at least two hundred feet away from me. "Breakfast. Break-fast." In my mind, I said, "Sam-u-el, Samu-el." But I didn't say that out loud.

He did not turn around. He lifted his hand in a gesture that pushed the sound of my voice away, indicating that he had heard me and that I was not to call him again. I sat down on the back steps to wait for him. Though the sun was up, it was cool in the yard. The air was filled with a delicate fragrance that came from all the flowering shrubs, from the cherry blossoms and the pear blossoms, and from the small plants—violets and daffodils. A song sparrow was singing somewhere close by. I told myself that if I were a maker of perfumes I would make one and call it Spring, and it would smell like this cool, sweet early-morning air and I would let only beautiful young brown girls use it, and if I could sing I would sing like the song sparrow and I would let only beautiful young brown boys hear me.

When we finally went into the house and sat down to breakfast, my father said (just as he did every spring) that the honeybees buzzed on one note and that it was

E flat just below middle C but with a difference. He said he had never been able to define this in the musical part of his mind and so had decided that it was the essential difference in the sound produced by the buzzing of a bee and the sound produced by a human voice lifted in song. He also said that he wouldn't want to live anywhere else in the world except right here in Wheeling, New York, in the building that housed our drugstore, with that big back yard with those cherry trees in it, so that in the spring of the year, when the trees were in full bloom, he could stand under them smelling that cherry-blossom sweet air and listening to those bees holding that one note—E flat below middle C. Then he said, "When I was out there just now, that first cherry tree was so aswarm with life, there were so many bees moving around bumping into the blossoms and making that buzzing sound, that hum . . ." He touched his forehead lightly with one of his big hands, as though he were trying to stimulate his thinking processes. "You know, I could have sworn that tree spoke to me."

I leaned toward him, waiting to hear what he was going to say. I did not believe the tree had said anything to him, but I wanted to know what it was he *thought* the tree had said. It seemed to me a perfect moment for this kind of revelation. We had just finished eating an enormous breakfast: grapefruit and oatmeal and scrambled eggs and sausage and hot corn-meal muffins. This delicious food and this sunny room in which we had eaten it were pleasant segments of the private part of our life, totally separated from the drugstore, which was the public part. I relished the thought that the steady stream of white customers who went in and out of our drugstore did not know what our dining room was like, did not even know if we had one. It was like having a concealed weapon to use against your enemy.

The dining room was a square-shaped, white-walled room on the east side of the building. The brilliant light of the morning sun was reflected from the walls so that the whole room seemed to shimmer with light and the walls were no longer white but a pale yellow. I thought my father looked quite handsome in this room. His skin was a deep reddish-brown, and he was freshly shaved. He had used an after-shaving lotion, and it gave his face a shiny look. He was bald-headed, and in this brilliantly sunlit room the skin on his face and on his head looked as though it had been polished.

The dining-room table was oak. It was square in shape, well suited to the square shape of the room. The chairs had tall backs and there was a design across the top of each one. The design looked as though it had been pressed into the wood by some kind of machine.

My mother sat at one end of the table and my father sat at the other end, in armchairs. I sat on one side of the table, and my Aunt Sophronia sat on the other side. She was my mother's youngest sister. She and my mother looked very much alike, though she was lighter in color than my mother. They were both short, rather small-boned women. Their eyes looked black, though they were a very dark brown. They wore their hair the same way—piled up on top of their heads. My mother's hair was beginning to turn gray, but Aunt Sophronia's was black. There was a big difference in their voices. Aunt Sophronia's voice was low-pitched, musical—a very gentle voice.

My aunt and my mother and father were drinking their second cups of coffee and I was drinking my second glass of milk when my father said he thought the cherry tree had spoken to him. They both looked at him in surprise.

I asked, "What did the tree say?"

"It bent down toward me and it said. . ." He paused, beckoned to me to lean toward him a little more. He lowered his voice. "The tree said, 'Child of the sun—' " He stopped talking and looked directly at me. In that sun-washed room, his eyes were reddish-brown, almost the same color as his skin, and I got the funny feeling that I had never really looked right at him before, and that he believed the tree had said something to him, and I was shocked. He whispered, "The tree said, 'It will soon be time to go and open the drugstore!' "

I scowled at him and he threw his head back and laughed, making a roaring, explosive sound. It was just as though he had said, "Got you, you idiot—you—ha, ha, ha." He opened his mouth so wide I could see his gums, red and moist, see the three teeth that he had left, one in the upper jaw and two in the lower jaw, even see his tonsils. I began muttering to him in my mind, "How do you chew your food, old toothless one with the red-brown skin and the bald head. Go up, thou bald head. Go up, thou bald-headed black man."

Right after breakfast, I helped my father open the

drugstore for the day. I was still annoyed that he had been able to fool me into thinking he believed a cherry tree had spoken to him, but I so enjoyed working in the drugstore that I would not deny myself that pleasure simply because he had deliberately talked nonsense and I had been stupid enough to believe him.

He swept the floor with a big soft-bristled broom. Then he went outside and swept off the long, wooden steps that ran all the way across the front of the building. He left the front door open, and the cool, sweet-smelling early-morning air dispelled the heavy odor of cigars, the sticky vanilla smell from the soda fountain, and the medicinal smell of the prescription room—part alcohol, part spicy things, part disinfectant.

I put change in both the cash registers—the one in the store proper and the one behind the fountain. The fountain was in a separate room, rather like a porch with a great many windows. I put syrups in the fountain—chocolate, Coca-Cola, root beer, lemon, cherry, vanilla. The chocolate syrup had a mouth-watering smell, and the cherry and lemon syrups smelled like a fruit stand on a hot summer day, but the root beer and the Coca-Cola syrups smelled like metal.

Our black-and-white cat sat in the doorway and watched my father. The cat yawned, opening his mouth wide, and I could see his wonderful flexible pink tongue and his teeth—like the teeth of a tiger, only smaller, of course. I wondered if cats ever became practically toothless, like my father. He wouldn't have cavities filled because he said all that silver or amalgam or gold or whatever it was, and all that X-raying that butterfingered dentists do, and all that use of Novocain

was what made people develop cancer of the jaw.
When his teeth hurt and the dentist said the pain was
due to a big cavity, he simply had the tooth pulled out
without an anesthetic. Once, I asked him if it hurt to
have teeth pulled without Novocain or gas. He said,
"Of course it hurts. But it is a purely temporary hurt.
The roots of my teeth go straight down and it is a very
simple matter to pull them out. I've pulled some of
them out myself."

I sorted the newspapers, looked at the headlines,
quickly skimmed the inside of the Buffalo *News*. I
saw a picture of a man, obviously an actor, wearing
a straw hat. I wanted the picture because of his tooth-
revealing grin, and I reminded myself to cut it out.
The newspapers that didn't sell were returned for
credit. Quite often I snipped out items that interested
me. I always hunted for articles that dealt with the
importance of chewing food thoroughly, and for pictures
of men with no teeth, and for pictures of very handsome men exposing a great many teeth. I intended
to leave this particular picture on the prescription
counter, where my father would be sure to see it.

When Aunt Sophronia came to work at nine o'clock,
the store was clean and it smelled good inside. Like
my father, she was a pharmacist, and when he was
not in the store, she was there. She wore dark skirts
and white shirtwaists when she was working, and she
put on a gray cotton store coat so that people would
know she worked in the store and would not think she
was a customer.

One other person worked in the drugstore—Pedro, a
twelve-year-old Portuguese boy. He was supposed to

arrive at nine on Saturdays and Sundays. He was always prompt, and the first stroke of the town clock had not yet sounded when he came hurrying into the store. He was a very sturdily built boy, with big dark eyes. He had an enormous quantity of tangled black hair. He couldn't afford to have his hair cut at the barbershop, so my father cut it for him. The first time I saw him cutting Pedro's hair out in the back room, I asked him if he knew how to cut hair.

He said, "No."

I said, "Well, how do you know what to do?"

"I don't," he said, snipping away with the scissors. "But I can shorten it some. Otherwise, he'll look like a girl."

Though Pedro was fond of all of us, he had a special feeling about my father. He told my father that he would like to stay in the store all the time—he could sleep in the back room, and all he needed was a blanket and a mattress and he could bring those from home, and he would provide his own food and clothes. There were eleven kids in his family, and I imagine he preferred being part of a family in which there were fewer people, and so decided to become a member of our family. My father wouldn't let him sleep in the back room, but Pedro did manage to spend most of his waking hours (when he wasn't in school, of course) at the store. He provided his own food. He ate oranges, sucking out the juice and the pulp. He hung a big smoked sausage from one of the rafters in the back room and sliced off pieces of it for his lunch. He loved fresh pineapple, and he was always saying that the only thing in the world he'd ever steal if he couldn't get it any other way would be a ripe pineapple.

At one minute after nine, my father went to the post office. When he left, he was holding some letters that he was going to mail. I thought his hand looked big and very dark holding all those white envelopes. I went to the door and watched him as he walked up the street, past the elm trees, past the iron urn on the village green, past the robins and the tender green young grass on each side of the gravel path. He had a stiff straw hat tilted just a little toward the back of his head. As he moved off up the street, he was whistling "Ain't goin' to study war no more, no more, no more."

We were so busy in the store that morning that I did not realize what time it was until my mother called up to find out why my father had not been home for his noon meal. There was such a sharp line of demarcation between house and store that my mother always telephoned the drugstore when she had a message for my father.

Aunt Sophronia answered the phone. I heard her say, "He's not in the store right now—he's probably in the cellar. We'll send him right along." After she hung up the receiver, she said, "See if your father is in the cellar unpacking stock or way down in the yard burning rubbish."

He wasn't in the cellar and he wasn't in the back yard. The burner was piled high with the contents of the wastebasket from the prescription room (junk mail, empty pillboxes, old labels) and the contents of the rubbish box from the fountain (straws, paper napkins, popsicle wrappers).

All three cherry trees were still filled with bees, and they were buzzing on their one note. I walked from one tree to the next, pausing to listen, looking up into the white blossoms, and the trees seemed to be alive in a strange way because of the comings and goings of the bees. As I stood there, I felt it would be very easy to believe that those trees could speak to me.

I went back to the drugstore, and Aunt Sophronia said, "You didn't see him?"

"No. And I don't think he ever came back from the post office. Each time someone asked for him, I thought he was in the back room or down in the cellar or outside in the yard. And each time, whoever it was wanted him said they'd come back later, and I never really had to look for him."

"I'll call the post office and ask if he's picked up our packages, and that way I'll find out if he's been there without actually saying that we're looking for him."

I could hear her end of the conversation, and obviously he hadn't been in the post office at all that morning. She hung up the telephone and called the railroad station and asked if Mr. Layen had been there to get an express package. The stationmaster had a big booming voice, and I could hear him say "No." Aunt Sophronia said, "You would have seen him if he had been at the station?" He said, "I certainly would."

Pedro and I wanted to go and look for my father. Aunt Sophronia snapped at us, saying, "Don't be foolish. Where would you look? In the river? In the taverns? Your father wouldn't kill himself, and he doesn't drink. . . ."

She frightened me. She had frightened Pedro, too; he was pale and his eyes looked bigger. I had thought my father was late for dinner because he had stopped somewhere to talk and got involved in a long-winded conversation, and that if Pedro and I had walked up or down the street we would have found him and told him his dinner was ready. Aunt Sophronia obviously thought something dreadful had happened to him. Now we began to think so, too.

We kept waiting on the customers just as though there was no crisis in our family. I kept saying to myself, "Your father dies, your mother dies, you break your leg or your back, you stand in a pool of cold sweat from a fever, you stand in a pool of warm blood from a wound, and you go out in the store and smile and say, 'Fine, just fine, we're all fine, nothin's ever wrong with us cull-ed folks.' "

Whenever the store was empty, my aunt would say nervously, "What could have happened to him?" And then clear her throat two or three times in quick succession—a sure sign that she was upset and frightened. Later in the afternoon she said in a queer way, just as though he had passed out of our lives and she was already reminiscing about him, "He did everything at exactly the same time every day. He always said that was the only way you could run a store—have a certain time for everything and stick to it."

This was true. He opened the drugstore promptly at eight, he went to get the mail promptly at nine, and he ate his dinner at twelve. At four in the afternoon, he drank a bottle of Moxie—the only soda pop that he regarded as fit for human consumption; he said if that were ever taken off the market he would have to drink tea, which upset his stomach because it was a drink suited to the emotional needs of the Chinese, the East Indians, the English, the Irish, and nervous American females, and it had, therefore, no value for him, representing as he did a segment of a submerged population group only a few generations out of Africa, where his ancestors had obviously been witch doctors.

On Sundays he went to church. He went in through the rear entrance and into the choir loft from the back about two minutes after the service started. There was a slight stir as the ladies of the choir and the other male singer (a tall, thin man who sang bass) rearranged themselves to make room for him. He sang a solo almost every Sunday, for he had a great big, beautiful tenor voice. On Sundays he smelled strongly of after-shave lotion, and on weekdays he smelled faintly of after-shave lotion.

My aunt kept saying, "Where would he go? Where would he go?"

I said, "Maybe he went to Buffalo." I didn't believe this, but she'd have to stop clearing her throat long enough to contradict me.

"What would he go there for? Why wouldn't he say so? How would he get there?"

"He could go on the bus," I said. "Maybe he went to get new eyeglasses. He buys his eyeglasses in the five-and-ten. He likes five-and-tens."

"He hates buses. He says they smell and they lurch."

I laughed. "He says they stink and they lurch in such a way they churn the contents of your belly upside down." She made no comment, so I said again, "He buys his glasses in the five-and-ten in Buffalo and—"

"What?" she said. "I don't believe it."

"It's true. You ask Mother. She said that the last time

they went to Buffalo. . ." I tried to remember how long
ago that would have been.

"Well?"

"Well, Mother said she wanted to get a new hat and
he said that he'd be in the five-and-ten. So after she
got the hat, she went down the street and went in
the five-and-ten, and there was Samuel and an old
colored man with him, and they were bent practically
double over a counter. She told me, 'Your father had a
piece of newspaper in his hand and he had on a pair
of glasses, and he was looking at this newspaper, saying, "No, not strong enough," and he moved on and
picked up another pair of glasses and put them on and
said, "Let's see. Ah! Fine!" Then he turned to this
old colored man, a dreadful-looking old man, ragged
and dirty and unshaven and smelling foully of whiskey,
and he said to him, "You got yours?" ' Mother said,
'Samuel, what ever are you doing?' Even when she told
it, she sounded horrified. He said, 'I'm getting my
glasses.' Then he asked the old man if he'd got his,
and the old man nodded and looked at Mother and sort
of slunk away. I suppose she had on one of those
flowered hats and white gloves. Mother said she
looked at the counter and there were rows and rows
of glasses and they were all fifty cents apiece. And
that's what Samuel uses—that's what he's always used.
He says that he doesn't need special lenses, that he
hasn't anything unusual the matter with his eyes. All
he needs is some magnifying glass so that he can see to
read small printed matter, and so that's why he buys
his glasses in the five-and-ten." I stopped talking.

My aunt didn't say anything. She frowned at me.

So I started again. "He gets two pair at a time. Sometimes he loses them. Sometimes he breaks them. You know he likes to push them up high on top of his forehead, out of the way when he isn't using them, and his bald head is always greasy or sweaty and the glasses slide off on the floor and quite often they break. Didn't you know that?"

She said, "No, and I wish you'd stop calling your father Samuel." She went to wait on a customer.

I sat down on the high stool in front of the prescription counter. I didn't believe that my father had gone to Buffalo. He wouldn't go away without leaving any message. I wondered if he'd been kidnapped, and dismissed the idea as ridiculous. Something must have happened to him.

My mother called the store again, and right afterward Aunt Sophronia told Pedro to go in through the kitchen door and get coffee and sandwiches that Mrs. Layen had made and bring them into the store. We ate in the back room, one at a time. We didn't eat very much. I didn't like the smell of the coffee. It has always seemed to me that the human liver doesn't like coffee, that it makes the liver shiver. But all my family drank coffee and so did Pedro, and they didn't like to have me tell them how I felt about it.

I sat in the back room with that liver-shivering smell in my nose and looked out the back door. It was a pleasant place to sit and eat. It was a big room, and the rafters in the ceiling were exposed. True, there was a lot of clutter—pots and pans and mops and brooms, and big copper kettles stuck in corners or hanging from the rafters, and piles of old newspapers and magazines stacked on empty cartons. The walls were lined with small boxes that contained herbs. Some wholesale druggist had thrown them out, and my father had said he'd take them, because a dried herb would be good a hundred years from now; if it were properly dried, it would not lose its special properties. The back room always smelled faintly of aromatic substances—a kind of sneeze-making smell. The door was open, and I could look out into the back yard and see the cherry trees and the forsythia and all the flowering shrubs and the tender new grass.

We were very busy in the store all that afternoon. At five o'clock my mother came in through the back door and sat down in the prescription room. She kept looking out of the window, toward the green. She had on a hat— a dark-blue straw hat with small white flowers across the front—and her best black summer suit and white gloves. She was obviously dressed for an emergency, for disaster, prepared to identify Samuel Layen in hospital or morgue or police station.

The customers came in a steady stream. They bought the afternoon papers, cigarettes, tobacco. Men on their way home from work stopped to get ice cream for dessert. As the afternoon wore along, the shadows from the elm trees lengthened until they were as long as the green was wide. The iron urn in the middle looked chalk white. As the daylight slowly diminished, the trunks of the trees—that great expanse of trunk without branches, characteristic of the elms—seemed to be darkening and darkening.

I turned on the lights in the store and the student lamp on the prescription counter. It wasn't really quite dark enough to justify turning on the lights and I thought my aunt would say this, but she didn't. She asked my mother if she would like a glass of ginger ale.

"That would be very nice, thank you," my mother said. Her voice was deeper and harsher, and its carrying quality seemed to have increased.

"Pedro, get Mrs. Layen a glass of ginger ale."

When Pedro brought the ginger ale, Mother took a sip of it and then put it on the window sill. It stayed there—bubbles forming, breaking, breaking, forming, breaking, until finally it was just a glass of yellowish liquid sitting forgotten on the window sill.

When there weren't any customers in the store, we all went into the prescription room and sat down and waited with my mother. We sat in silence—Pedro and Aunt Sophronia and my mother and I. I kept thinking, But my father wouldn't leave us of his own free will. Only this morning at breakfast he said he wouldn't want to live anywhere else in the world except right here where we live. It could be suicide, or he could have been murdered. Certainly not kidnapped for ransom. What do we own? We don't own a car. There's the old building where we live and there's the store with its ancient mahogany-colored fixtures and glass-enclosed cases and the fountain room. But if it were all put together with our clothes and our household goods—pots and pans and chairs and tables and sofas and beds and mirrors—it wouldn't add up to anything to kidnap a man for.

Then I thought, Perhaps he left my mother for another

woman. Preposterous. He was always saying that the
first time he saw her she was sixteen and he decided
right then and there he was going to marry her; she
had big, black, snappy eyes, and her skin was so
brown and so beautiful. His friends said he would be
robbing the cradle, because he was twenty-four. He
did marry her when she was eighteen. He said that
whenever he looked at her he always thought, Black
is the color of my true love's hair.

Aunt Sophronia said, "Perhaps we should put
something in the newspaper—something. . ."

My mother said, "No," harshly. "The Layens would
descend like a horde of locusts, crying 'Samuel! Samuel!
Samuel!' No. They all read the Buffalo *Recorder* and
they would be down from Buffalo before we could turn
around twice. Sometimes I think they use some form of
astral projection. No. We won't put anything in the
newspapers, not even if . . ."

I knew she was going to say, or had stopped herself
from saying, "even if he is dead," though I did not see
how she could keep an account of his death out of the
newspapers.

My mother said my father's family was like a separate and warlike tribe—arrogant, wary, hostile. She
thought they were probably descended from the Watusi.
In Buffalo, they moved through the streets in groups of
three or four. She always had the impression they were
stalking something. Their voices were very low in
pitch, almost guttural, and unless you listened closely
you got the impression they were not speaking English
but were simply making an accented sound—uh-uh-uh-
uh—that only they could understand.

Whenever my great-grandfather, the bearded patriarch of the family, went out on the streets of Buffalo, he was accompanied by one of his grandsons, a boy about fourteen, tall, quick-moving. The boy was always given the same instructions: "Anything happen to your grandfather, anybody say anything to him, you come straight back here, straight back here." "Anybody say anything to him" meant if anyone called him "out of his name." If this occurred, my mother said the boy would go straight home with the old man and emerge in the company of Uncle Joe, Uncle Bill, Uncle Bobby, Uncle John, Uncle George, my father, Aunt Kate, and Aunt Hal—all of them hellbent on vengeance.

They had lived in New Jersey—they always said "Jersey"—at the foot of a mountain they called Sour Mountain. When they first came to New York State, they lived in Albany. The whole clan—Great-Grandma, Great-Grandpa, Grandma and Grandpa, and all eight children including my father, Samuel, and a baby—came to Albany on one of the Hudson River boats. They had six ducks in wooden cages going splat all over the deck, a huge, woolly black dog—ancestry unknown, temper vicious—and six painted parlor chairs that Great-Grandma insisted on bringing with her. The men and boys wore black felt hats, and the skin on their faces and hands was almost as dark as the felt of the hats. They wore heavy black suits that Great-Grandma had made for them. Whenever anyone approached them on the boat, they executed a kind of flanking motion and very quickly formed a circle, the men facing the outside, the women on the inside.

My mother once told me she knew all the details

about the arrival of these black strangers in Albany, because her family had known a colored man who worked on the Hudson River boats and he had told her father about it. When the boat approached the dock, it had to be maneuvered into position, and so it started to move back down the river. It did not go very far, but there was an ever-increasing length of water between the boat and the dock. The sun was out, the brass railings gleamed in the sunlight, and the white paint sparkled as the boat edged away from the dock. The dark-skinned, fierce-looking men held a conference. The old bearded man who was my great-grandfather gave a cry—a trumpeting kind of cry—and took a long running leap off the boat and landed on the dock. He began walking up and down the dock, hitting it with his cane and bellowing, "You ain't takin' us back now, you know! Throw that baby down to me! Throw that baby down to me!" There were outraged cries from the people on the deck. One of the Layens threw the baby down to the old man and he caught it. He glared up at the scowling deckhands and the staring people and shouted, "Ain't goin' to take us back now, you know! We paid to get here. Ain't goin' to take us back now. Jump!" he roared. "All of you, jump!"

My mother said the colored man told her father this story, and he ended it by saying, "You know, those people jumped off that boat—even the women. They picked up all their stuff, even those damn ducks and that vicious dog and those chairs and they took these long running leaps and landed on the dock. I never saw anything like it. And that old bearded black man kept walking up and down on the dock, hitting it with his cane, and he's got this baby, dangling it by one foot, and he's hollering out and hollering out, 'We paid to get here! Ain't goin' to take us back now, you know!' "

I sat in the prescription room staring at my mother and thinking again, If my father died, she would not tell his family? Even if he died? She would be afraid to tell them for fear they would arrive in Wheeling and attack all the inhabitants—they would be as devastating as a gang of professional stranglers. Old as he was now, my great-grandfather wouldn't ride in an automobile and he didn't like trains, so he would probably walk down to Wheeling from Buffalo, muttering to himself, intractable, dangerous, his beard quivering with rage, his little eyes blazing with the light of battle.

Customers kept coming into the store. Pedro and I waited on them. Once, when we were both behind the tobacco counter, he said, "I could just walk around in the town and look for him. I wouldn't tell people he was lost."

I shook my head. "Aunt Sophronia wouldn't like it."

Each time the phone rang, I answered it. I left the door of the phone booth open, so they could all hear what I said, in case it was some kind of news about my father. It never was. It was always somebody who wanted some of his chocolate syrup, or his special-formula cold cream, or his lotion for acne. I kept saying the same thing in reply. "He isn't here right now. We expect him, we expect him. When? Later. We expect him later."

There was an automatic closing device on the screen

door which kept it from banging shut. It made a hissing sound when the door was opened. Each time we heard that hiss, we all looked toward the door expectantly, thinking perhaps this time it would be Samuel. Finally, Aunt Sophronia turned on a small radio on the prescription counter. There was a great deal of static, voices came in faintly, and there was a thin thread of music in the background—a confusion of sounds. I had never known my aunt to turn on the radio in the store. My father said that only certain kinds of decaying drugstores had radios blatting in them, and that the owners turned them on hoping to distract the customers' attention away from the leaks in the roof, the holes in the floor, the flyblown packages, and the smell of cat.

Aunt Sophronia sat on the high stool in front of the prescription counter, bent forward a little, listening. We all listened. My mother looked down at her hands, Pedro looked at the floor, Aunt Sophronia looked at the black-and-white linoleum on the counter. I thought, We're waiting to hear one of those fudge-voiced announcers say that a short, thick-bodied colored man has been found on the railroad track, train gone over him, or he's been found hanging or shot or drowned. Why drowned? Well, the river's close by.

I practiced different versions of the story. "Young woman finds short, thick-bodied unidentified colored man." "Schoolchildren find colored druggist in river." "Negro pharmacist lost in mountains." "Black man shot by white man in love duel." Colored druggist. Negro pharmacist. Black man. My father? I hovered in the doorway listening to the radio—world-news roundup, weather, terrible music. Nothing about unidentified colored men.

Aunt Sophronia turned toward my mother and said something in a low voice.

"Police?" my mother said in a very loud voice, and repeated it. "Police?"

"He's been gone since nine o'clock this morning. What else can we do except call the police?"

"No!" My mother's voice was louder and harsher than I had ever heard it. "There's no need to go to the police. We don't know where Samuel is, but if we wait patiently we'll find out." Her eyes were open very wide and they glistened. It occurred to me that they might be luminous in the dark, like a cat's eyes.

"He might have had an accident."

"We would have been informed," my mother said firmly. "His name is engraved on the inside of his watch. His name is on his shirt and on his underwear and his handkerchiefs. I mark everything with indelible ink."

"But if it happened in Buffalo—"

"If what happened? What are you talking about?"

Aunt Sophronia began to cry. Right there in the prescription room. She made so much noise you could hear her out in the store. I was appalled. The private part of our life had suddenly and noisily entered the public part—or perhaps it was the other way around. When people cry and try to talk at the same time, their words come out jerkily and they have to speak between the taking of big convulsive breaths, and so they cannot control the volume of their speech and they shout, and that is what my quiet-voiced Aunt Sophronia was doing.

She was shouting right there in the drugstore. Someone came into the store and turned to look toward the prescription room to see what was going on. Pedro ran out of the room to wait on the customer.

"I'm just as fond of him as you are!" Aunt Sophronia shouted between sobs and gasps and agonized-sounding crying noises. "Just as worried as you are! You can't just sit there and let him disappear! And not do anything about it!"

My mother stood up, looked at me, and said, "Call a taxi." Then she turned to my aunt and said, "We will go to the Tenyeck Barracks and discuss this with the state police." Her voice was pitched so low and it was so loud that it sounded like a man's voice.

When the town taxi came, I stood in the doorway and watched them go down the front steps. It was perfectly obvious that my aunt had been crying, for her eyelids were red and swollen. My mother looked ill. They both seemed to have shrunk in size. They were bent over and so looked smaller and shorter than they actually were. When they reached the sidewalk, they turned and glanced up at me. I felt like crying, too. The flowered hat had slipped so far back on my mother's head that it made her look as though she were bald. Aunt Sophronia had a yellow pencil stuck in her hair, and she had put on an old black coat that hung in the back room. The coat was too big for her; the sleeves were too long, and it reached almost to her ankles. Under it she was still wearing the gray cotton store coat. They looked like little old women—humble, questing, moving slowly. When they turned, I could see the white part of their eyes under the irises, and I had to look away from them.

Aunt Sophronia said, "If there are any prescriptions,

I'll fill them later." Then she took my mother by the arm and they went toward the taxi. The driver got out and held the door open for them and closed it behind them.

I wondered what my mother would say to the state police. "My husband is missing. He is a short, broad-shouldered colored man, bald-headed, forty-eight years old"? Would the state police snicker and say, "Yes, we would hardly expect you, with your dark-brown skin, to be married to a white man. Wearing what when last seen?" "Light-gray summer suit and polka-dot bow tie, highly polished black shoes." The gravel path that bisects the village green was very dry this morning—no mud. So there would still have been polish on his shoes. But not if he were drowned. But who would drown him, and why? Might have drowned himself. Drowned himself? Surely she will say that he has only three teeth, three teeth only—one in the upper jaw and two in the lower jaw.

Then I thought, But why did they have to *go* to the police? Why couldn't they have telephoned? Because someone might have overheard the conversation. So what difference would that make? Did they think the police would send out a silent and invisible bloodhound to hunt for the colored druggist from Wheeling? Did they think the police would send out invisible men to search the morgues in Buffalo, to fish for a fresh colored corpse in the streams and coves and brooks in and around Wheeling?

We didn't even hunt for him the way white people would have hunted for their father. It was all indirect. Has he been to the post office? . . . "Oh, oh, oh." Has he been to the railroad station to pick up an express package? . . . "I see, I see, I see."

Between customers, I thought, We've even infected Pedro, who is Portuguese, with this disease, whatever it is. Why did we have to hunt for my father this way? Because there is something scandalous about a disappearance, especially if it is a colored man who disappears. Could be caused by a shortage of funds (What funds? His own?), a shortage of narcotics, unpaid bills, a mistake made in a prescription—scandal, scandal, scandal. Colored druggist, mixed up with police, disappears. Mixed up with police.

It wasn't until Miss Rena Randolph handed me an empty prescription bottle to be refilled that I realized what my aunt had done. I held the sticky bottle in my hand, the label all over gravy drips, as my father was wont to say, and I thought, Why, I'm in charge of the drugstore and I am only fifteen. The only other person working in the store is Pedro, and he is only twelve. All my life I'd heard conversations about "uncovered" drugstores—drugstores without a pharmacist on the premises. For the first time, our store was "uncovered." Suppose something happened. . . .

Miss Randolph leaned against the counter and coughed and coughed and coughed. "I won't need it until morning," she said, pointing at the bottle that I held. "I have more at home. I always keep two bottles ahead."

My father told me once that he thought she looked as though she had just been dug up out of her grave. She was a very unhealthy-looking old woman. She was tall and very thin. Her skin was gray, her clothes were gray, and her hair was gray. But her teeth were yellow. She wore eyeglasses with no rims. Just last week when my father was refilling this same prescription for her, he said, "I don't know what Doc keeps giving her this stuff for. Perfectly obvious what's the matter with her, and this isn't going to cure it."

"What *is* the matter with her?" I asked.

He shrugged his shoulders and said evasively, "Your guess is just as good as mine—or Doc's."

"I can get it in the morning," she repeated now.

"Yes, Ma'am. It will be ready in the morning."

"Quiet in here tonight. Where's your aunt?"

"Outside," I said, and the way I said it made it sound as though I meant "transported" or "sold down the river."

She looked around the store as though she were a stranger, seeing it for the first time. She said, "It's a nice night. I suppose she's working in the garden."

After Miss Randolph left, I looked around the store, too. What had she seen that made her say it was a nice night and that my aunt would be working in the garden? You couldn't really see what was on the shelves—just the gleam of bottles and jars inside the dark-mahogany, glass-enclosed cases. The corners lay in deep shadow. It might have been a conjurer's shop, except, of course, for the cigarettes and the candy and the soda fountain. The bottles gleaming darkly along the walls could have held wool of bat and nose of Turk, root of the mandrake and dust of the toad. I went out in the back room and looked into the yard. It seemed to go on forever, reaching into a vast, mysterious distance, unexplored, silent—not even the twitter of a bird. It was pitch black. I couldn't see the blossoms on the cherry trees, I couldn't tell what shape the yard was. But I now knew what was wrong with Miss Rena Randolph. She was crazy.

As the evening wore along, we got fewer and fewer customers. They bought cigarettes and cigars, candy, magazines. Very few cars went past. The town clock struck nine, and this surprised me, because I hadn't realized it was so late. My father always closed the store at nine-thirty. I had never closed it—or opened it, for that matter. I did not know where the keys to the front door were kept. I watched the clock, wondering what I should do at nine-thirty.

At quarter past nine, there was only one customer in the store—a woman who had purchased a box of candy. I was wrapping it up for her when someone pulled the screen door open with an abrupt, yanking movement and Pedro said, "Ah—"

I looked up and saw my father standing in the doorway, swaying back and forth, his arms extended. As I watched, he reached out and supported himself by leaning against the doorjamb. His appearance was so strange, he seemed so weak, so unlike himself, that I thought, He's been wounded. I peered at him, hunting for bruises on his face or his hands. As he entered the store, he kept looking around, blinking. He was wearing his light-gray suit, and his newest boater hat, and the bow tie that I remembered. But the tie was twisted around to one side and it was partly untied, and his suit looked rumpled and so did his shirt.

I escorted the customer to the door, held it open for her, and then went to my father and said, "We—we didn't know where you were. Are you all right?"

He patted my hand. He said, "Look," and he smiled, revealing a set of glittering, horrible, wolfish-looking false teeth. There was a dribble of dried blood at the corner of his mouth. "I got my teeth."

I could barely understand what he said. He sounded as though he were speaking through or around a formidable obstruction that prevented his tongue and his lips from performing their normal function. The teeth glistened like the white porcelain fixtures in the downstairs bathroom.

I said, "Oh," weakly.

Pedro patted my father's arm. He said, "I worried—"

"Am I always going to sound like this?"

"I don't think so," I said.

He went into the prescription room and sat down in the chair by the window. Pedro stood beside him. I sat down on the high stool in front of the counter.

"Where's Sophy?"

I jumped off the stool. "They've gone to the police. I must telephone them—"

"Police? Police?" He made whistling noises when he said this. "Jesus Christ! For what?"

"They thought you were lost. I've got to call the Barracks—"

"Lawth?" he said, angrily. "Loweth?" he roared. "Lowerth? How could I be lowerth?" He stopped talking, reached up and took out the new false teeth, and wrapped them in his handkerchief. When he spoke again, he sounded just like himself. "I read about this place in Norwich where they take all your teeth out at once and put the false teeth in—make them for you and put them in all the same day. That's where I was. In Norwich. Getting my teeth. How could I get lost?"

"Oh!" I said and put my hand over my mouth, keeping the pain away. "Didn't it hurt? Don't the teeth hurt?"

"Hurt?" he shouted. "Of course they hurt!"

"But why didn't you tell Mother you were going?"

"I didn't think I'd be gone more than two hours. I got on a bus up at the corner, and it didn't take long to get there. They pulled the teeth out. Then they took impressions. They wouldn't let me have the teeth right away, said they had to wait to make sure the jaw had stopped bleeding, and so the whole process took longer than I thought it would."

"What made you finally get false teeth?" I didn't think it was pictures of the Valentino types, with their perfect white teeth, that I'd left around for him to see, and I didn't think it was the sight of Gramps Fender, the old man who took care of the house next door and whose false teeth hung loose in his mouth, or the fact that my Aunt Sophronia and my mother kept talking about the importance of chewing as an aid to the digestion of food. So if it wasn't any of these things, then what was it?

He sighed and said that that morning, while he was shaving, he had run through a solo he was to sing in church on Sunday. He stood in front of that new plate-glass mirror in the downstairs bathroom under all that brilliant white light, and he opened his mouth wide, and he saw himself in the mirror—the open mouth all red and moist inside, and the naked gums with a tooth here and there, and it was the mouth of an idiot out of Shakespeare, it was the mouth of the nurse in "Romeo and Juliet," the mouth of the gravediggers in "Hamlet," but, most shocking of all, it was the mouth of Samuel Layen. This was what the congregation looked at and into on Sunday mornings. He said he couldn't bear the thought that that was what all those white people saw when he sang a solo. If he hadn't seen his mouth wide open like that in the new mirror under that new light. . . .

I thought, But the congregation couldn't possibly see the inside of his mouth—he's in the choir loft when he sings, and he's much too far away from them. But I didn't say this.

He said it was while he was standing under the first cherry tree, looking up at the sky and listening to the hum of the bees, that he decided he would take a bus and head for Norwich and get himself some false teeth that very day without saying anything about it to anyone. He put the teeth back in his mouth and turned to Pedro and said, in that mumbling, full-of-pebbles voice, "How do I look?," and he smiled.

Pedro said, "You look beautiful, Mr. Layen," and touched him gently on the shoulder.

I went into the phone booth and closed the door. I started to dial the number of the state police. It was on a card up over the phone, along with the telephone numbers of the local doctors and the firehouse. I hesitated. The phone booth smelled of all its recent users—of cigar smoke, perfume, sweat. I felt as constrained as though all of these people were in the booth with me: politicians, idle females, workmen. I couldn't imagine myself saying, "We thought my father was missing. He's been gone all day and my mother and my aunt have now reported him as missing, but he's back." Why didn't I feel free to say this? Was it the presence of those recent users of the phone booth, who might ask, "Where'd he go?" "Has he done this before?" "Has he got a girl friend?" I dialled the number, and a gruff voice said, "State police. Tenyeck Barracks. Officer O'Toole speaking."

I didn't know what to say to him, so I didn't say anything.

The voice sounded loud, impatient, in my ear. "*Hu*llo! *He*llo? Speak up! Speak up!"

If I said that we thought my father was missing but he isn't, he's found, he's back, then wouldn't this Officer O'Toole want to know where he'd been? I said, "Well—"

The voice said, "Hello? Hello?" and "Yes?" and "What is it?" It was a very gruff voice, and it had a barking quality.

I shook my head at the voice. I was not free to speak openly to that gruff policeman's voice. I thought, Well, now, perhaps the reason my father hadn't wanted to replace his teeth was that one of the images of the black man that the white man carries around with him is of white teeth flashing in a black and grinning face. So my father went toothless to destroy that image. But then there is toothless old Uncle Tom, and my old black mammy with her head rag is toothless, too, and without teeth my father fitted *that* image of the black man, didn't he?

So he was damned either way. Was he not? And so was I. And so was I.

Then I thought, Why bother? Why not act just like other people, just this once, just like white people—come right out and say the lost is found. My hand, my own hand, had in response to some order from my subconscious reached for a pencil that was securely fastened to a nail in the booth, tied there by a long red string. The pencil hung next to a big white pad. This was where we wrote down telephone orders. I was doodling on the big white pad. The skin on my hand was so dark in contrast to the white pad that I stared, because it was the second time that day that I had taken a good look at the color of my skin against something stark white. I looked at my dark-brown hand and thought, Throw that baby down to me, you ain't goin' to take us back now, you know; all of us people with this dark skin must help hold the black island inviolate. I said, "This is Mr. Layen's daughter, at Layen's Drugstore in Wheeling. Mrs. Layen and her sister, Miss Bart, are on their way over there. Will you tell them that Mr. Layen found his watch—"

"Found his watch? He lost it, did he? Valuable watch, I suppose. Wait a minute. They're just coming up the steps now, just coming in the door. Wait a minute. I'll let you talk to Mrs. Layen yourself."

Everybody knew us for miles and miles around. We were those rare laboratory specimens the black people who ran the drugstore in the white town of Wheeling, New York, only black family in town except for the Granites, who, ha, ha, ha—

"Wait a minute," the gruff, barking voice said again.

I closed my eyes and I could see my mother and my aunt—two bent-over little colored women, going up the steps of the state-police barracks in Tenyeck, humble, hesitant, the whites of their eyes showing under the irises.

My mother's voice sounded in my ear. "Yes?" Harsh, loud.

I said, "Father is so happy. He found his watch. He thinks he dropped it in Norwich, where he went to get his new false teeth." It sounded as though he'd always had false teeth—or, at least Officer O'Toole, who was undoubtedly listening in, would think so.

S.A. Williams

Tell martha not to moan

Shirley A. Williams, who writes under the name S. A. Williams, was born in Central Valley, California, and was graduated from Fresno State College; she has been a teacher and administrator of Black Studies programs in Washington, D.C. and Georgia, as well as in her home state. She has also worked in Alabama as an administrative intern in the office of the president of Mills College in Birmingham.

In "Tell Martha Not to Moan," she delineates with compassion for her characters and a meticulous ear for their language one of the trials faced, and often triumphed over, by Black women.

My mama a big woman, tall and stout and men like her cause she soft and fluffy looking. When she round them it all smiles and dimples and her mouth be looking like it couldn't never be fixed to say nothing but darling and honey.

They see her now, they sho see something different. I should not even come today. Since I had Larry things ain't been too good between us. But—that's my mamma and I know she gon be there when I need her. And sometime when I come, it okay. But this ain't gon be

114

one a them times. Her eyes looking all ove me and I
know it coming. She snort cause she want to say god
damn but she don't cuss. "When it due, Martha?"

First I start to say, what. But I know it ain't no use.
You can't fool old folks bout something like that, so I tell
her.

"Last part of November."

"Who the daddy?"

"Time."

"That man what play piano at the Legion?"

"Yeah."

"What he gon do bout it?"

"Mamma, it ain't too much he can do, now is it? The
baby on its way."

She don't say nothing for a long time. She sit looking
at her hands. They all wet from where she been washing dishes and they all wrinkled like yo hands be when
they been in water too long. She get up and get a dish
cloth and dry em, then sit down at the table. "Where
he at now?"

"Gone."

"Gone? Gone where?" I don't say nothing and she
start cussing then. I get kinda scared cause mamma
got to be real mad foe she cuss and I don't know who
she cussing—me or Time. Then she start talking to me.
"Martha, you just a fool. I told you that man wan't no

good first time I seed him. A musician the worst kind
of man you can get mixed up with. Look at you. You ain't
even eighteen years old yet, Larry just barely two and
here you is pregnant again." She go on like that for a
while and I don't say nothing. Couldn't no way. By the
time I get my mouth fixed to say something, she done
raced on so far ahead that what I got to say don't have
nothing to do with what she saying right then. Finally
she stop and ask, "What you gon do now? You want to
come back here?" She ain't never like me living with
Orine and when I say no, she ask, "Why not? It be
easier for you."

I shake my head again. "If I here, Time won't know
where to find me, and Time coming; he be back. He gon
to make a place for us, you a see."

"Hump, you just played the fool again, Martha."

"No mamma, that not it at all; Time want me."

"Is that what he say when he left?"

"No, but. . ."

Well, like the first night we met, he come over to
me like he knowed me for a long time and like I been
his for awmost that long. Yeah, I think that how it
was. Cause I didn' even see him when we come in the
Legion that first night.

Me and Orine, we just got our checks that day. We
went downtown and Orine bought her some new dresses.
But the dress she want to wear that night don't look
right so we go racing back to town and change it. Then
we had to hurry home and get dressed. It Friday night
and the Legion crowded. You got to get there early on
the week-end if you want a seat. And Orine don't want

just any seat; she want one right up front. "Who gon see you way back there? Nobody. They can't see you, who gon ask you to dance? Nobody. You don't dance, how you gon meet people? You don't meet people, what you doing out?" So we sit up front. Whole lots a people there that night. You can't even see the bandstand cross the dance floor. We sharing the table with some more people and Orine keep jabbing me, telling me to sit cool. And I try cause Orine say it a good thing to be cool.

The set end and people start leaving the dance floor. That when I see Time. He just getting up from the piano. I like him right off cause I like men what look like him. He kind of tall and slim. First time I ever seed a man wear his hair so long and it nappy—he tell me once it an African Bush—but he look good anyway and he know it. He look round all cool. He step down from the bandstand and start walking toward me. He come over to the table and just look. "You," he say, "you my Black queen." And he bow down most to the floor.

Ah shit! I mad cause I think he just trying to run a game. "What you trying to prove, fool?" I ask him.

"Ah man," he say and it like I cut him. That the way he say it. "Ah man. I call this woman my Black queen— tell her she can rule my life and she call me a fool."

"And sides what, nigga," I tell him then, "I ain't black." And I ain't, I don't care what Time say. I just a dark woman.

"What's the matter, you shamed of being Black? Ain't nobody told you Black is pretty?" He talk all loud and people start gathering round. Somebody say, "Yeah, you tell her bout it, soul." I embarrassed and I look over at Orine. But she just grinning, not saying nothing. I guess she waiting to see what I gon do so I stand up.

"Well if I is black, I is a fine black." And I walk over to the bar. I walk just like I don't know they watching my ass, and I hold my head up. Time follow me right on over to the bar and put his arm round my shoulder.

"You want a drink?" I start to say no cause I scared. Man not supposed to make you feel like he make me feel. Not just like doing it—but, oh, like it right for him to be there with me, touching me. So I say yes. "What's your name?" he ask then.

I smile and say, "They call me the player." Orine told a man that once in Berkeley and he didn't know what to say. Orine a smart woman.

"Well they call me Time and I know yo mamma done told you Time ain't nothing to play with." His smile cooler than mine. We don't say nothing for a long while. He just stand there with his arm round my shoulder looking at us in the mirror behind the bar. Finally he say, "Yeah, you gon be my Black queen." And he look down at me and laugh. I don't know what to do, don't know what to say neither, so I just smile.

"You gon tell me your name or not?"

"Martha."

He laugh. "That a good name for you."

"My mamma name me that so I be good. She name all us kids from the Bible," I tell him laughing.

"And is you good?"

I nod yes and no all at the same time and kind of

mumble cause I don't know what to say. Mamma really did name all us kids from the Bible. She always saying, "My mamma name me Veronica after the woman in the Bible and I a better woman for it. That why I name all my kids from the Bible. They got something to look up to." But mamma don't think I'm good, specially since I got Larry. Maybe Time ain't gon think I good neither. So I don't answer, just smile and move on back to the table. I hear him singing soft-like, "Oh Mary don't you weep, tell yo sister Martha not to moan." And I kind of glad cause most people don't even think bout that when I tell em my name. That make me know he really smart.

We went out for breakfast after the Legion close. Him and me and Orine and German, the drummer. Only places open is on the other side of town and at first Time don't want to go. But we finally swade him.

Time got funny eyes, you can't hardly see into em. You look and you look and you can't tell nothing from em. It make me feel funny when he look at me. I finally get used to it, but that night he just sit there looking and don't say nothing for a long time after we order.

"So you don't like Black?" he finally say.

"Do you?" I ask. I think I just ask him questions, then I don't have to talk so much. But I don't want him to talk bout that right then, so I smile and say, "Let's talk bout you."

"I am not what I am." He smiling and I smile back, but I feel funny cause I think I supposed to know what he mean.

"What kind of game you trying to run?" Orine ask.

Then she laugh. "Just cause we from the country don't mean we ain't hip to niggas trying to be big-time. Ain't that right, Martha?"

I don't know what to say, but I know Time don't like that. I think he was going to cuss Orine out, but German put his arm round Orine and he laugh. "He just mean he ain't what he want to be. Don't pay no mind to that cat. He always trying to blow some shit." And he start talking that talk, rapping to Orine.

I look at Time. "That what you mean?"

He all lounged back in the seat, his legs stretched way out under the table. He pour salt in a napkin and mix it up with his finger. "Yeah, that's what I mean. That's all about me. Black is pretty, Martha." He touch my face with one finger. "You let white people make you believe you ugly. I bet you don't even dream."

"I do too."

"What you dream?"

"Huh?" I don't know what he talking bout. I kind of smile and look at him out the corner of my eye. "I dreams bout a man like you. Why, just last night, I dream—"

He start laughing. "That's all right. That's all right."

The food come then and we all start eating. Time act like he forgot all bout dreams. I never figure out how he think I can just sit there and tell him the dreams I have at night, just like that. It don't seem like what I dream bout at night mean as much as what I think bout during the day.

We leaving when Time trip over this white man's feet. That man's feet all out in the aisle but Time don't never be watching where he going no way. "Excuse me," he say kind of mean.

"Say, watch it buddy." That white man talk most as nasty as Time. He kind of old and maybe he drunk or an Okie.

"Man, I said excuse me. You the one got your feet in the aisle."

"You," that man say, starting to get up, "you better watch yourself, boy."

And what he want to say that for? Time step back and say real quiet, "No, motherfucker. You the one. You better watch yourself and your daughter too. See how many babies she gon have by boys like me." That man get all red in the face, but the woman in the booth with him finally start pulling at him, telling him to sit down, shut up. Cause Time set to kill that man.

I touch Time's arm first, then put my arm round his waist. "Ain't no use getting messed behind somebody like that."

Time and that man just looking at each other, not wanting to back down. People was gon start wondering what going on in a few minutes. I tell him, " 'Got something for you, baby,' " and he look down at me and grin. Orine pick it up. We go out that place singing, " 'Good loving, good, good loving, make you feel so clean.' "

"You like to hear me play?" he ask when we in the car.

"This the first time they ever have anybody here that sound that good."

"Yeah," Orine say. "How come you all staying round a little jive-ass town like Ashley?"

"We going to New York pretty soon," Time say kind of snappy.

"Well, shit, baby, you—"

"When you going to New York?" I ask real quick. When Orine in a bad mood, can't nobody say nothing right.

"Couple of months." He lean back and put his arm round me. "They doing so many things with music back there. Up in the City, they doing one maybe two things. In L. A. they doing another one, two things. But, man, in New York, they doing everything. Person couldn't never get stuck in one groove there. So many things going on, you got to be hip, real hip to keep up. You always growing there. Shit, if you 'live and playing, you can't help but grow. Say, man," he reach and tap German on the shoulder, "let's leave right now."

We all crack up. Then I say, "I sorry but I can't go, got to take care of my baby."

He laugh, "Sugar, you got yo baby right here."

"Well, I must got two babies then."

We pull up in front of the partment house then but don't no one move. Finally Time reach over and touch my hair. "You gon be my Black queen?"

I look straight ahead at the night. "Yeah," I say. "Yeah."

We go in and I check first on Larry cause sometimes that girl don't watch him good. When I come in some nights, he be all out the cover and shivering but too sleepy to get back under em. Time come in when I'm pulling the cover up on Orine two kids.

"Which one yours?" he ask.

I go over to Larry bed. "This my baby," I tell him.

"What's his name?"

"Larry."

"Oh, I suppose you name him after his daddy?"

I don't like the way he say that, like I was wrong to name him after his daddy. "Who else I gon name him after?" He don't say nothing and I leave him standing there. I mad now and I go in the bedroom and start pulling off my clothes. I think, that nigga can stand up in the living room all night, for all I care; let Orine talk to German and him, too. But Time come in the bedroom and put his arms round me. He touch my hair and my face and my tittie, and it scare me. I try to pull away but he hold me too close. "Martha," he say, "Black Martha." Then he just stand there holding me, not saying nothing, with his hand covering one side on my face. I stand there trembling but he don't notice. I know a woman not supposed to feel the way I feel bout Time, not right away. But I do.

He tell me things nobody ever say to me before. And I want to tell him that I ain't never liked no man much as I like him. But sometime you tell a man that and he go cause he think you liking him a whole lot gon hang him up.

"You and me," he say after we in bed, "we can make it together real good." He laugh. "I used to think all I needed was that music, but it take a woman to make that music sing, I think. So now stead of the music and me, it be the music and me and you."

"You left out Larry," I tell him. I don't think he want to hear that. But Larry my baby.

"How come you couldn't be free," he say real low. Then, "How you going when I go if you got a baby?"

"When you going?"

He turn his back to me. "Oh, I don't know. You know what the song say, 'When a woman take the blues,

She tuck her head and cry. But when a man catch the blues, He grab his shoes and slide.' Next time I get the blues," he laugh a little, "next time the man get too much for me, I leave here and go someplace else. He always chasing me. The god damn white man." He turn over and reach for me. "You feel good. He chasing me and I chasing dreams. You think I'm crazy, huh? But I'm not. I just got so many, many things going on inside me I don't know which one to let out first. They all want out so bad. When I play—I got to be better, Martha. You gon help me?"

"Yes, Time, I help you."

"You see," and he reach over and turn on the light and look down at me, "I'm not what I am. I up tight on the inside but I can't get it to show on the outside. I don't know how to make it come out. You ever hear Coltrane blow? That man is together. He showing on the outside what he got on the inside. When I can do that, then I be somewhere. But I can't go by myself. I need a woman. A Black woman. Them other women steal your soul and don't leave nothing. But a Black woman—" He laugh and pull me close. He want me and that all I care bout.

Mamma come over that next morning and come right on in the bedroom, just like she always do. I kind of shamed for her to see me like that, with a man and all, but she don't say nothing cept scuse me, then turn away. "I come to get Larry."

"He in the other bedroom," I say starting to get up.

"That's okay; I get him." And she go out and close the door.

I start to get out the bed anyway. Time reach for his cigarettes and light one. "Your mamma don't believe in knocking, do she?"

I start to tell him not to talk so loud cause mamma a hear him, but that might make him mad. "Well, it ain't usually nobody in here with me for her to walk in on." I standing by the bed buttoning my house coat and Time reach out and pull my arm, smiling.

"I know you ain't no tramp, Martha. Come on, get back in bed."

I pull my arm way and start out the door. "I got to get Larry's clothes together," I tell him. I do got to get them clothes together cause when mamma come for Larry like that on Sadday morning, she want to keep him for the rest of the weekend. But—I don't know. It just don't seem right for me to be in the bed with a man and my mamma in the next room.

I think Orine and German still in the other bedroom. But I don't know; Orine don't too much like for her mens to stay all night. She say it make a bad impression on her kids. I glad the door close anyway. If mamma gon start talking that "why don't you come home" talk the way she usually do, it best for Orine not to hear it.

Orine's two kids still sleep but mamma got Larry on his bed tickling him and playing with him. He like that. "Boy, you sho happy for it to be so early in the morning," I tell him.

Mamma stop tickling him and he lay there breathing hard for a minute. "Big mamma," he say laughing and pointing at her. I just laugh at him and go get his clothes.

"You gon marry this one?" Every man I been with since I had Larry, she ask that about.

"You think marrying gon save my soul, Mamma?" I sorry right away cause mamma don't like me to make fun of God. But I swear I gets tired of all that. What I want to marry for anyway? Get somebody like daddy always coming and going and every time he go leave a baby behind. Or get a man what stay round and beat me all the time and have my kids thinking they big shit just cause they got a daddy what stay with them, like them saddity kids at school. Shit, married or single they still doing the same thing when they goes to bed.

Mamma don't say nothing else bout it. She ask where he work. I tell her and then take Larry in the bathroom and wash him up.

"The older you get, the more foolish you get, Martha. Them musicians ain't got nothing for a woman. Lots sweet talk and babies, that's all. Welfare don't even want to give you nothing for the one you got now, how you gon—" I sorry but I just stop listening. Mamma run her mouth like a clatterbone on a goose ass sometime. I just go on and give her the baby and get the rest of his things ready.

"So your mamma don't like musicians, huh?" Time say when I get back in the bedroom. "Square-ass people. Everything they don't know about, they hate. Lord deliver me from a square-ass town with square-ass people." He turn over.

"You wasn't calling me square last night."

"I'm not calling you square now, Martha."

I get back in the bed then and he put his arm round me. "But they say what they want to say. Long as they don't mess with me things be okay. But that's impossible. Somebody always got to have their little say about your life. They want to tell you where to go, how to play, what to play, where to play it—shit, even who to fuck and how to fuck em. But when I get to New York—"

"Time, let's don't talk now."

He laugh then, "Martha, you so Black." I don't know what I should say so I don't say nothing, just get closer and we don't talk.

That how it is lots a time with me and him. It seem like all I got is lots little pitchers in my mind and can't tell nobody what they look like. Once I try to tell him bout that, bout the pitchers, and he just laugh. "Least your head ain't empty. Maybe now you got some pictures, you get some thoughts." That make me mad and I start cussing, but he laugh and kiss me and hold me. And that time, when we doing it, it all—all angry and like he want to hurt me. And I think bout that song he sing that first night bout having the blues. But that the only time he mean like that.

Time and German brung the piano a couple days after that. The piano small and all shiny black wood. Time cussed German when German knocked it against the front door getting it in the house. Time want to put it in the bedroom but I want him to be thinking bout me, not some damn piano when he in there. I tell him he put it in the living room or it don't come in the house. Orine don't want it in the house period, say it too damn noisy—that's what she tell me. She don't say nothing to Time. I think she half-way scared of him. He pretty good bout playing it though. He don't never play it when the babies is sleep or at least he don't play loud as he can. But all he thinking bout when he playing is that piano. You talk to him, he don't answer; you touch him, he don't look up. One time I say to him, "pay me some tention," but he don't even hear. I hit his hand, not hard, just playing. He look at me but he don't stop playing. "Get out of here, Martha." First I start to tell him he can't tell me what to do in my own self's house, but he just looking at me. Looking at me and playing and not saying nothing. I leave.

His friends come over most evenings when he home, not playing. It like Time is the leader. Whatever he say go. They always telling him how good he is. "Out of sight, man, the way you play." "You ought to get out of this little town so somebody can hear you play." Most times, he just smile and don't say nothing, or he just say thanks. But I wonder if he really believe em. I tell him, sometime, that he sound better than lots a them men on records. He give me his little cool smile. But I feel he glad I tell him that.

When his friends come over, we sit round laughing and talking and drinking. Orine like that cause she be playing up to em all and they be telling her what a fine ass she got. They don't tell me nothing like that cause Time be sitting right there, but long as Time telling me, I don't care. It like when we go to the Legion, after Time and German started being with us. We all the time get in free then and get to sit at one a the big front tables. And Orine like that cause it make her think she big time. But she still her same old picky self; all the time telling me to "sit cool, Martha," and "be cool, girl." Acting like cool the most important thing in the world. I finally just tell her, "Time like me just the way I am, cool or not." And it true; Time always saying that I be myself and I be fine.

Time and his friends, they talk mostly bout music, music and New York City and white people. Sometime I get so sick a listening to em. Always talking bout how they gon put something over on the white man, gon take something way from him, gon do this, gon do that. Ah shit! I tell em. But they don't pay me no mind.

German say, one night, "Man, this white man come asking if I want to play at his house for—"

"What you tell him, man, 'Put money in my purse?'" Time ask. They all crack up. Me and Orine sit there quiet. Orine all swole up cause Time and them running some kind of game and she don't know what going down.

"Hey, man, yo all member that time up in Frisco when we got fired from that gig and wan't none of our old ladies working?" That Brown, he play bass with em.

"Man," Time say, "all I remember is that I stayed high most of the time. But how'd I stay high if ain't nobody had no bread? Somebody was putting something in somebody's purse." He lean back laughing a little. "Verna's mamma must have been sending her some money till she got a job. Yeah, yeah man, that was it. You remember the first time her mamma sent that money and she gave it all to me to hold?"

"And what she wanna do that for? You went out and gambled half a it away and bought pot with most of the rest." German not laughing much as Time and Brown.

"Man, I was scared to tell her, cause you remember how easy it was for her to get her jaws tight. But she was cool, didn't say nothing. I told her I was going to get food with the rest of the money and asked her what she wanted, and—"

"And she say cigarettes," Brown break in laughing, "and this cat, man, this cat tell her, 'Woman, we ain't wasting this bread on no non-essentials!'" He doubled over laughing. They all laughing. But I don't think it that funny. Any woman can give a man money.

"I thought the babe was gon kill me, her jaws was so tight. But even with her jaws tight, Verna was still cool. She just say, 'Baby, you done fucked up fifty dollars on non-essentials; let me try thirty cents.'"

That really funny to em. They all cracking up but me. Time sit there smiling just a little and shaking his head. Then, he reach out and squeeze my knee and smile at me. And I know it like I say; any woman can give a man money.

German been twitching round in his chair and finally he say, "Yeah, man, this fay dude want me to play at his house for fifty cent." That German always got to hear hisself talk. "I tell him take his fifty cent and shove it up his ass—oh scuse me. I forgot that baby was here—but I told him what to do with it. When I play for honkies, I tell him, I don't play for less than two hundred dollars and he so foolish he gon pay it." They all laugh, but I know German lying. Anybody offer him ten cent let lone fifty, he gon play.

"It ain't the money, man," Time say. "They just don't know what the fuck going on." I tell him Larry sitting right there. I know he ain't gon pay me no mind, but I feel if German can respect my baby, Time can too. "Man they go out to some little school, learn a few chords, and they think they know it all. Then they come round to the clubs wanting to sit in with you. Then, if you working for a white man, he fire you and hire him. No, man, I can't tie shit from no white man."

"That where you wrong," I tell him. "Somebody you don't like, you supposed to take em for everything they got. Take em and tell em to kiss yo butt."

"That another one of your pictures, I guess," Time say. And they all laugh cause he told em bout that, too, one time when he was mad with me.

"No, no," I say. "Listen, one day I walking downtown and this white man offer me a ride. I say okay and get in the car. He start talking and hinting round and finally he come on out and say it. I give you twenty dollars, he say. I say okay. We in Chinatown by then and at the next stop light he get out his wallet and give me a twenty dollar bill. 'That what I like bout you colored women,' he say easing all back in his seat just like he already done got some and waiting to get some more. 'Yeah,' he say, 'you all so easy to get.' I put that money in my purse, open the door and tell him, 'Motherfucker, you ain't got shit here,' and slam the door."

"Watch your mouth," Time say, "Larry sitting here." We all crack up.

"What he do then?" Orine ask.

"What could he do? We in Chinatown and all them colored folks walking round. You know they ain't gon' let no white man do nothing to me."

Time tell me after we go to bed that night that he kill me if he ever see me with a white man.

I laugh and kiss him. "What I want with a white man when I got you?" We both laugh and get in the bed. I lay stretched out waiting for him to reach for me. It funny, I think, how colored men don't never want no colored women messing with no white mens but the first chance he get, that colored man gon be right there in that white woman's bed. Yeah, colored men sho give colored womens a hard way to go. But I know if Time got to give a hard way to go, it ain't gon be for no scaggy fay babe, and I kinda smile to myself.

"Martha—"

"Yeah, Time," I say turning to him.

"How old you—eighteen?—what you want to do in life? What you want to be?"

What he mean? "I want to be with you," I tell him.

"No, I mean really. What you want?" Why he want to know I wonder. Everytime he start talking serious-like, I think he must be hearing his sliding song.

"I don't want to have to ask nobody for nothing. I want to be able to take care of my own self." I won't be no weight on you, Time, I want to tell him. I won't be no trouble to you.

"Then what you doing on the Welfare?"

"What else I gon do? Go out and scrub somebody else's toilets like my mamma did so Larry can run wild like I did? No. I stay on Welfare a while, thank you."

"You see what the white man have done to us, is doing to us?"

"White man my ass," I tell him. "That was my no good daddy. If he'd got out and worked, we woulda been better off."

"How he gon work if the man won't let him?"

"You just let the man turn you out. Yeah, that man got yo mind."

"What you mean?" he ask real quiet. But I don't pay no tention to him.

"You always talking bout music and New York City, New York City and the white man. Why don't you forget all that shit and get a job like other men? I hate that damn piano."

He grab my shoulder real tight. "What you mean, 'got my mind?' What you mean?" And he start shaking me. But I crying and thinking bout he gon leave.

"You laugh cause I say all I got in my mind is pitchers but least they better than some old music. That all you ever think bout, Time."

"What you mean? What you mean?"

Finally I scream. "You ain't going no damn New York City and it ain't the white man what gon keep you. You just using him for a scuse cause you scared. Maybe you can't play." That the only time he ever hit me. And I cry cause I know he gon leave for sho. He hold me and say don't cry, say he sorry, but I can't stop. Orine bamming on the door and Time yelling at her to leave us lone and the babies crying and finally he start to pull away. I say, "Time . . ." He still for a long time, then he say, "Okay. Okay, Martha."

No, it not like he don't want me no more, he—

"Martha. Martha. You ain't been listening to a word I say."

"Mamma." I say it soft cause I don't want to hurt her. "Please leave me lone. You and Orine—and Time too, sometime—yo all treat me like I don't know nothing. But just cause it don't seem like to you that I know what I'm doing, that don't mean nothing. You can't see into my life."

"I see enough to know you just get into one mess after nother." She shake her head and her voice come kinda slow. "Martha, I named you after that woman in

the Bible cause I want you to be like her. Be good in the
same way she is. Martha, that woman ain't never
stopped believing. She humble and patient and the Lord
make a place for her." She lean her hands on the
table. Been in them dishes again, hands all wrinkled
and shiny wet. "But that was the Bible. You ain't got
the time to be patient, to be waiting for Time or no one
else to make no place for you. That man ain't no good. I
told you—"

Words coming faster and faster. She got the cow by
the tail and gon on down shit creek. It don't matter
though. She talk and I sit here thinking bout Time.
"You feel good . . . You gon be my Black queen? . . . We
can make it together . . . You feel good . . ." He be back.

Martin Hamer

Sarah

The blues have been described by Ralph Ellison
as "an impulse to keep the painful details and
episodes of a brutal experience alive in one's
aching consciousness, to finger its jagged
grain, and to transcend it, not by the consola-
tion of philosophy but by squeezing from it a
near-tragic, near-comic lyricism." Martin Hamer's Sarah suffers that impulse and fingers that
jagged grain, and she searches for and loses the
hard-to-find good man. Sarah is unable to transcend, but Hamer's sensitive account reaches
that lyricism.

When Martin Hamer, who was born in New
York City and grew up in Harlem, dropped
out of the City College of New York, he did so
to write. But jobs (editor, director of market-
ing for a large publishing house, director of an
art gallery) diverted him from his chosen path.
At his home in Westport, Connecticut, he has
returned to writing fulltime. One of his projects is a trip to Africa to research a new book
about the Afro-A-Kom, the sacred statue of the
Cameroons.

It snowed on Thanksgiving Day. With the wonder of
all the preparations and the knowledge that a man was
coming to visit, the snow was more than Clyde could

bear. "It's snowing!" he screamed. "Mama, it's snowing!" In a frenzy he ran into the kitchen to tell his mother the news. He was in the way; he was sent back into
the living room. He came sneaking back, frightening
his Aunt Bea with a loud "Boo!" He ran out again and
opened the window. The snow was falling in great silver
flakes. He took what he could catch in his hands and
blew it across the room. "Snow! Snow!" he cried. He was
placed in a chair and given a magazine.

Bea Boyce had come early to help out. She was a ro-
tund woman, forty-six years of age, with a romantic
air and quick brown eyes. As she moved around and
around, setting the open-leafed table, her taffeta dress
swished and swirled about her and she hummed in a
very high key. She placed the silverware with elaborate
care and folded the linen napkins into white fluffed
caps. When she remembered that the shoes she wore
were open at the toes, she said aloud to no one in particular that she hoped Mr. Boyce would think to bring her
rubbers. Then she began to whistle "The Twelve Days
of Christmas," the wobbly sound coming from between
her large, pursed lips, the effort hollowing her cheeks
and arching her penciled-in eyebrows. Sarah called
from the kitchen that house whistling was bad luck.

"It's not Christmas, anyway," Clyde said. "It's
Thanksgiving!" His aunt rolled her eyes at him, and he
pushed himself into the farthest corner of the chair
and tried to roll his eyes at her.

"You're getting too cute," she said. "Mr. George will
fix you, though. He's going to fix your wagon, but good!"

"Don't frighten the boy," said Sarah. She came from
the kitchen with the water glasses tinkling in her

slender hands, and after placing them on the table she viewed herself solemnly in the mirror. Her hair was drawn straight back from her oval face, and her pierced ears showed tiny pearl earrings to match the necklace hanging in the fullness of her breast. Unlike her sister's, her brown pupils moved slowly. Her expression was apprehensive, and there was the suggestion of a clown's sorrow about her mouth where the lipstick had been drawn boldly onto the dark facial skin of her upper lip. Turning her body from side to side, she smoothed her purple dress about her hips and asked Bea, "How do I look?"

"Like a belle of the ball," said Bea.

Sarah frowned. "A belle of the ball at forty. A real belle of the ball." She placed one leg out in front of her and pressed a hand to its knee. "I think this dress is too short."

"What do you mean, too short? Look at mine!"

"Yours is too short too," Sarah said.

"Well, honey, that's the style these days."

"Dress like this will only put ideas in his head."

"And that ain't what you want?"

"I most certainly do *not*. Getting a man means about as much to me as getting an ice-cream cone."

"Which is why," said Bea, "you're making all this fuss about dinner." She went back to the table and fluffed a fallen napkin. "You just better pray that Ann's not in one of her moods. 'Cause, child, she'll sure mess things up for you."

"She'd better not," said Sarah angrily. "She'd just better be on her *p*'s and *q*'s if she knows what's good for her."

"I can't see why you even invited her. You know how she is."

"I invited her for the same reason I invited you—you're family."

"Well," said Bea, "remember what Papa used to say: Ain't nothing worse—Ain't nothing worse than family."

"I just wish you'd shut up," said Sarah, "for once!"

The doorbell rang, and Clyde scrambled into the hallway calling, "Who is it? Who is it?"

"It's me!"

"It's me!"

"It is I," shouted the final and strongest voice from far below, and his Aunt Ann's three boys came thundering up the four flights to the landing. They swept past him, shaking snow, fists, and tongues in his face. When Ann appeared on the landing, she took his small bewildered form in her arms and pressed him deep into the damp fur collar of her coat. Before they were inside, the bell rang again and Mr. Boyce came up the stairs puffing. A great wool muffler swathed his neck, and his mustache sparkled with melting snow. Bea Boyce made it clear to everyone that he had not thought enough to bring her rubbers.

Ann sat near the oilstove and warmed her bony frame in its shimmering heat. She was dressed in black, and the huge iron cross that hung about her neck made her corner of the room solemnly remote. Mr. Boyce sprawled on the couch, hung one hand on his vest pocket in the manner of a train conductor, and caressed his bushy mustache with the other. His wife fluttered

among the children like a bird. "The boys have grown,"
she said. "They give no trouble," replied Ann. In less
than ten minutes, thought Sarah, they've used Clyde's
caps, broken his gun, crushed a plastic soldier, and rolled
most of his marbles under the piano. "Well," she
said loudly, "you all just make yourselves comfortable."
"Gimme that!" said Ann's oldest. Without looking up,
Ann said, "Now, now." Then she reached into her purse
and took out her Bible. Sarah picked up a cigarette from
the table and started to light it. Mr. Boyce brought out
a fat cigar. "I hope you're not going to light that thing
before dinner," said Bea. He glowered at her, rolling
the fat cigar between his jaundiced-looking fingers.
He harrumphed and placed it back in his pocket. Sarah's
match popped loudly, and Mr. Boyce watched as a cloud
of smoke obscured her. "Blow a smoke ring. Aunt Sarah!
Blow a smoke ring!" Bea frowned, the doorbell rang,
and everyone became silent. When a light rap sounded
at the door, Bea crossed her legs and whispered to Mr.
Boyce to sit straight. Ann took one hand from her Bible
and began to finger her cross. Her boys gaped stupidly
at the door, and Clyde moved cautiously toward his
mother. Sarah closed her eyes and prayed: Please, Lord,
don't let anything go wrong. "Come in!" she called.
"Come in!"

A huge man entered, his black coat glistening with
melted snow, and immediately a chilled air, heavy with
the pungent odor of stale tobacco, spread about the
room. "Come in, Mr. George," said Sarah. "Come in and
meet the folks." He removed his coat and stood before
them in a neat but tattered blue suit, a bright new white
shirt, and a faded maroon-colored tie. His gaze moved

easily from face to face; his slightly graying hair and soft features made him appear calm, but there was the indication of surprise in his manner, and his brow was drawn and deeply furrowed. Sarah introduced him to Mr. Boyce. "How do you do, sir," said Mr. George. Mr. Boyce was flattered. He pumped the tall man's arm, mumbling that it was a pleasure to meet a gentleman. Bea was squirming on the couch all the while, and by the time she was introduced her skirts were so high you could see where her stockings ended. When Sarah saw that Mr. George had noticed, she said, "Now, you wouldn't think she was the oldest, would you?" Everyone was silent. "And," Sarah went on loudly, "over here's my other sister, Ann."

Ann extended her left hand, holding on to her cross with her right. "I've heard a lot about you," she said.

"Thank you," said Mr. George warmly.

"I wouldn't be so quick to say thank you if I were you. You're not at all what I expected."

Mr. George stopped smiling. Sarah quickly said, "These are all her boys, except one. This one." She pushed Clyde forward. "This is Clyde. Well," she said to the boy, "what do you say?" Clyde stared at Mr. George and then retreated back behind Sarah.

"Boy sure needs to be taught," said Ann. "I've never seen a child so backward."

The fire could be heard burning in the oilstove, and Sarah closed her eyes to pray to God. "I brought you these," said Mr. George awkwardly. When Sarah turned, he was handing her two brown-paper-wrapped packages. Embarrassed, she mumbled "Thank you" and looked toward the floor. He was standing in a small puddle of dark water. "One of you boys fetch a piece of newspaper," she said loudly. "And one of you come take the gentleman's coat." Ann's boys moved furiously about the room. "The paper's in there," she screamed. "Take the coat in there, and the rest of you go get washed! Bea! Come help me in the kitchen." Bea rose like a princess, the swishing sound of her dress adding to the confusion. "Hurry up now, you boys," Sarah screamed. "Put those things up! Get washed! Dinner's almost ready." She turned to leave the room: she turned back. "Oh, have a seat, Mr. George. Do have a seat."

"And, dear Lord," droned Ann, asking the blessing, "help those of us who have erred from your path of right-eousness and who are even now sittin' in your house, at your table, eatin' your food without your grace." One of her boys snickered. A loud pop echoed in the silence, and as Ann continued the boy whimpered softly, the short, gurgling wheeze of his breath punctuating his sobs. "God, we thank you for this food which we are about to receive, for the nourishin' of the body, and for Christ's sake"—she looked up—"Amen."

"Amen," they all chorused.

"Leg or breast?" asked Sarah. "Just let me know." She carved the turkey, and the plates were passed in silence, filled with turnips, rice, and bread stuffing. Clyde poured the gravy on his plate for so long that Mr. Boyce quipped, "That bird can't swim, son." Everyone laughed; Bea frowned; then she went out of her way to pass Mr. George the bread. Struggling to cut her share of the bird, Sarah took time to make note. I'm going to have to speak to her before this day is over.

"How many churches, Mr. George," Ann began slowly, "do they have out there in Queens?" She rested her fork on her plate, the effort of the question distracting her from eating.

"What kind of churches?" asked Mr. George.

"Baptist," came the reply.

"Wouldn't know," he said curtly. "I'm Episcopalian."

Mr. Boyce grinned. Ann stiffened her bony frame until it loomed like a cattail over her boys. "How many of those do you have, then?"

Mr. George hesitated and looked toward the ceiling. In the interim Mr. Boyce belched. Sarah waited for him to excuse himself; then she asked Mr. George, "Did you know that the Boyces are business people? They own that candy store at the corner, one of the nicest in the neighborhood."

"Is that so?" said Mr. George.

"You in business too?" asked Mr. Boyce.

"No, not me," he said. "Don't you know I work with Sarah?"

"I thought you met in a dance hall," said Ann.

"I just read in the paper," said Mr. Boyce, "about two people who got married."

"What's that got to do with anything?" asked Bea.

"If you'd let me finish." He wiped his mouth. "I was going to say they got married in a dance hall."

"Couldn't be no worse sin," said Ann. She placed a finger in her mouth, and to Clyde's wonder and Sarah's chagrin removed a small bone covered with masticated food.

"Is that the wishbone?" Clyde asked.

"If it is," chimed Mr. Boyce, "better give it to his mama." He chuckled; Sarah banged her fork onto her plate, rose, and announced that she was going for dessert. In the kitchen she leaned against the cupboard and cried. They were all against her, and Bea was even trying to make time with him. Nothing's worse than family. Nothing's worse. Oh, Papa! Why'd you have to be right? She moved to get the dessert plates and saw the packages on the table. Unwrapping them carefully, she found the first was a bottle of Scotch; the second, a fuzz-covered monkey in a red velvet suit. It played a blue metal drum and raised a plastic bowler while marching to the sound of an unsteady, tinny beat. I don't know what he sees in me. Lord! I sure don't know what he sees in me. But if You let him go on seeing it, I'll treat him well, I swear it. I'll treat him well.

She re-entered the room and was pleased to see that Mr. George had become the center of attention. He had grown up not far from them on St. Nicholas Avenue, and he was telling them how nice Harlem was in those days. "Curtains at all the foyer windows," he said. "And I used to make my money by going around polishing the mailboxes."

"Yeah," said Mr. Boyce, "those were really the days. Really the days——"

"Now, out in Queens, where I am now——" he went on.

Sarah thought of Queens. Beautiful Queens. That's where she'd like to live. Throw out all this junk and move to Queens. Only thing I'd keep—she looked about the room—is the piano; Clyde will have to learn to play someday. And maybe the couch. It needs a new cover.

With a new cover it won't look so bad. She straightened her shoulders, walked to the table, and handed Clyde the monkey. "Say thank you to Mr. George," she prompted.

"Is that his father?" asked Ann's youngest.

"Hush!" said Ann.

"That's all right," Mr. George said. "Children don't know any better."

"You sure have a fine sense for the pumps in life," said Bea.

"Bumps!" corrected Mr. Boyce.

"Bumps, pumps!" screamed Bea. "No matter what you call it, you ain't got it!"

Mr. Boyce harrumphed and looked down at the table-cloth.

"Can't get together, get apart," said Ann sweetly. "Man's a worse worry than hell."

"Is that why you ain't got one?"

"Okay, now, you all," said Sarah.

"Okay yourself," screamed Bea. "You ain't much better. Different one every time you turn around!"

"Why don't you shut up!"

"Look to God," said Ann. "You all better learn to look to God for your happiness. Better put your faith in the Lord—"

Tears blurred Sarah's vision. I'm going to move to Queens, she thought. Beautiful Queens. And I'm not going to see any of them again.

The dessert was eaten in silence. Afterward, Bea announced that she would do the dishes, and Ann offered to help. Sarah sat with Mr. George on the couch while Ann's boys, who had overeaten, moved more or less circuitously about the room. They stumbled into

furniture and relatives like doped flies until finally
the two younger ones crashed into one another and
fell to the floor and to sleep. The oldest one continued
to traverse the route for about five more minutes, and
then, on receiving a sudden call from nature, he departed for the bathroom. He was found some time
later, asleep on the stool. Clyde, no longer finding it
necessary to protect his monkey, fell asleep near the
stove, and in the big chair nearby, Mr. Boyce, his belt
and shoes undone, began to snore. Soft shadows moved
across the cracked plaster walls of the green room.
Only an occasional clatter of a dish or piece of silverware from the kitchen interrupted the silence. Mr.
George yawned, stretched, and let his big hand fall
lightly on Sarah's thigh. She jumped. "What do you
think I am?" she said.

"We're finished," said Ann, entering the room.
"Well, will you look at this." She motioned toward
her boys and Bea's husband. "Child, what did you put in
that food? All right now, c'mon"—she clapped her hands.
"Everybody up and out! Dinner's over, day's over, time
to go home and to bed!"

The confusion began again. Mr. Boyce wanted Mr.
George's address; Sarah could not find a pencil. Bea
came back from the window with the news that so
much snow had fallen none of them would be able to get
home. "Then you all better hurry now," said Sarah,
"before it gets worse." She could not find a pencil, so
Mr. Boyce stood in the middle of the room and repeated
Mr. George's phone number over and over again until
all of the boys were shouting it at the top of their lungs.
Finally Sarah got them all to the door. "Good-by." "Good-

by." "Gimme that!" "So long." "You must come by the store sometime." "Mama! He took my—— " "Whenever you stop here, stop there." "Fine dinner, Sarah," said Mr. Boyce. "Why don't you come to church sometime?" "Gimme!" "Will you two behave! Give him back his monkey!" "So long, Mr. George," said Mr. Boyce. "Don't come crying to me," said Ann. "Stop it! You're pulling my clothes off." "Good-by." "Good-by." "So long." They left. Sarah watched them from the window, a huddled group of people in the cold night and the snow. "The world is a beautiful place," she said softly.

"What'd you say?" asked Mr. George.

"I said the world is a beautiful place."

"Only sometimes," he said. "Only sometimes."

Sarah sighed, discouraged that he could not feel what she felt, and began to tidy the room. She cleaned around Clyde, who had fallen asleep in a chair. She emptied the ashtrays and picked up bits of paper from the floor. Then she put the lights out, leaving the oilstove to light the room, and sat down on the couch next to Mr. George. "There's something I'd like to tell you," she said.

"What beats me," he interrupted, "is why you invited your whole family. I thought it was just going to be me, you, and the boy."

"You had to meet them sometime," she said, annoyed. "Anyway, I love my family—"

"Do they always act like that?" he asked.

"Like what?"

"Never mind," he said, and was silent.

She leaned back on the couch. "There's something I

have to tell you. Mr. George, I have to know how you feel about something I have to tell you."

He drew in his mouth reflectively and slapped a hand to his knee. "OK," he said, "I'm listening."

"Once I made a mistake," she went on slowly, "of not telling a fellow all about me. When people come to find out things about you later, they sometimes come to hate you. I want to tell you the worst things about me. That way, if you can't understand, we can quit and neither of us will be the worse off for it. If we stay together, I don't want to have any secrets from you."

"Sort of like a test, huh?" said Mr. George.

"Sort of," said Sarah. "I just hope I pass."

"Well, listen now, Sarah, I don't care about—"

"Hush! I've got to tell you this! Just like I had to have you meet my family—no matter how they treat me. You'll just have to understand. I want to tell you about Clyde's father." She paused, and when he remained quiet, she went on. "I met him in a museum five years ago when I was doing daywork on Fifty-seventh Street. I used to walk past that museum every day. They had this fence made out of wooden slats, and inside was a garden, a beautiful garden with a black stone pool and statues and everything. After a while I got to thinking that one day I was going to go there. Can you imagine that? Me, going to that museum. Well, one day I did." She stopped and listened. It was the wind gently rattling the sashes and tapping the snow lightly against the panes. "I'll never forget that day. It was a Sunday in August, and I had on my blue cotton dress, the one with the paisley print, and my white heels and white gloves. I was really dressed to kill. Really dressed to kill. I left my madam at two that afternoon, went straight there, and when I got inside I went to the lunchroom, ordered myself a glass of iced tea, and took it straight to the patio. I can't begin to tell you how I felt. There I was inside, sitting down, and I could see the place where I used to look through. Do you understand what I'm trying to say? Do you?"

"Sort of," said Mr. George. He stared steadily into the fire, rubbing the tips of his thumbs together.

"Well," Sarah said, "after a while I felt like I'd been there all my life. In fact, I was even getting a little bored, and then this fellow came up. He came over to my table and sat down. Just like that. He came over, sat down, and started to talk. We went together that same afternoon, and we stayed together after, for a year. I was really a fool." She shook her head sadly. "Some fool. But I loved him. I loved him because I could respect him. But I guess I respected him too much. I started being honest with him, and he started to hate me."

"What were you honest about?" asked Mr. George.

"I told him about the men I'd known. I never loved any of them, but I was hurt plenty, and even though it was in the past I had to tell him."

"Why?"

"I don't know. I guess it made me feel better. I don't know. The important thing is that he couldn't stand knowing I'd been with other men. And when I got pregnant, we broke up." She paused. "Ain't you going to say nothing?"

"What's there to say?" said Mr. George. He rested his head on the back of the couch and touched her shoulder with his hand. She stood up. "I'd better get Clyde to bed, and I think I'm getting a little sleepy too."

"You're——"

"Clyde! Get up and go to bed." He rose, half asleep, leaving his monkey balanced precariously in the chair, and left the room.

"You're sure making it hard for me," said Mr. George.

"Not if you're a man, I ain't making it hard. A man is supposed to understand a woman's weakness."

"That's not what I'm——"

"He's supposed to understand anything."

"OK!" shouted Mr. George. "I understand. Now, for the love of God, let's talk about something else."

"I wish I could! I wish I could meet somebody who could make me forget about him. Somebody with just a little of his good side. You know, he took me to more places in that one year than I've ever been before—or since! And please, don't get the idea that I'm saying we don't go out. I just mean he took me downtown, to places we can't afford to go to."

Mr. George stood. "Sarah, what do you want?"

She was silent for a while, and then she answered, "I don't know."

"Well," he said, "since you had your say tonight, maybe I'd better have mine." He paused while she sat down on the couch. "I like you." He turned from her and watched the shadows on the wall. "As far as anything else goes, I guess I ain't happy and I ain't sad. I'm sure not rich—but I ain't poor either. I ain't ugly and I ain't good-looking, and I don't like going downtown among white folks. They make me nervous."

The fire in the stove had burned low. The room was

almost dark, and he could barely see her face in the remaining light. "Will you look see how much oil's left in the stove?" she asked. He stooped and then kneeled, peering about the hot metal carefully. "Not much," he finally said. "Looks like it's on *E*."

"Well then, you'd better turn it out." He fumbled about for the knob while she went on talking in a low voice. "I've been on pins and needles all day," she said. "I wanted everything to go right. I even prayed to God." She went over to him. He was still fumbling about the stove, and when she touched him he tried to rise, almost knocking it over. "Damn it! I've never known a man to be so clumsy." His slap sent her crashing into the chair. "Oh, God," she cried, "aren't there any men left anywhere in this world!"

"*Chica, chica, chica, chi—ca, chi—ca, chi—ca.*" The fuzz-covered monkey in his red velvet suit stopped drumming when he bumped into her leg. She reached down, picked it up, and hurled it at him in the darkness.

R. J. Meaddough

Poppa's story

R. J. Meaddough, a native New Yorker, is a
member of the Harlem Writer's Guild, a
workshop which has produced many notable
writers. He is the author of *A White Negro with
a Button Down Mind,* a collection of short
stories.

"Poppa's Story" is unlike the other stories
in this collection. It is not even like other
stories by R. J. Meaddough. The story does not
seem to be a piece of the Black experience
in America. What, after all, does a futuristic
story about a man and a machine say about
Black people? To hint briefly—in 1793 a Yankee
tinkerer named Eli Whitney invented a
machine called the cotton gin. Remember?

The helicopter, following landing instructions closely,
set down on the Pan Am Heliport at precisely 9:57 a. m.
The fifth of several executives that alighted and scurried
toward the elevators was Leslie Turner, a heavy-set
black man with huge jowls—symbols of bourgeois plea-
sures past and present—too preoccupied, at the moment,
to be readily accessible. He waved in a perfunctory
manner at the landing personnel and the elevator
operator, secretly thrilled that they had a continuing
recognition of him, although he had ridden the same
helicopter from Scarsdale lo these past three years.

151

His tread, enshrined in handmade, spit-shined, Italian leather, continental-style shoes, was deliberate, almost ponderous in nature, and the full head of white hair added a distinguished contrast to his mahogany coloring.

Or was it four years? he thought, still distant in his analyses and computations. Let's see, the firm moved to the Pan Am building in 1963 and private helicopter service was provided immediately, and it had been in effect——

"Forty-seventh floor, Dr. Turner."

—in effect for four years prior to that, which made it a total of seven years——

"Dr. Turner! Forty-seventh floor, sir!"

"Oh! Oh, thank you *so much*."

He handled the vicuña overcoat carefully, seeing to it that it was draped just so on the wooden coat hanger, flicking a piece of lint that had had the audacity, the temerity, the effrontery to soil its appearance. Then, satisfied, he strode aggressively into his office, seated himself and pressed the button energizing the machines.

"Hail deux," he said, sarcastically, raising his arm in salute. *The machine pulsed, enigmatically.*

Automatically he pressed the CLEAR button, the first thing he did every morning, and the machine checked and cleared its circuits. *R-R-Rat-tat-tat-tat-tat-tat-tat! R-R-Rat tat-tat-tat! R-R-Rat-tat! R-R-Rat-tat! R-R-Rat-tat-tat-tat!* It paused, gurgled once, then shut itself off with a smooth self-satisfied *gluck*. Dials flickered briefly with surges of current, subsiding as regulating elements warmed up and began to take control.

"Mark IX, '65 series-mod. 1," he said, briefly, into the dictaphone. He pressed a button on the control panel and a small white *O* appeared in the upper right sector of the screen. The machine pulsed, *confidently*.

These '65 series were much better than the old Mark II: '57 or '58 series. Much more sophisticated, these were, more control, more gain, less error. The loss factor on these was 99 44/100; on the older ones, well, a man had room to swing. And there were rewards for winning.

Of course, he didn't know all that when he went into the interview. There was this telegram asking him to come to Williams Street at 5:30 p. m. Very urgent, the telegram said. So he went to their plush, air-conditioned offices and sat in one of their sterile, "modern" cubicles until this guy came in, beaming and smiling like he just ate shit and it didn't taste bad at all.

"Yes, Mr. Turner. We have your file right here." No preamble, no introduction. "Born 1910, Styx, Illinois, outside of Chicago. Attended Carver High School, graduated 1928; valedictorian of class. Attended City College of New York, 1928-1934. Received B. S. Degree in Electrical Engineering, graduated eighth in class of 113. Attended Columbia Graduate School of Engineering, 1934-1943. Received M. S. in Electrical Engineering. Received Doctorate in Electrical Engineering in June, 1955. Doctoral Thesis: 'Chip Theory: The Application of Integrated Circuits to the Social Sciences.'

"Experience: Systems Operations Research—Flaffstaf Breweries, Inc., 1934 to present. Assistant Director for Research, 1945 to present. Married, three children; I hospitalized. Activities: Congress of Racial Equality——

Tch! Tch!" he murmured, "resigned after two days and joined the National Urban League." He beamed. "You're hired, of course. Starting salary is twenty-six thousand per annum."

"Who," he said, pointedly, "are you?"

"Oh, I'm so sorry, forgive me. My name's Johnston, Personnel Director, and this is the Fail-Safe Amusement Corporation, we're very big in the West. Naturally you'll have all the standard executive benefits— stock options, paid-up pension plan, expense account, you know, all the normal goodies. When can you start?"

"Well," Leslie said, dazed. "I guess I can start in two weeks. This will be electronic research?"

"Yes, of course. Frankly, we've been very anxious to get someone of your caliber on board."

He walked out on his own cloud, stunned, disbelieving, uncomfortable. Twenty-six thousand; five hundred dollars a week! It opened the way to all the things Marion wanted. All the things the kids needed and a few extras besides. An acre in Scarsdale, room for the kids to play in. And grass, green grass, not park straw. A new car, a BMW or Mercedes-Benz, a Rolls-Royce maybe, but nothing American, the sloppy bastards. He caught sight of an American flag snapping roguishly in the wind and he smiled happily. Now it had meaning, now it had value, and beauty, sheer beauty against the blue sky. He barely restrained himself from saluting.

The machine pulsed, impatiently. He pressed another button and an *O* appeared in the lower left sector of the screen. There was an investigation, of course; the organization handled many defense contracts. There was the standard check of background, associates, and affiliations, plus several oral examinations. It normally took eight to twelve weeks for the process, but Johnston put through a Priority I request and they did it in ten days. The result was that he was granted the top clearance: "Q Clearance—Green." It was not clear whether he had the approval of the country, the Irish, or J. Edgar Von Hoover, but the manual said that he was cleared to attend top secret planning conferences—on an advisory basis, of course.

The machine pulsed, apathetically. What the hell was wrong? Leslie checked the time pulse of the next move from the time he pressed his button to the point that the machine reacted and an X appeared on the top center sector of the screen. Two and nine-tenths seconds, much too slow. He measured grid current into the main circuit, but everything seemed satisfactory. He hooked an "O-scope" into the circuit at the primary stage and analyzed the sine curve. It curved slightly on the lead edge; it should have been square. Hastily, he consulted the schematic. The 6JW8, the oscillator gate, must be opening late. Rapidly he put figures and information into the console computer, pushing the buttons to energize their circuits, and the wheels and dials began their passion dance in the name of science. They stopped suddenly, complete, reporting a consensus of the activity. Three to the negative twelfth power, three *mickey-mikes*. He consulted another chart to determine the power resistor he needed, pulled the oscillator unit and performed the needed surgery. *The machine pulsed, aggressively.*

Now came the whole snow job. They weren't content to have a home in Scarsdale. No sir, not my family, they wanted to keep a co-op apartment down in Harlem. Everybody trying to get *out* of Harlem and here they are breaking their butts to get *in*. Damn, he thought, we ain't ready. On second thought, though, somebody should write a book on the subtleties of prejudice in suburbia—dogs trained to crap on nobody's lawn but yours; people that build brick walls on either side of you; or when you catch a chill walking down the street—and it's summer.

Leslie paused, pulling out a special key for opening the bottom left drawer of the desk, which was always locked. Ancient bottles of Canadian Club stared up at him and he selected one, opened it, poured himself a drink on the rocks with the handy accouterments and downed it quickly; by God, that was good stuff.

Now there was the time, he laughed, when Marion was invited down the street to meet the neighbors and got introduced to the servants.

"Snotty bitches," Marion muttered, certainly out of character.

And how does one explain to kids why they were not invited to the party next door? It had been a revelation to him to see how the "other half" lived, such that he now felt supremely safe in the midst of Harlem. You could predict what motivated an action in Harlem; these people operated out of a different mechanism.

The machine pulsed, petulantly. He made a move and observed with satisfaction that the machine now took only one and five-tenths seconds to respond. He took a second drink, slowly this time, gazing at the pictures of Marion and the children on the desk. Roosevelt was in the hospital now, would be from now on. Too bad. Sandy was growing up like a beansprout, turning into a little heartbreaker like her mother. It was Wesley that bothered him. Wild, he was, and stubborn too. Thought he might learn something hanging out with David Giles, but that didn't last long. Young Giles had a head on his shoulders. Wesley'd rather drown than admit he couldn't swim.

God it's lonely here, he thought. Research doesn't have much of a communal element like some of the other divisions. Everybody's in his own cubicle; sort of individual team spirit, whatever the hell that is.

He pressed another button, checked the screen to make sure it would be a draw, then cleared the machine for another game, consulting a Book of Random Numbers to select his opening sequence. Then, on impulse, he switched circuits to force the machine to make the first move. An *X* appeared in the center sector of the screen.

The bottle was half empty now. He observed it with a measure of unsteadiness. His radio picked up a record by Lawrence Welk, and he roused himself and walked slowly toward the center of the cubicle. The curved banks of equipment left a six-foot square in the center of the room and he danced, slowly, to the music. *The machine pulsed, sinisterly.* He hummed it faintly to himself. It was a nice tune, hadn't heard it since 'forty-two or three, or whatever. But the room began to spin of its own volition and the dance floor, the dance floor seemed much smaller to him now. Surely his eyes played tricks upon him for the machines were anchored securely to the wall. He looked up at them, stacked nine feet high into air. The dials and the scales seemed to vibrate excessively and the normal hum of the motors took on a much higher whine. The fluorescent lighting flickered dismally in the background, adding a certain chiaroscuro to the scene and he stumbled backward, hand raised in fear, beginning to fall.

The machine pulsed, maliciously. The console computer began to chatter incessantly. *R-Rat-tat-tat-tat-tat! R-Rat-tat-tat-tat-tat! R-Rat-tat! R-Rat-tat! R-Rat-tat-tat-tat-tat!* Current appeared to be shooting wildly, sending gauge needles dancing and scurrying across their dials, and the machine banks seemed to be moving toward him.

"No, God, no," Leslie said, "NO-O-O-O!" he screamed. He got a hand under himself and pushed himself upright, dared not touch the walls, and made his way back to the desk, back to the console, and sat down with a sigh of relief. *The machine pulsed, disappointedly.*

He glanced up, after a moment, mopping perspiration from his face and neck. The machine showed no more than the normal activity, and the noise was at its normal hum.

It took him several minutes to distinguish the various buttons on the control panel, and to see the extent of the game on the screen. He was about to select a button when he recoiled, horrified. Pressing that button would have ruined the game, and he would have lost.

Naturally, they didn't mention what happened to the

man whose place he took until later. He lost a game to the machine and that was that. The machine, which had been programmed for this event, promptly went berserk. Alarms went off all over the building, bringing people on the double to witness the event. Alarms were also sounded throughout the city, the country, the world; and reporters from the major wire services, newspapers, magazines, and TV were on hand to cover the ceremony. At that time the culprit was introduced and denounced before the entire world. He couldn't play the game, the accusation would read, and he was banished forever from the counsels of men. And the law required that he affix the letter *B* to his signature: for Bitter.

Leslie had hoped, at one time, to get out of the game completely. The BOBI Organization had contacted him, very informally, about a position. Buckets of Blood Incorporated was a new Negro outfit looking for an electronic systems man familiar with the very latest techniques in the field. Unfortunately, they had been unable to meet his salary demands—they could only pay twenty thousand and no man wants to take a cut in salary to change positions. Still, they were a Black organization; maybe they would be a credit and a service to the race. It would mean pulling in the belt a notch, but well worth the effort. Then he got a call to drop in and see Johnston that afternoon.

"Ah, Turner," Johnston said, smiling broadly, "we'd like you to take over the research division now that old Slicdicht is retiring. You know the field as well or better than anyone else around; no reason you shouldn't get paid for it." He smiled happily. "Oh yes, the official title of the position is Senior Opponent and carries a salary of fifty-two thousand. And there's an automatic Responsible Cluster for your Leadership Pin."

He had stumbled out, grateful, all thoughts of resignation forever banished from his mind. *The machine pulsed, indifferently.*

But there was one other time when a major change was in the offing. Not a resignation, nothing as important as that. It had to do with Adam.

Now everybody knew Adam; he had IOU's afloat all over town. Adam was a good electronics engineer, too; fought the machine to a standstill every time. But Adam loved life more than he loved work. He had a place or a business, or someone in just about every important town in the world. He was known at all the best night-spots, always where the action was, a *bon vivant* who was the life of every party, who lied, cheated and stole from all parties with equal aplomb. But on this one day he asked Adam if he knew the answer. Could the new machines be beaten? Or were they forever doomed to these lousy six by six cubicles within the organization? With respect to the machines, must they always have a button-down mind?

Adam paused, blowing a smoke ring which he studied carefully to its point of dissipation. Then he smiled, slyly, "Hell, you're not supposed to win, just don't lose." *The machine pulsed, pragmatically.*

It was nearly five, time to go. Leslie cleared his screen for the next day and shrugged unsteadily into his overcoat. He glanced around once, making sure that everything was in order, that the bottles were locked up, and paused briefly in the doorway.

"Hail deux," he murmured, waving his fingers weakly once or twice, then he staggered out the door.

The machine pulsed, implacably.

Ernest Gaines

Three men

Ernest Gaines was born on a Louisiana plantation, which remains his spiritual home and the inspiration for the locale and many of the characters and episodes of his fiction. When he was fifteen years old, a family move to California took him from the fields in which he spent his childhood working. He was graduated from San Francisco State College in 1957 and won the Wallace Stegner Creative Writing Fellowship at Stanford University. A year later, he was the recipient of the Joseph Henry Jackson Literary Award. His first novel, *Catherine Carmier* (1964), has been followed by two other novels, *Of Love and Dust* and *The Autobiography of Miss Jane Pittman,* and by a collection of short stories, *Bloodline.*

The prison is both the reality of and the metaphor for the Black experience in America. "Let my people go," the spiritual says. "This jail is full of blues, I know they'll come down on me," Leroy Carr sings. And William Wells Brown describes his own slave narrative as "a voice from the prison-house unfolding the deeds of darkness which are these perpetuated."

Two of them was sitting in the office when I came in
there. One was sitting in a chair behind the desk, the
other one was sitting on the end of the desk. They looked
at me, but when they saw I was just a nigger they went
back to talking like I wasn't even there. They talked like
that two or three more minutes before the one behind the
desk looked at me again. That was T. J. I didn't know
who the other one was.

"Yeah, what you want?" T. J. said.

They sat inside a little railed-in office. I went closer
to the gate. It was one of them little gates that swung
in and out.

"I come to turn myself in," I said.

"Turn yourself in for what?"

"I had a fight with somebody. I think I hurt him."

T. J. and the other policeman looked at me like I was
crazy. I guess they had never heard of a nigger doing
that before.

"You Procter Lewis?" T. J. said.

"Yes, sir."

"Come in here."

I pushed the little gate open and went in. I made sure
it didn't swing back too hard and make noise. I stopped
a little way from the desk. T. J. and the other policeman
was watching me all the time.

"Give me some papers," T. J. said. He was looking up at me like he was still trying to figure out if I was crazy. If I wasn't crazy, then I was a smart aleck.

I got my wallet out my pocket. I could feel T. J. and the other policeman looking at me all the time. I wasn't supposed to get any papers out, myself, I was supposed to give him the wallet and let him take what he wanted. I held the wallet out to him and he jerked it out of my hand. Then he started going through every-thing I had in there, the money and all. After he looked at everything, he handed them to the other policeman. The other one looked at them, too; then he laid them on the desk. T. J. picked up the phone and started talking to somebody. All the time he was talking to the other person, he was looking up at me. He had a hard time making the other person believe I had turned myself in. When he hung up the phone, he told the policeman on the desk to get my records. He called the other police-man "Paul." Paul slid away from the desk and went to the file cabinet against the wall. T. J. still looked at me. His eyes was the color of ashes. I looked down at the floor, but I could still feel him looking at me. Paul came back with the records and handed them to him. I looked up again and saw them looking over the records together. Paul was standing behind T. J., looking over his shoulder.

"So you think you hurt him, huh?" T. J. asked, looking up at me again.

I didn't say anything to him. He was a mean, evil sonofabitch. He was big and red and he didn't waste time kicking your ass if you gived him the wrong answers. You had to weigh every word he said to you. Sometimes

you answered, other times you kept your mouth shut.
This time I passed my tongue over my lips and kept quiet.

It was about four o'clock in the morning, but it must've
been seventy-five in there. T. J. and the other policeman had on short-sleeve khaki shirts. I had on a white
shirt, but it was all dirty and torn. My sleeves was
rolled up to the elbows, and both of my elbows was
skinned and bruised.

"Didn't I bring you in here one time, myself?"
Paul said.

"Yes, sir, once, I think," I said. I had been there two or
three times, but I wasn't go'n say it if he didn't. I had
been in couple other jails two or three times, too, but
I wasn't go'n say anything about them either. If they
hadn't put it on my record that was they hard luck.

"A fist fight," Paul said. "Pretty good with your fists,
ain't you?"

"I protect myself," I said.

It was quiet in there for a second or two. I knowed
why; I hadn't answered the right way.

"You protect yourself, what?" T. J. said.

"I protect myself, *sir*," I said.

They still looked at me. But I could tell Paul wasn't
anything like T. J. He wasn't mean at all, he just had
to play mean because T. J. was there. Couple Sundays
ago I had played baseball with a boy who looked just
like Paul. But he had brown eyes; Paul had blue eyes.

"You'll be sorry you didn't use your fists this time,"
T. J. said. "Take everything out your pockets."

I did what he said.

"Where's your knife?" he asked.

"I never car' a knife," I said.

"You never car' a knife, what, boy?" T. J. said.

"I never car' a knife, *sir*," I said.

He looked at me hard again. He didn't think I was crazy for turning myself in, he thought I was a smart aleck. I could tell from his big, fat, red face he wanted to hit me with his fist.

He nodded to Paul and Paul came toward me. I moved back some.

"I'm not going to hurt you," Paul said.

I stopped, but I could still feel myself shaking. Paul started patting me down. He found a pack of cigarettes in my shirt pocket. I could see in his face he didn't want take them out, but he took them out, anyhow.

"Thought I told you empty your pockets?" T. J. said.

"I didn't know—"

"Paul, if you can't make that boy shut up, I can," T. J. said.

"He'll be quiet," Paul said, looking at me. He was telling me with his eyes to be quiet or I was go'n get myself in a lot of trouble.

"You got one more time to butt in," T. J. said. "One more time now."

I was getting a swimming in the head, and I looked down at the floor. I hoped they would hurry up and lock me up so I could have a little peace.

"Why'd you turn yourself in?" T. J. asked.

I kept my head down. I didn't answer him.

"Paul, can't you make that boy talk?" T. J. said. "Or do I have to get up and do it?"

"He'll talk," Paul said.

"I figured y'all was go'n catch me sooner or later—sir."

"That's not the reason you turned yourself in," T. J. said

I kept my head down.

"Look up when I talk to you," T. J. said.

I raised my head. I felt weak and shaky. My clothes was wet and sticking to my body, but my mouth felt dry as dust. My eyes wanted to look down again, but I forced myself to look at T. J.'s big red face.

"You figured if you turned yourself in, Roger Medlow was go'n get you out, now, didn't you?"

I didn't say anything—but that's exactly what I was figuring on.

"Sure," he said. He looked at me a long time. He knowed how I was feeling; he knowed I was weak and almost ready to fall. That's why he was making me stand there like that. "What you think we ought to do with niggers like you?" he said. "Come on now—what you think we ought to do with you?"

I didn't answer him.

"Well?" he said.

"I don't know," I said. "Sir."

"I'll tell you," he said. "See, if I was gov'nor, I'd run every damned one of you off in that river out there. Man, woman and child. You know that?"

I was quiet, looking at him. But I made sure I didn't show in my face what I was thinking. I could've been killed for what I was thinking then.

"Well, what you think of that?" he said.

"That's up to the gov'nor, sir," I said.

"Yeah," he said. "That's right. That's right. I think I'll write him a little telegram and tell him 'bout my idea. Can save this state a hell of a lot trouble."

Now he just sat there looking at me again. He wanted to hit me in the mouth with his fist. Not just hit me, he wanted to beat me. But he had to have a good excuse. And what excuse could he have when I had already turned myself in.

"Put him in there with Munford," he said to Paul.

We went out. We had to walk down a hall to the cell block. The niggers' cell block was on the second floor. We had to go up some concrete steps to get there. Paul turned on the lights and a woman hollered at him to turn them off. "What's this supposed to be—Christmas?" she said. "A person can't sleep in this joint." The women was locked up on one end of the block and the men was at the other end. If you had a mirror or a piece of shiny tin, you could stick it out the cell and fix it so you could see the other end of the block.

The guard opened the cell door and let me in, then he locked it back. I looked at him through the bars.

"When will y'all ever learn?" he said, shaking his head.

He said it like he meant it, like he was sorry for me. He kept reminding me of that boy I had played baseball with. They called that other boy Lloyd, and he used to show up just about every Sunday to play baseball with us. He used to play the outfield so he could do a lot of running. He used to buy Cokes for everybody after the game. He was the only white boy out there.

"Here's a pack of cigarettes and some matches," Paul said. "Might not be your brand, but I doubt if you'll mind it too much in there."

I took the cigarettes from him.

"You can say 'Thanks,' " he said.

"Thanks," I said.

"And you can say 'sir' sometimes," he said.

"Sir," I said.

He looked at me like he felt sorry for me, like he felt sorry for everybody. He didn't look like a policeman at all.

"Let me give you a word of warning," he said. "Don't push T. J. Don't push him, now."

"I won't."

"It doesn't take much to get him started—don't push him."

I nodded.

"Y'all go'n turn out them goddamn lights?" the woman hollered from the other end of the block.

"Take it easy," Paul said to me and left.

After the lights went out, I stood at the cell door till my eyes got used to the dark. Then I climbed up on my bunk. Two other people was in the cell. Somebody on the bunk under mine, somebody on the lower bunk 'cross from me. The upper bunk 'cross from me was empty.

"Cigarette?" the person below me said.

He said it very low, but I could tell he was talking to me and not to the man 'cross from us. I shook a cigarette out the pack and dropped it on the bunk. I could hear the man scratching the match to light the cigarette. He cupped his hands close to his face, because I didn't see too much light. I could tell from the way he let that smoke out he had wanted a cigarette very bad.

"What you in for?" he said, real quiet.

"A fight," I said.

"First time?"

"No, I been in before."

He didn't say any more and I didn't, either. I didn't feel like talking, anyhow. I looked up at the window on my left, and I could see a few stars. I felt lonely and I felt like crying. But I couldn't cry. Once you started that in here you was done for. Everybody and his brother would run over you.

The man on the other bunk got up to take a leak. The toilet was up by the head of my bunk. After the man had zipped up his pants, he just stood there looking at me. I tightened my fist to swing at him if he tried any funny stuff.

"Well, hello there," he said.

"Get your ass back over there, Hattie," the man below me said. He spoke in that quiet voice again. "Hattie is a woman," he said to me. "Don't see how come they didn't put him with the rest of them whores."

"Don't let it worry your mind," Hattie said.

"Caught him playing with this man dick," the man below me said. "At this old flea-bitten show back of town there. Up front—front row—there he is playing with this man dick. Bitch."

"Is that any worse than choking somebody half to death?" Hattie said.

The man below me was quiet. Hattie went back to his bunk.

"Oh, these old crampy, stuffy, old ill-smelling beds," he said, slapping the mattress level with the palm of his hand. "How do they expect you to sleep." He laid down. "What are you in for, honey?" he asked me. "You look awful young."

"Fighting," I said.

"You poor, poor thing," Hattie said. "If I can help you in any way, don't hesitate to ask."

"Shit," the man below me said. I heard him turning over so he could go to sleep.

"The world has given up on the likes of you," Hattie said. "You jungle beast."

"Bitch, why don't you just shut up," the man said.

"Why don't both of y'all shut up," somebody said from another cell.

It was quiet after that.

I looked up at the window and I could see the stars going out in the sky. My eyes felt tired and my head started spinning, and I wasn't here any more, I was at the Seven Spots. And she was there in red, and she had two big dimples in her jaws. Then she got up and danced with him, and every time she turned my way she looked over his shoulder at me and smiled. And when she turned her back to me, she rolled her big ass real slow and easy—just for me, just for me. Grinning Boy was sitting at the table with me, saying: "Poison, poison—nothing but poison. Look at that; just look at that." I was looking, but I wasn't thinking about what he was saying. When she went back to that table to sit down, I went there and asked her to dance. That nigger sitting there just looked at me, rolling his big white eyes like I was supposed to break out of the joint. I didn't pay him no mind, I was looking at that woman. And I was looking down at them two big pretty brown things poking that dress way out. They looked so soft and warm and waiting, I wanted to touch them right there in front of that ugly nigger. She shook her head, because he was sitting there, but little bit later when she went back in the kitchen, I went back there, too. Grinning Boy tried to stop me, saying, "Poison, poison, poison," but I didn't pay him no mind. When I came back in the kitchen, she was standing at the counter ordering a chicken sandwich. The lady back of the counter had to fry the chicken, so she had to wait a while. When she saw me, she started smiling. Them two big dimples came in her jaws. I smiled back at her.

"She go'n take a while," I said. "Let's step out in the cool till she get done."

She looked over her shoulder and didn't see the nigger peeping, and we went outside. There was people talking out there, but I didn't care, I had to touch her.

"What's your name?" I said.

"Clara."

"Let's go somewhere, Clara."

"I can't. I'm with somebody," she said.

"That nigger?" I said. "You call him somebody?"

She just looked at me with that little smile on her face—them two big dimples in her jaws. I looked little farther down, and I could see how them two warm, brown things was waiting for somebody to tear that dress open so they could get free.

"You must be the prettiest woman in the world," I said.

"You like me?"

"Lord, yes."

"I want you to like me," she said.

"Then what's keeping us from going?" I said. "Hell away with that nigger."

"My name is Clara Johnson," she said. "It's in the book. Call me tomorrow after four."

She turned to go back inside, but just then that big sweaty nigger bust out the door. He passed by her like she wasn't even there.

"No, Bayou," she said. "No."

But he wasn't listening to a thing. Before I knowed it, he had cracked me on the chin and I was down on my back. He raised his foot to kick me in the stomach, and I rolled and rolled till I was out of the way. Then I jumped back up.

"I don't want fight you, Bayou," I said. "I don't want fight you, now."

"You fight or you fly, nigger," somebody else said. "If you run, we go'n catch you."

Bayou didn't say nothing. He just came in swinging. I backed away from him.

"I wasn't doing nothing but talking to her," I said.

He rushed in and knocked me on a bunch of people. They picked me clear off the ground and throwed me back on him. He hit me again, this time a glancing blow on the shoulder. I moved back from him, holding the shoulder with the other hand.

"I don't want fight you," I told him. "I was just talking to her."

But trying to talk to Bayou was like trying to talk to a mule. He came in swinging wild and high, and I went under his arm and rammed my fist in his stomach. But it felt like ramming your fist into a hundred-pound sack of flour. He stopped about a half a second, then he was right back on me again. I hit him in the face this time, and I saw the blood splash out of his mouth. I was still backing away from him, hoping he would quit, but the nigger kept coming on me. He had to, because all his friends and that woman was there. But he didn't know how to fight, and every time he moved in I hit him in the face. Then I saw him going for his knife.

"Watch it, now, Bayou," I said. "I don't have a knife. Let's keep this fair."

But he didn't hear a thing I was saying; he was listening to the others who was sicking him on. He kept moving in on me. He had both of his arms way out—that blade in his right hand. From the way he was holding it, he didn't have nothing but killing on his mind.

I kept moving back, moving back. Then my foot touched a bottle and I stooped down and picked it up. I broke it against the corner of the building, but I never took my eyes off Bayou. He started circling me with the knife, and I moved round him with the bottle. He made a slash at me, and I jumped back. He was all opened and I could've gotten him then, but I was still hoping for him to change his mind.

"Let's stop it, Bayou," I kept saying to him. "Let's stop it, now."

But he kept on circling me with the knife, and I kept on going round him with the bottle. I didn't look at his face any more, I kept my eyes on that knife. It was a Texas jack with a pearl handle, and that blade must've been five inches long.

"Stop it, Bayou," I said. "Stop it, stop it."

He slashed at me, and I jumped back. He slashed at me again, and I jumped back again. Then he acted like a fool and ran on me, and all I did was stick the bottle out. I felt it go in his clothes and in his stomach and I felt the hot, sticky blood on my hand and I saw his face all twisted and sweaty. I felt his hands brush against mine when he throwed both of his hands up to his stomach. I started running. I was running toward the car, and Grinning Boy was running there, too. He got there before me and jumped in on the driving side, but I pushed him out the way and got under that ste'r'n wheel. I could hear that gang coming after me, and I shot that Ford out of there a hundred miles an hour. Some of them ran up the road to cut me off, but when they saw I wasn't stopping they jumped out of the way. Now, it was nobody but me, that Ford and that gravel road. Grinning Boy was sitting over there crying, but I wasn't paying him no mind. I wanted to get much road between me and Seven Spots as I could.

After I had gone a good piece, I slammed on the brakes and told Grinning Boy to get out. He wouldn't get out. I opened the door and pushed on him, but he held the ste'r'n wheel. He was crying and holding the wheel with both hands. I hit him and pushed on him and hit him and pushed on him but he wouldn't turn it loose. If they was go'n kill me, I didn't want them to kill him, too, but he couldn't see that. I shot away from there with the door still opened, and after we had gone a little piece, Grinning Boy reached out and got it and slammed it again.

I came out on the pave road and drove three or four miles 'long the river. Then I turned down a dirt road and parked the car under a big pecan tree. It was one of these old plantation quarters and the place was quiet as a graveyard. It was pretty bright, though, because the moon and the stars was out. The dust in that long, old road was white as snow. I lit a cigarette and tried to think. Grinning Boy was sitting over there crying. He was crying real quiet with his head hanging down on his chest. Every now and then I could hear him sniffing.

"I'm turning myself in," I said.

I had been thinking and thinking and I couldn't think of nothing else to do. I knowed Bayou was dead or hurt pretty bad, and I knowed either that gang or the law was go'n get me, anyhow. I backed the car out on the pave road and drove to Bayonne. I told Grinning Boy to let my uncle know I was in trouble. My uncle would go to Roger Medlow—and I was hoping Roger Medlow would get me off like he had done once before. He owned the plantation where I lived.

"Hey," somebody was calling and shaking me. "Hey, there, now; wake up."

I opened my eyes and looked at this old man standing by the head of my bunk. I'm sure if I had woke up anywhere else and found him that close to me I would've jumped back screaming. He must've been sixty; he had reddish-brown eyes, and a stubby gray beard. 'Cross his right jaw, from his cheekbone to his mouth, was a big shiny scar where somebody had gotten him with a razor. He was wearing a derby hat, and he had it cocked a little to the back of his head.

"They coming," he said.

"Who?"

"Breakfast."

"I'm not hungry."

"You better eat. Never can tell when you go'n eat again in this joint."

His breath didn't smell too good either, and he was

standing so close to me, I could smell his breath every time he breathed in and out. I figured he was the one they called Munford. Just before they brought me down here last night, I heard T. J. tell Paul to put me in there with Munford. Since he had called the other one Hattie, I figured he was Munford.

"Been having yourself a nice little nightmare," he said. "Twisting and turning there like you wanted to fall off. You can have this bunk of mine tonight if you want."

I looked at the freak laying on the other bunk. He looked back at me with a sad little smile on his face.

"I'll stay here," I said.

The freak stopped smiling, but he still looked sad— like a sad woman. He knowed why I didn't want get down there. I didn't want no part of him.

Out on the cell block, the nigger trustee was singing. He went from one cell to the other one singing, "Come and get it, it's hot. What a lovely, lovely day, isn't it? Yes, indeed," he answered himself. "Yes, indeed . . . Come and get it, my children, come and get it. Unc' Toby won't feel right if y'all don't eat his lovely food."

He stopped before the cell with his little shiny push-cart. A white guard was with him. The guard opened the cell door and Unc' Toby gived each one of us a cup of coffee and two baloney sandwiches. Then the guard shut the cell again and him and Unc' Toby went on up the block. Unc' Toby was singing again.

"Toby used to have a little stand," Munford said to me. "He think he still got it. He kinda loose up here," he said, tapping his head with the hand that held the sandwiches.

"They ought to send him to Jackson if he's crazy."

"They like keeping him here," Munford said. "Part of the scheme of things."

"You want this?" I asked.

"No, eat it," he said.

I got back on my bunk. I ate one of the sandwiches and drank some of the coffee. The coffee was nothing but brown water. It didn't have any kind of taste—not even bitter taste. I drank about half and poured the rest in the toilet.

The freak, Hattie, sat on his bunk, nibbling at his food. He wrapped one slice of bread round the slice of baloney and ate that, then he did the same thing with the other sandwich. The two extra slices of bread, he dipped down in his coffee and ate it like that. All the time he was eating, he was looking at me like a sad woman looks at you.

Munford stood between the two rows of bunks, eating and drinking his coffee. He pressed both of the sandwiches together and ate them like they was just one. Nobody said anything all the time we was eating. Even when I poured out the coffee, nobody said anything. The freak just looked at me like a sad woman. But Munford didn't look at me at all—he was looking up at the window all the time. When he got through eating, he wiped his mouth and throwed his cup on his bunk.

"Another one of them smokes," he said to me.

The way he said it, it sounded like he would've took it if I didn't give it to him. I got out the pack of cigarettes and gived him one. He lit it and took a big draw. I was laying back against the wall, looking up at the window; but I could tell that Munford was looking at me.

"Killed somebody, huh?" Munford said, in his quiet, calm voice.

"I cut him pretty bad," I said, still looking up at the window.

"He's dead," Munford said.

I wouldn't take my eyes off the window. My throat got tight, and my heart started beating so loud, I'm sure both Munford and that freak could hear it.

"That's bad," Munford said.

"And so young," Hattie said. I didn't have to look at the freak to know he was crying. "And so much of his life still before him—my Lord."

"You got people?" Munford asked.

"Uncle," I said.

"You notified him?"

"I think he knows."

"You got a lawyer?"

"No."

"No money?"

"No."

"That's bad," he said.

"Maybe his uncle can do something," Hattie said. "Poor thing." Then I heard him blowing his nose.

I looked at the bars in the window. I wanted them to leave me alone so I could think.

"So young, too," Hattie said. "My Lord, my Lord."

"Oh shut up," Munford said. "I don't know why they didn't lock you up with the rest of them whores."

"Is it too much to have some feeling of sympathy?" Hattie said, and blowed his nose again.

"Morris David is a good lawyer," Munford said. "Get him if you can. Best for colored round here."

I nodded, but I didn't look at Munford. I felt bad and I wanted them to leave me alone.

"Was he a local boy?" Munford asked.

"I don't know," I said.

"Where was it?"

I didn't answer him.

"Best to talk 'bout it," Munford said. "Keeping it in just make it worse."

"Seven Spots," I said.

"That's a rough joint," Munford said.

"They're all rough joints," Hattie said. "That's all you have—rough joints. No decent places for someone like him."

"Who's your uncle?" Munford asked.

"Martin Baptiste. Medlow plantation."

"Martin Baptiste?" Munford said.

I could tell from the way he said it, he knowed my uncle. I looked at him now. He was looking back at me with his left eye half shut. I could tell from his face he didn't like my uncle.

"You same as out already," he said.

He didn't like my uncle at all, and now he was studying me to see how much I was like him.

"Medlow can get you out of here just by snapping his fingers," he said. "Big men like that run little towns like these."

"I killed somebody," I said.

"You killed another old nigger," Munford said. "A nigger ain't nobody."

He drawed on the cigarette, and I looked at the big scar on the side of his face. He took the cigarette from his mouth and patted the scar with the tip of one of his fingers.

"Bunch of them jumped on me one night," he said. "One caught me with a straight razor. Had the flesh hanging so much, I coulda ripped it off with my hands if I wanted to. Ah, but before I went down you shoulda seen what I did to the bunch of 'em." He stopped and thought a while. He even laughed a little to himself. "I been in this joint so much, everybody from the judge on down know me. 'How's it going, Munford?' 'Well, you back with us again, huh, Munt?' 'Look, y'all, old Munt's back with us again, just like he said he'd be.' They all know me. All know me. I'll get out little later on. What time is it getting to be—'leven? I'll give 'em till twelve and tell 'em I want get out. They'll let me out. Got in Saturday night. They always keep me from Saturday till Monday. If it rain, they keep me till Tuesday—don't want me get out and catch cold, you know. Next Saturday, I'm right back. Can't stay out of here to save my soul."

"Places like these are built for people like you," Hattie said. "Not for decent people."

"Been going in and out of these jails here, I don't know how long," Munford said. "Forty, fifty years. Started out just like you—kilt a boy just like you did last night. Kilt him and got off—got off scot free. My pappy worked for a white man who got me off. At first I didn't know why he had done it—I didn't think; all I knowed was I was free, and free is how I wanted to be. Then I got in trouble again, and again they got me off. I kept on getting in trouble, and they kept on getting me off. Didn't wake up till I got to be nearly old as I'm is now. Then I realized they kept getting me off because they needed a Munford Bazille. They need me to prove they human—just like they need that thing over there. They need us. Because without us, they don't know what they is—they don't know what they is out there. With us around, they can see us and they know what they ain't. They ain't us. Do you see? Do you see how they think?''

I didn't know what he was talking about. It was hot in the cell and he had started sweating. His face was wet, except for that big scar. It was just laying there smooth and shiny.

"But I got news for them. They us. I never tell them that, but inside I know it. They us, just like we is ourselves. Cut any of them open and you see if you don't find Munford Bazille or Hattie Brown there. You know what I mean?''

"I guess so.''

"No, you don't know what I mean," he said. "What I mean is not one of them out there is a man. Not one. They think they men. They think they men 'cause they got me and him in here who ain't men. But I got news for them—cut them open; go 'head and cut one open— you see if you don't find Munford Bazille or Hattie Brown. Not a man one of them. 'Cause face don't make a man—black or white. Face don't make him and fucking don't make him and fighting don't make him—neither killing. None of this prove you a man. 'Cause animals can fuck, can kill, can fight—you know that?''

I looked at him, but I didn't answer him. I didn't feel like answering.

"Well?'' he said.

"Yeah.''

"Then answer me when I ask you a question. I don't like talking to myself.''

He stopped and looked at me a while.

"You know what I'm getting at?"

"No," I said.

"To hell if you don't," he said. "Don't let Medlow get you out of here so you can kill again."

"You got out," I said.

"Yeah," he said, "and I'm still coming back here and I'm still getting out. Next Saturday I'm go'n hit another nigger in the head, and Saturday night they go'n bring me here, and Monday they go'n let me out again. And Saturday after that I'm go'n hit me another nigger in the head—'cause I'll hit a nigger in the head quick as I'll look at one."

"You're just an animal out the black jungle," Hattie said. "Because you have to hit somebody in the head every Saturday night don't mean he has to do the same."

"He'll do it," Munford said, looking at me, not at Hattie. "He'll do it 'cause he know Medlow'll get him out. Won't you?"

I didn't answer him. Munford nodded his head.

"Yeah, he'll do it. They'll see to that."

He looked at me like he was mad at me, then he looked up at the bars in the window. He frowned and rubbed his hand over his chin, and I could hear the gritty sound his beard made. He studied the bars a long time, like he was thinking about something 'way off; then I saw how his face changed; his eyes twinkled and he grinned to himself. He turned to look at Hattie laying on the bunk.

"Look here," he said. "I got a few coppers and a few minutes—what you say me and you giving it a little whirl?"

"My God, man," Hattie said. He said it the way a

young girl would've said it if you had asked her to
pull down her drawers. He even opened his eyes wide
the same way a young girl would've done it. "Do you
think I could possibly ever sink so low?" he said.

"Well, that's what you do on the outside," Munford
said.

"What I do on the outside is absolutely no concern
of yours, let me assure you," the freak said. "And fur-
thermore, I have friends that I associate with."

"And them 'sociating friends you got there—what they
got Munford don't have?" Munford said.

"For one thing, manners," Hattie said. "Of all the
nerve."

Munford grinned at him and looked at me.

"You know what make 'em like that?" he asked.

"No."

He nodded his head. "Then I'll tell you. It start in
the cradle when they send that preacher there to chris-
ten you. At the same time he's doing that mumbo-jumbo
stuff, he's low'ing his mouth to your little nipper to suck
out your manhood. I know, he tried it on me. Here, I'm
laying in his arms in my little white blanket and he suppose to be christening me. My mammy there, my pappy
there; uncle, aunt, grandmammy, grandpappy; my nan-
nane, my pa-ran—all of them standing there with they
head bowed. This preacher going, 'Mumbo-jumbo,
mumbo-jumbo,' but all the time he's low'ing his mouth
toward my little private. Nobody else don't see him,
but I catch him, and I haul 'way back and hit him right
smack in the eye. I ain't no more than three months old
but I give him a good one. 'Get your goddamn mouth
away from my little pecker, you no-teef, rotten, egg-

sucking sonofabitch. Get away from here, you sister-jumper, God-calling, pulpit-spitting, mother-huncher. Get away from here, you chicken-eating, catfish-eating, gin-drinking sonofabitch. Get away, goddamn it, get away . . .' ''

I thought Munford was just being funny, but he was serious as he could ever get. He had worked himself up so much, he had to stop and catch his breath.

"That's what I told him," he said. "That's what I told him . . . But they don't stop there, they stay after you. If they miss you in the cradle, they catch you some other time. And when they catch you, they draw it out of you or they make you a beast—make you use it in a brutish way. You use it on a woman without caring for her, you use it on children, you use it on other men, you use it on yourself. Then when you get so disgusted with everything round you, you kill. And if your back is strong, like your back is strong, they get you out so you can kill again." He stopped and looked at me and nodded his head. "Yeah, that's what they do with you—exactly . . . But not everybody end up like that. Some of them make it. Not many—but some of them do make it."

"Going to the pen?" I said.

"Yeah—the pen is one way," he said. "But you don't go to the pen for the nigger you killed. Not for him—he ain't worth it. They told you that from the cradle—a nigger ain't worth a good gray mule. Don't mention a white mule: fifty niggers ain't worth a good white mule. So you don't go to the pen for killing the nigger, you go for yourself. You go to sweat out all the crud you got in your system. You go, saying, 'Go fuck yourself, Roger

Medlow, I want to be a man, and by God I will be a man. For once in my life I will be a man.' "

"And a month after you been in the pen, Medlow tell them to kill you for being a smart aleck. How much of a man you is then?"

"At least you been a man a month—where if you let him get you out you won't be a man a second. He won't 'low it."

"I'll take that chance," I said.

He looked at me a long time now. His reddish-brown eyes was sad and mean. He felt sorry for me, and at the same time he wanted to hit me with his fist.

"You don't look like that whitemouth uncle of yours," he said. "And you look much brighter than I did at your age. But I guess every man must live his own life. I just wish I had mine to live all over again."

After a while, he looked back at Hattie on the bunk.

"You not thinking 'bout what I asked you?" he said.

Hattie looked up at him just like a woman looks at a man she can't stand.

"Munford, if you dropped dead this second, I doubt if I would shed a tear."

"Put all that together, I take it you mean no," Munford said.

Hattie rolled his eyes at Munford the way a woman rolls her eyes at a man she can't stand.

"Well, I better get out of here," Munford said. He passed his hand over his chin. It sounded like passing your hand over sandpaper. "Go home and take me a shave and might go out and do little fishing," he said. "Too hot to pick cotton."

He looked at me again.

"I guess I'll be back next week or the week after—but I suppose you'll be gone to Medlow by then."

"If he come for me—yes."

"He'll come for you," Munford said. "How old you is—twenty?"

"Nineteen."

"Yeah, he'll come and take you back. And next year you'll kill another old nigger. 'Cause they grow niggers just to be killed, and they grow people like you to kill 'em. That's all part of the—the culture. And every man got to play his part in the culture, or the culture don't go on. But I'll tell you this; if you was kin to anybody else except that Martin Baptiste, I'd stay in here long enough to make you go to Angola. 'Cause I'd break your back 'fore I let you walk out of this cell with Medlow. But with Martin Baptiste blood in you, you'll never be worth a goddamn no matter what I did. With that, I bid you adieu."

He tipped his derby to me, then he went to the door and called for the guard. The guard came and let him out. The people on the block told him good-bye and said they would see him when they got out. Munford waved at them and followed the guard toward the door.

"That Munford," Hattie said. "Thank God we're not all like that." He looked up at me. "I hope you didn't listen to half of that nonsense."

I didn't answer the freak—I didn't want have nothing to do with him. I looked up at the window. The sky was darkish blue and I could tell it was hot out there. I had always hated the hot sun, but I wished I was out there now. I wouldn't even mind picking cotton, much as I hated picking cotton.

I got out my other sandwich: nothing but two slices of
light bread and a thin slice of baloney sausage. If I
wasn't hungry, I wouldn't 'a' ate it at all. I tried to think
about what everybody was doing at home. But hard as
I tried, all I could think about was here. Maybe it was
best if I didn't think about outside. That could run you
crazy. I had heard about people going crazy in jail. I
tried to remember how it was when I was in jail before.
It wasn't like this if I could remember. Before, it was
just a brawl—a fight. I had never stayed in more than a
couple weeks. I had been in about a half dozen times, but
never more than a week or two. This time it was different, though. Munford said Roger Medlow was go'n
get me out, but suppose Munford was wrong. Suppose
I had to go up? Suppose I had to go to the pen?

Hattie started singing. He was singing a spiritual and
he was singing it in a high-pitched voice like a woman.
I wanted to tell him to shut up, but I didn't want have
nothing to do with that freak. I could feel him looking
at me; a second later he had quit singing.

"That Munford," he said. "I hope you didn't believe
everything he said about me."

I was quiet. I didn't want to talk to Hattie. He saw
it and kept his mouth shut.

If Medlow was go'n get me out of here, why hadn't he
done so? If all he had to do was snap his fingers,
what was keeping him from snapping them? Maybe he
wasn't go'n do anything for me. I wasn't one of them
Uncle Tom-ing niggers like my uncle, and maybe he
was go'n let me go up this time.

I couldn't make it in the pen. Locked up—caged. Walking round all day with shackles on my legs. No woman,

no pussy—I'd die in there. I'd die in a year. Not five years—one year. If Roger Medlow came, I was leaving. That's how old people is: they always want you to do something they never did when they was young. If he had his life to live all over—how come he didn't do it then? Don't tell me do it when he didn't do it. If that's part of the culture, then I'm part of the culture, because I sure ain't for the pen.

That black sonofabitch—that coward. I hope he didn't have religion. I hope his ass burn in hell till eternity.

Look how life can change on you—just look. Yesterday this time I was poon-tanging like a dog. Today—that black sonofabitch—behind these bars maybe for the rest of my life. And look at me, look at me. Strong. A man. A damn good man. A hard dick—a pile of muscles. But look at me—locked in here like a caged animal.

Maybe that's what Munford was talking about. You spend much time in here like he done spent, you can't be nothing but a' animal.

I wish somebody could do something for me. I can make a phone call, can't I? But call who? That ass-hole uncle of mine? I'm sure Grinning Boy already told him where I'm at. I wonder if Grinning Boy got in touch with Marie. I suppose this finish it. Hell, why should she stick her neck out for me. I was treating her like a dog, anyhow. I'm sorry, baby; I'm sorry. No, I'm not sorry; I'd do the same thing tomorrow if I was out of here. Maybe I'm a' animal already. I don't care who she is, I'd do it with her and don't give a damn. Hell, let me stop whining; I ain't no goddamn animal. I'm a man, and I got to act and think like a man.

I got to think, I got to think. My daddy is somewhere

up North—but where? I got more people scattered around, but no use going to them. I'm the black sheep of this family—and they don't care if I live or die. They'd be glad if I died so they'd be rid of me for good.

That black sonofabitch—I swear to God. Big as he was, he had to go for a knife. I hope he rot in hell. I hope he burn—goddamn it—till eternity come and go.

Let me see, let me see, who can I call? I don't know a soul with a dime. Them white people out there got it, but what do they care 'bout me, a nigger. Now, if I was a' Uncle Tom-ing nigger—oh, yes, they'd come then. They'd come running. But like I'm is, I'm fucked. Done for.

Five years, five years—that's what they give you. Five years for killing a nigger like that. Five years out of my life. Five years for a rotten, no good sonofabitch who didn't have no business being born in the first place. Five years . . . .

Maybe I ought to call Medlow myself . . . But suppose he come, then what? Me and Medlow never got along. I couldn't never bow and say, "Yes sir," and scratch my head. But I'd have to do it now. He'd have me by the nuts and he'd know it; and I'd have to kiss his ass if he told me to.

Oh Lord, have mercy . . . They get you, don't they. They let you run and run, then they get you. They stick a no-good, trashy nigger up there, and they get you. And they twist your nuts and twist them till you don't care no more.

I got to stop this, I got to stop it. My head'll go to hurting after while and I won't be able to think anything out.

"Oh, you're so beautiful when you're meditating," Hattie said. "And what were you meditating about?"

I didn't answer him—I didn't want have nothing to do with that freak.

"How long you're going to be in here, is that it?" he said. "Sometimes they let you sit for days and days. In your case they might let you sit here a week before they say anything to you. What do they care—they're in-human."

I got a cigarette out of the pack and lit it.

"I smoke, too," Hattie said.

I didn't answer that freak. He came over and got the pack out of my shirt pocket. His fingers went down in my pocket just like a woman's fingers go in your pocket.

"May I?" he said.

I didn't say nothing to him. He lit his cigarette and laid the pack on my chest just like a woman'd do it.

"Really, I'm not all that awful," he said. "Munford has poisoned your mind with all sorts of notions. Let go—relax. You need friends at a time like this."

I stuffed the pack of cigarettes in my pocket and looked up at the window.

"These are very good," the freak said. "Very, very good. Well, maybe you'll feel like talking a little later on. It's always good to let go. I'm understanding; I'll be here."

He went back to his bunk and laid down.

Toward three o'clock, they let the women out of the cells to walk around. Some of the women came down the block and talked to the men through the bars. Some of them even laughed and joked. Three-thirty, the guard locked them up and let the men out. From the way the guard looked at me, I knowed I wasn't going anywhere. I didn't want to go anywhere, either, because I didn't want people asking me a pile of questions. Hattie went out to stretch, but few minutes later he came and laid back down. He was grumbling about some man on the block trying to get fresh with him.

"Some of them think you'll stoop to anything," he said.

I looked out of the window at the sky. I couldn't see too much, but I liked what I could see. I liked the sun, too. I hadn't ever liked the sun before, but I liked it now. I felt my throat getting tight, and I turned my head.

Toward four o'clock, Unc' Toby came on the block with dinner. For dinner, we had stew, mashed potatoes, lettuce and tomatoes. The stew was too soupy; the mashed potatoes was too soupy; the lettuce and tomatoes was too soggy. Dessert was three or four dried-up prunes with black water poured over them. After Unc' Toby served us, the guard locked up the cell. By the time we finished eating, they was back there again to pick up the trays.

I laid on my bunk, looking up at the window. How long I had been there? No more than about twelve hours. Twelve hours—but it felt like three days, already.

They knowed how to get a man down. Because they had me now. No matter which way I went—plantation or pen—they had me. That's why Medlow wasn't in any hurry to get me out. You don't have to be in any hurry when you already know you got a man by the nuts.

Look at the way they did Jack. Jack was a man, a good man. Look what they did him. Let a fifteen-cents Cajun bond him out of jail—a no-teeth, dirty, overall-wearing Cajun get him out. Then they broke him. Broke him down to nothing—to a grinning, bowing fool. . . . We loved Jack. Jack could do anything. Work, play ball, run women—anything. They knowed we loved him, that's why they did him that. Broke him—broke him the way you break a wild horse. . . . Now everybody laughs at him. Gamble with him and cheat him. He know you cheating him, but he don't care—just don't care any more. . . .

Where is my father? Why my mama had to die? Why they brought me here and left me to struggle like this? I used to love my mama so much. Her skin was light brown; her hair was silky. I used to watch her powdering her face in the glass. I used to always cry when she went out —and be glad when she came back because she always brought me candy. But you gone for good now, Mama; and I got nothing in this world but me.

A man in the other cell started singing. I listened to him and looked up at the window. The sky had changed some more. It was lighter blue now—gray-blue almost.

The sun went down, a star came out. For a while it was the only star; then some more came to join it. I watched all of them. Then I watched just a few, then just one. I shut my eyes and opened them and tried to find the star again. I couldn't find it. I wasn't too sure which one it was. I could've pretended and choosed either one, but I didn't want lie to myself. I don't believe in lying to myself. I don't believe in lying to nobody else, either. I believe in being straight with a man. And I want a man to be straight with me. I wouldn't 'a' picked up that bottle for nothing if that nigger hadn't pulled his knife. Not for nothing. Because I don't believe in that kind of stuff. I believe in straight stuff. But a man got to protect himself . . . But with stars I wasn't go'n cheat. If I didn't know where the one was I was looking at at first, I wasn't go'n say I did. I picked out another one, one that wasn't too much in a cluster. I measured it off from the bars in the window, then I shut my eyes. When I opened them, I found the star right away. And I didn't have to cheat, either.

The lights went out on the block. I got up and took a leak and got back on my bunk. I got in the same place I was before and looked for the star. I found it right away. It was easier to find now because the lights was out. I got tired looking at it after a while and looked at another one. The other one was much more smaller and much more in a cluster. But I got tired of it after a while, too.

I thought about Munford. He said if they didn't get you in the cradle, they got you later. If they didn't suck all the manhood out of you in the cradle, they made you use it on people you didn't love. I never messed with a woman I didn't love. I always loved all these women I ever messed with. . . . No, I didn't love them. Because I didn't love her last night—I just wanted to fuck her. And I don't think I ever loved Marie, either. Marie just had the best pussy in the world. She had the best—still got the best. And that's why I went to her, the only reason I went. Because God knows she don't have any kind a face to make you come at her. . . .

Maybe I ain't never loved nobody. Maybe I ain't never loved nobody since my mama died. Because I loved her. I know I loved her. But the rest—no, I never loved the rest. They don't let you love them. Some kind of way they keep you from loving them. . . .

I have to stop thinking. That's how you go crazy—thinking. But what else can you do in a place like this—what? I wish I knowed somebody. I wish I knowed a good person. I would be good if I knowed a good person. I swear to God I would be good.

All of a sudden the lights came on, and I heard them bringing in somebody who was crying. They was coming toward the cell where I was; the person was crying all the way. Then the cell door opened and they throwed him in there and they locked the door again. I didn't look up—I wouldn't raise my head for nothing. I could tell nobody else was looking up, either. Then the footsteps faded away and the lights went out again.

I raised my head and looked at the person they had throwed in there. He was nothing but a little boy—fourteen or fifteen. He had on a white shirt and a pair of dark pants. Hattie helped him up off the floor and laid him on the bunk under me. Then he sat on the bunk 'side the boy. The boy was still crying.

"Shhh now, shhh now," Hattie was saying. It was just like a woman saying it. It made me sick a' the stomach. "Shhh now, shhh now," he kept on saying.

I swung to the floor and looked at the boy. Hattie was sitting on the bunk, passing his hand over the boy's face.

"What happened?" I asked him.

He was crying too much to answer me.

"They beat you?" I asked him.

He couldn't answer.

"A cigarette?" I said.

"No—no—sir," he said.

I lit one, anyhow, and stuck it in his mouth. He tried to smoke it and started coughing. I took it out.

"Shhh now," Hattie said, patting his face. "Just look

at his clothes. The bunch of animals. Not one of them is
a man. A bunch of pigs—dogs—philistines."

"You hurt?" I asked the boy.

"Sure, he's hurt," Hattie said. "Just look at his clothes,
how they beat him. The bunch of dogs."

I went to the door to call the guard. But I stopped; I
told myself to keep out of this. He ain't the first one they
ever beat and he won't be the last one, and getting in it
will just bring you a dose of the same medicine. I turned
around and looked at the boy. Hattie was holding the boy
in his arms and whispering to him. I hated what Hattie
was doing much as I hated what the law had done.

"Leave him alone," I said to Hattie.

"The child needs somebody," he said. "You're going to
look after him?"

"What happened?" I asked the boy.

"They beat me," he said.

"They didn't beat you for nothing, boy."

He was quiet now. Hattie was patting the side of his
face and his hair.

"What they beat you for?" I asked him.

"I took something."

"What you took?"

"I took some cakes. I was hungry."

"You got no business stealing," I said.

"Some people got no business killing, but it don't keep
them from killing," Hattie said.

He started rocking the boy in his arms the way a
woman rocks a child.

"Why don't you leave him alone?" I said.

He wouldn't answer me. He kept on.

"You hear me, whore?"

"I might be a whore, but I'm not a merciless killer," he said.

I started to crack him side the head, but I changed my mind. I had already raised my fist to hit him, but I changed my mind. I started walking. I was smoking the cigarette and walking. I walked, I walked, I walked. Then I stood at the head of the bunk and look up at the window at the stars. Where was the one I was looking at a while back? I smoked on the cigarette and looked for it—but where was it? I threw the cigarette in the toilet and lit another one. I smoked and walked some more. The rest of the place was quiet. Nobody had said a word since the guards throwed that little boy in the cell. Like a bunch of roaches, like a bunch of mices, they had crawled in they holes and pulled the cover over they head.

All of a sudden I wanted to scream. I wanted to scream to the top of my voice. I wanted to get them bars in my hands and I wanted to shake, I wanted to shake that door down. I wanted to let all these people out. But would they follow me—would they? Y'all go'n follow me? I screamed inside. Y'all go'n follow me?

I ran to my bunk and bit down in the cover. I bit harder, harder, harder. I could taste the dry sweat, the dry piss, the dry vomit. I bit harder, harder, harder . . .

I got on the bunk. I looked out at the stars. A million little white, cool stars was out there. I felt my throat hurting. I felt the water running down my face. But I gripped my mouth tight so I wouldn't make a sound. I didn't make a sound, but I cried. I cried and cried and cried.

I knowed I was going to the pen now. I knowed I was going, I knowed I was going. Even if Medlow came to get me, I wasn't leaving with him. I was go'n do like Munford said. I was going there and I was go'n sweat it and I was go'n take it. I didn't want have to pull cover over my head every time a white man did something to a black boy—I wanted to stand. Because they never let you stand if they got you out. They didn't let Jack stand —and I had never heard of them letting anybody else stand, either.

I felt good. I laid there feeling good. I felt so good I wanted to sing. I sat up on the bunk and lit a cigarette. I had never smoked a cigarette like I smoked that one. I drawed deep, deep, till my chest got big. It felt good deep down in me. I jumped to the floor feeling good.

"You want a cigarette?" I asked the boy.

I spoke to him like I had been talking to him just a few minutes ago, but it was over an hour. He was laying in Hattie's arms quiet like he was half asleep.

"No, sir," he said.

I had already shook the cigarette out of the pack.

"Here," I said.

"No sir," he said.

"Get up from there and go to your own bunk," I said to Hattie.

"And who do you think you are to be giving orders?"

I grabbed two handsful of his shirt and jerked him up and slammed him 'cross the cell. He hit against that bunk and started crying—just laying there, holding his side and crying like a woman. After a while he picked himself up and got on that bunk.

"Philistine," he said. "Dog—brute."

When I saw he wasn't go'n act a fool and try to hit me, I turned my back on him.

"Here," I said to the boy.

"I don't smoke—please, sir."

"You big enough to steal?" I said. "You'll smoke it or you'll eat it." I lit it and pushed it in his mouth. "Smoke it."

He smoked and puffed it out. I sat down on the bunk 'side him. The freak was sitting on the bunk 'cross from us, holding his side and crying.

"Hold that smoke in," I said to the boy.

He held it in and started coughing. When he stopped coughing I told him to draw again. He drawed and held it, then he let it out. I knowed he wasn't doing it right, but this was his first time, and I let him slide.

"If Medlow come to get me, I'm not going," I said to the boy. "That means T. J. and his boys coming, too. They go'n beat me because they think I'm a smart aleck trying to show them up. Now you listen to me, and listen good. Every time they come for me I want you to start praying. I want you to pray till they bring me back in this cell. And I don't want you praying like a woman, I want you to pray like a man. You don't even have to get on your knees; you can lay on your bunk and pray. Pray quiet and to yourself. You hear me?"

He didn't know what I was talking about, but he said, "Yes, sir," anyhow.

"I don't believe in God," I said. "But I want you to believe. I want you to believe He can hear you. That's the only way I'll be able to take those beatings—with you praying. You understand what I'm saying?"

"Yes, sir."

"You sure, now?"

"Yes, sir."

I drawed on the cigarette and looked at him. Deep in me I felt some kind of love for this little boy.

"You got a daddy?" I asked him.

"Yes, sir."

"A mama?"

"Yes, sir."

"Then how come you stealing?"

" 'Cause I was hungry."

"Don't they look after you?"

"No, sir."

"You been in here before?"

"Yes, sir."

"You like it in here?"

"No, sir. I was hungry."

"Let's wash your back," I said.

We got up and went to the facebowl. I helped him off with his shirt. His back was cut from where they had beat him.

"You know Munford Bazille?" I asked him.

"Yes, sir. He don't live too far from us. He kin to you?"

"No, he's not kin to me. You like him?"

"No, sir, I don't like him. He stay in fights all the time, and they always got him in jail."

"That's how you go'n end up."

"No, sir, not me. 'Cause I ain't coming back here no more."

"I better not ever catch you in here again," I said. "Hold onto that bunk—this might hurt."

"What you go'n do?"

"Wash them bruises."

"Don't mash too hard."

"Shut up," I told him, "and hold on."

I wet my handkerchief and dabbed at the bruises. Every time I touched his back, he flinched. But I didn't let that stop me. I washed his back good and clean. When I got through, I told him to go back to his bunk and lay down. Then I rinched out his shirt and spread it out on the foot of my bunk. I took off my own shirt and rinched it out because it was filthy.

I lit a cigarette and looked up at the window. I had talked big, but what was I going to do when Medlow came? Was I going to change my mind and go with him? And if I didn't go with Medlow, I surely had to go with T. J. and his boys. Was I going to be able to take the beatings night after night? I had seen what T. J. could do to your back. I had seen it on this kid and I had seen it on other people. Was I going to be able to take it?

I don't know, I thought to myself. I'll just have to wait and see.

Mike Thelwell

Bright an' mownin' star

Mike Thelwell's output, though distinguished, is, unfortunately, limited. His short stories began to collect awards and favorable notices while he was still a student at Howard University. His analysis of Styron's *Confessions of Nat Turner,* "Mr. William Styron and the Reverend Turner," should outlast the novel because of Thelwell's incisive commentary on Black language and Black thought. His other essays, whether dealing with Black Studies programs or with recollections of the Mississippi Delta, reveal an equally constant intelligence and keen perception.

Although Thelwell was born in Jamaica, West Indies, and did not come to the United States until 1959 to study at Howard, most of his writing is rooted in the Black American experience. Thelwell has had an intimate acquaintance with the Mississippi Delta through his association with the Student Non-Violent Coordinating Committee (SNCC) and the Mississippi Freedom Party.

Traveling south from Memphis on Highway 49, one crosses over the last rolling hill and the Mississippi Delta stretches before you like the sea, an unbroken monotony of land so flat as to appear unnatural. So pervasive is this low-ceilinged, almost total flatness that one loses all other dimensions of space and vision. An endless succession of cotton and soybean fields surround the road.

A few weather-greyed shacks, stark, skeletal and abrasively ugly perch in a precarious oasis hacked out in the narrow, neutral strip between the road and the encroaching fields. Contemptuous of weather, time and gravity, they stand apparently empty, long-abandoned and sheltering nothing but the wind. Then some appear, no different in point of squalor and decrepitude from the others, except that people stand before them.

At one point a single huge tree, off in a cotton field a distance, breaks the horizon. It is the first tree of any size that has appeared. This tree is an oak that bears small, gnarled acorns so bitter that there is no animal that will eat them. Its wood is very hard, but is knotty, faulted, and with a grain so treacherous and erratic that it cannot easily be worked. It is used for nothing more durable than a weapon. In this region they are called blackjacks, from the sootlike darkness of the bark, and find utility mainly in conversation as a metaphor of hardness, "tougher'n a blackjack oak."

This one is unusual beyond its mere presence and size, having both name and history. Its appearance, too, is unusual. The trunk and lower limbs are fire-charred to a dull black. These limbs are leafless and dead, but the top-most branches in the center of the tree continue to grow. In a strange inharmony the living oak flourishes out of the cinders of its own corpse. White folk call this tree the Nigger Jack, while Negroes speak of it hardly at all, save on those Sundays when the tree becomes the central symbol in some hell-fire sermon, for it is widely known that the flames that burned the oak roasted the bodies of slaves judged dangerous beyond redemption or control.

Once, it is said, some young black men from the county, returned from defeating the Kaiser, resolved to fell and burn the tree. On the night before this event was to take place, a huge and fiery cross was seen to shine at the base of the tree, burning through the night and into the next day.

For many years—the space of three generations—the land around this tree has lain fallow, producing annually only a tangled transient jungle of rabbit grass and myriad nameless weeds, for no Negro could be found who might be bribed, persuaded, or coerced into working there.

Lowe Junior grunted deep in his chest as the heavy, broad-bladed chopping hoe hit into the dry black earth. He jerked it up, sighted on the next clump of wire-grass and weeds, and drove the hoe-blade into the furrow just beyond the weeds, and with the same smooth motion pulled the blade towards his body and slightly upwards, neatly grubbing out the intruder in a little cloud of dust, without touching the flanking cotton plants.

"Sho do seem like the grass growin' faster'n the cotton." He leaned on the hoe handle and inspected the grubbed-up weed. "Hit be greener an' fatter'n the cotton evrahtime. Heah hit is, middle o' June, an hit ain't sca'cely to mah knee yet." He ran his glance over the rows of stunted plants, already turning a dull brownish green, then squinted down the row he was chopping, estimating the work left. He saw much "grass" wrestling its way around and between the cotton. "Finish dishyer after dinner," he said, noting that the sun had already cleared the tip of the blackjack oak which stood some ten rows into the middle of the field. Dragging his hoe he started towards the tree's shade.

Lowe Junior was tall, a gaunt, slightly-stooped figure as he shambled with the foot-dragging, slightly pigeon-toed, stiff-backed gait that a man develops straddling new-turned furrows while holding down the jerking, bucking handle of a bull-tongue plow. His boots and the dragging hoe raised a fine powder of dust around his knees. When he reached the tree he leaned his tool against the trunk and stretched himself. He moved his shoulders, feeling the pull of the overalls where the straps had worn into his flesh during the morning's work. Holding the small of his back, he arched his middle forward to ease the numb, cramping ache that hardly seemed to leave the muscles in his back. Then he straightened up and stood for a while looking out over his cotton.

Then Lowe Junior turned to the tree and took a pail which hung from one of the broken stubs. He touched the blackened trunk, running his hands over the rough cinders. "Thet fiah oney toughed yo' up, thass all . . . an there ain't nothin' wrong with thet." There was something familiar, almost affectionate, in his voice and action. When he first started working this section, he had carefully avoided the tree, sitting on the hot earth in the rows to eat and rest. But he had become accustomed to the tree now, was grateful for its shade, and he found himself accepting it as the only other living thing he encountered during the day. After all, he assured himself, "Hit cain't be no harm to no tree, fo' a certain fack."

He eased himself down ponderously, almost painfully, like a man too old or too fat, and began to eat. In the pail were butter beans boiled with country peppers, wild onions, and slabs of salted fatback. This stew was tepid, almost perceptibly warm from the midday heat. The coating of pork grease that had floated to the top had not congealed. Lowe Junior briefly debated making a small fire but decided against taking the time. He ate quickly, stirring the stew and scooping it into his mouth with a thin square of cornbread, biting into the gravy-soaked bread, then chewing and swallowing rapidly. Finishing his meal he drank deeply from a kerosene tin filled with water and covered with burlap (wet in the morning but now bone dry), which stood among the roots of the tree.

He stretched himself again, yawned, belched, spat, and braced himself firmly against the tree. He lay there limply, his eyes closed as though to shut out the rows and rows of small, drying-out plants that represented the work of his hands, every day, from can see to can't, since early in the spring.

"Ef hit would jes' rain some . . . seems like the mo' a man strain, hits the harder times git. Li'l rain now, an' the cotton be right up, but soon'll be too late." Weariness spread in him and the effort even of thinking was too great. He just lay there inert, more passive even than the tree, which at least stood. Even if by some miracle this cotton in the section he was "halfing" for Mr. Riley Peterson survived the drought, rains coming in August or September would turn the dust into mud and rot whatever cotton was ripening in the bolls—or else wash it into the mud.

A sudden panic came upon Lowe Junior, stretched beneath the tree. He could hardly feel his body, which was just a numbness. He felt that he could not rise, could not even begin, for his body would not obey him. For a brief moment he was terrified of making the effort lest he fail. Then he sat up suddenly, almost falling over forward from the violence of his effort. "Better study out whut t' do. No profit to layin' here scarin' m'se'f. Quarter section be a lot o' farmin' fo' a man. Sho ain't be able to keep t' grass outen the cotton by myse'f."

This was a problem for him, had been ever since he had asked Mr. Peterson to give him this quarter section. He was young but a good worker; still Mr. Peterson might not have given it to him had it not been for the fact that no other tenant would take it. Lowe Junior did not want to ask for help with the chopping because, in "halfing," the cost of the seed, fertilizer, ginning, and any hired help came out of the tenant's half. Already most of his half belonged to Mr. J. D. Odum, the merchant in Sunflower who had "furnished" him. He knew that he would have to have help with the picking, and did not want to hire any help before then, when he would at least have an idea of the crop's potential. "Man can en' up with nothin' thet way," he muttered. "Hit'll happen anyways, tho'. Figured to put in eight mebbe even nine bale fo' my share come the crop . . . now be the grace o' the good Gawd ef ah makes fo' . . . man doan feel much even t' keep on . . . Lawd, hit be better t' die, than t' live so hard." He found little comfort in those grim lines from the old Blues to which his grandmother was so partial. She was always incanting that song as though it had a special meaning for her.

After his father died, and his mother went off to the north to find work, it was the old woman, pious and accepting, who had told him the old stories, raised him in the Church, and interpreted for him the ways of their world. He remembered her story of how God had put two boxes into the world, one big and the other small. The first Negro and the first white man had seen the boxes at the same time and run towards them, but the Negro arrived first and greedily appropriated for himself the larger box. Unfortunately this box contained a plough, a hoe, a cop-axe, and a mule, while the smaller box contained a pen, paper, and a ledger book. "An' thass why," the old woman would conclude, her face serious, "the Nigger been aworkin' evah since, an' the white man he reckon up the crop; he be sittin' theah at crop time, jes' afigurin' an' areckonin'; he say

> Noughts a nought,
> Figgers a figger,
> All fo' us folks,
> None fo' the Nigger.

He had been fifteen before he even began to doubt the authenticity of this explanation. Now the old lady was ailing and very old. But she had not lost her faith in the ultimate justice of the Lord or her stoic acceptance of whatever He sent. It was a joke among the neighbors that when the good sisters of the Church went in to see the old lady, now failing in sight and almost bedridden, her answer to the question, "How yo' keepin', Miz Culvah?" invariably was "Porely, thank d' Lawd." Lowe Junior chuckled, got up, dusted off his clothes, and went out into the sun.

That evening he stopped work early, just as the sun was setting, and started home, trudging slowly over the flat dusty road past fields, a few as parched and poor as his own, and large ones where elaborate machinery hurled silvery sprays over rows of tall lush plants. A wind swept the fine cool spray into the road. He felt the pleasant tickling points of coldness on his face and saw the grayish dust coating his overalls turn dark with the moisture. Minute grains of mud formed on his skin. He looked into the dazzling spray and saw a band of color where the setting sun made a rainbow.

> *D'Lawd give Noah d' rainbow sign,*
> *No mo' watah, d' fiah nex' time.*

"Thass whut the ol' woman would say, an tell evrahbody thet she seen d' Lawd's sign. Be jes' sun an' watah, tho'." He did not look at the green fields. Looking straight ahead into the dust of the road, he increased his pace. He wanted only to get home.

Just where the dust road meets the highway, at the very edge of a huge field, was the shack. Tin-roofed with gray clapboard sides painted only with the stain of

time and weather, it had two small rooms. As Lowe
Junior came up the road, it seemed to be tossed and balanced on a sea of brown stalks, the remains of last year's
bean crop which came up to the back door.

In the front, the small bare yard was shaded by a pecan
tree already in blossom. Small lots, well-kept and tidy,
grew okra, butter-bean and collard green plants on both
sides of the yard. Lowe Junior walked around the shack
to a standpipe in back of the stoop. He washed the dust
from his head and arms, filled his pail and drank. The
water was brown, tepid, and rusty-tasting. He sprinkled
the okra and bean plants, then entered the shack. The
fire was out, and the huge pot hanging over the fire, from
which he had taken his dinner that morning, had not
been touched.

"Mam, Mam," he called softly, "Yo' awright?" There
was no answer, and he went into the old woman's
room. The room was stifling-hot as the tin roof radiated
the day's heat. The air was heavy with the smell of stale
urine, old flesh, and night sweat. The old lady lay against
the wall, partially covered by an old quilt. A ray of sunlight beamed through a small knothole and lighted up
the lined and creasing skin pattern on one side of her
face. A single fly buzzed noisily around her open mouth
and lighted on the tuft of straggling white hairs on her
chin. Her eyes stared at a framed picture of the bleeding heart of Jesus, violent red and surrounded by a
wreath of murderous-looking thorns and a hopeful glow,
which hung on the opposite wall above the motto, "The
Blood of Jesus Saves."

Lowe Junior searched his pockets slowly, almost absently, for two coins to place over her eyes. His gaze

never left her face and, as he looked, the ray of sunlight
gradually diminished, seeming to withdraw reluctantly
from the face, finally leaving it to shadow.

Failing to find any coins, he straightened the limbs,
pulled the quilt over the face, and went to tell the neighbors.

When he returned, the thick purple Delta darkness had
descended with a tropical suddenness. He added more
beans, fatback and water to the stew, and started the
fire. Then he lit a kerosene lantern and took it into the
yard to a spot beneath the pecan tree. He hung the
lantern on a branch and began to dig.

The neighbors found him still digging when they began
to arrive in the little yard. The first small group of women was led by Sister Beulah, a big, imposing, very
black woman with a reputation for fierce holiness.
She stood out from the worn and subdued group not only
because of the crisp whiteness of her robe and bandanna
but in her purposeful, almost aggressive manner. She
led the women to the side of the hole.

"Sho sorry t' heah 'bout Sistah Culvah, but as you knows
. . . ," she began.

"She inside," Lowe Junior said without looking up,
"an' ah thanks yo' all fo' comin'."

Interrupted in mid-benediction, Beulah stood with
her mouth open. She had failed to officiate at buryings
in the community only twice in the past twenty years,
and then only because she had been holding revivals at
the other end of the state. She had never quite forgiven
the families of the deceased for not awaiting her return.

She resented Lowe Junior's thanks, the first she had ever received for doing what she thought of as an indispensable service. May as well thank the grave.

"Thet boy sho actin' funny," she murmured, and swept into the shack to take charge of preparations.

More neighbors straggled into the yard. Another lantern was brought and hung in the tree, widening the chancy and uncertain perimeter of light in the otherwise enveloping blackness of the Delta night. Each man arriving offered to help Lowe Junior with the digging. Some had even brought tools, but Lowe Junior stonily refused all offers.

"Ah be finished time the box git heah," he answered without looking at the men. "Sho do thank yo', tho'."

So the men sat and smoked, speaking only in murmurs and infrequently. The women passed out steaming plates of stew and tins of coffee bitter with chicory. Lowe Junior declined all food. The plates in the shack were emptied and rotated until all were fed. After a muttered consultation,.one of the men approached Lowe Junior. He was old, his hair very white against his skin. He was very neat and careful of himself, moving with great dignity. His faded overalls were clean and shiny from the iron. He stood quietly at the side of the hole until Lowe Junior stopped work and looked up at him. Then he spoke, but so softly that the other men could not make out his words. The yard was very silent.

"Brothar Culvah. The peoples ain't easy in min'. They come to he'p yo' an heah yo' takin' no he'p." Lowe Junior said nothing.

"In time o' grief, praise Jesus, folks, they wants t', an' mo'n thet, they needs, t' he'p . . . they come t' pay respeck t' the daid an' share the burden an' sarrow o' d' livin'. Thass how hits allus bin . . . Son, when folks offer comfort an' he'p, a man mus' accep' hit, 'caus hit's mebbe all they got."

Lowe Junior looked at the old man.

"Yo' unnerstan' what ah'm asayin', son?" he asked gently. "The peoples doan feel like as if they got any- thang t' do heah, anythang thet they needs t' be adoin'."

Lowe Junior looked into the darkness. His voice was low and without inflection. "Hit ain't no he'p to give, ain't no sarrow t' share. Hits jes' thet the ol' woman was ol', an now she daid. Ain't no sarrow in thet."

They became aware of a sound. It came from the shack and at first did not seem to intrude or in any way chal- lenge the dark silence. It began as a deep sonorous hum, close in pitch to the sound of silence. Then it grew, ca- denced and inflected, gathering power and volume un- til it filled the yard and was present, physical and real. The men picked up the moan and it became a hymn.

hhhmmmmmmmmMMMAY THE CIRCLE . . . BE UN-
BROKEN BYE AN BYE, LAWD . . . BYE ANNNN BYE

"Peoples can sang," Lowe Junior said. "Praise Jesus, they can allus do thet."

The old man walked away silent. He sat on the stoop ignoring the questioning looks of the others. He hunched over, his frail body gently rocking back and forth, as though moved against his will by the throbbing cadences of the singing. He sat there in isolation, his eyes looking into the darkness as at his own approaching end, his face etched with lines of a private and unnamable old man's sorrow. Deep and low in his chest he began to hum the dirge melody.

Lowe Junior chopped viciously at the earth. The people intoned the old and troubled music that they were born to, which, along with a capacity to endure, was their only legacy from the generations that had gone before, the music that gathered around them, close, warm and personal as the physical throbbing of their natural life.

When the hole was to Lowe Junior's chin, the Haskell boys came into the yard carrying the coffin. It was of green pitchpine, the boards rough-planed so that all depressions on the surface of the boards were sticky with sap. The men also brought two boxes so that the coffin would not rest on the ground. The Haskells stood by the hole, wiping their gummy hands on their overalls.

"Yo' reckon hit'll be awright?" Ben Haskell asked.

"Sholey. Sho, hit'll be jes fine. Yo' done real good; hits a coffin, ain't hit?" Lowe Junior still had not looked at the coffin, which was surrounded by the neighbor men. The Haskells stood silent, looking at him.

" 'Sides, ol' woman . . . allus was right partial t' scent o' pine. Yassuh, hit'll be right fine," Lowe Junior said. Ben Haskell smiled, a diffident embarrassed stretching of his mouth. "Yo' said cedar, but see, quick as yo' needed hit, pine wuz all we could git."

"Thass right," his brother assented.

Leastwise, Lowe Junior thought, Mist' Odum wouldn' give yo' all cedar fo' credit. He repeated softly, "Yo' done good, real good," The Haskells beamed, relieved, and expressed again their sympathy before moving away.

The yard was now full, some twenty persons stood,

hunkered, or sat around. Set on the boxes in the center of the group, the raw white coffin dominated the scene like an altar, filling the air with the pungent odor of crude turpentine.

Lowe Junior walked around the coffin and approached the steps of the shack. The neighbors' eyes followed him. Sister Beulah met him at the door. He saw the faces of the other women peering down at him from behind her. All conversation ceased.

"Brothah Culvah, this yer ah'm agonna say ain't strickly mah business. Some would say hit rightly ain't *none* o' mah concern atall." She paused, looking at Lowe Junior and the men in the yard. Nothing was said, and she continued. "But lookin' at hit anothah way, hit what ah'm gonna say, *is* mah business. Hits bin troublin' mah min', an hits lotsa othah folks heah, what ah *knows* feel d' same way." When she paused again, there was a faint assenting Ahmen from the people.

"So ah'm agonna say hit . . . Now, yo' all knows me, bin apreachin' an aservin' the Lawd in these parts fo' thutty year, an live heah thutty year befo' thet." Murmurs of "Thass right" came from the group.

"Yas, thass the Lawd's truth, an ah knows Sistah Culvah, Miss Alice we used t' call her, from the fust come off t' plantation, an' nobody evah had a word o' bad to say 'bout her, praise Jesus. Yas, an' ah know yo' po' mothah, an yo' se'f, Brothah Culvah, from evah since." The murmurs from the neighbors were stronger now. Encouraged, Sister Beulah continued. She was now speaking louder than anyone had spoken in the yard all evening.

"She wuz a good woman, a go-o-d woman, she knowed Jesus an' she wuz saved. Hits true, towards the las' when she wuz porely an' gittin' up in age, she couldn't git to meetin' to praise her Gawd, but yo' all knows she *lo-oved* the Church." She took a deep breath. "Now, ah knows thet back then, in slavery times, when the ol' folks could' do no bettah, an' had to hol' buryin's an' Chris'nin' an' evrah-thang at night. But, thank Jesus, them days is gone. They's gone. Hit ain't fittin' an' hit ain't right an' propah t' hol' no buryin' at night, leas' hit ain't bin done herebouts. The body o' the good sistah, now called t' Glorah, ain't even bin churched. Yo' knows thet ain't right. Ah knows thet, effen she could have somepin t' say, she'd want hit done right at the las'! Ah *kno-o-ows* in mah heart she would."

"Yas, yas, ahah, praise Jesus." The neighbors agreed.

"An Brothah Culvah, yo' a young man, yo' a Gawd-fearin' man, an' ah knows yo' wants t' do right. Cause . . . yo' know hit says . . . the longes' road mus' ha' some endin', but a good name endureth fo'evah." On this dramatic and veiled note of warning the huge white-draped woman ended.

Everyone was quiet, but there was a faint expectant shuffling of feet as the people looked at Lowe Junior.

"'Tain't no call t' fret yo'se'f," he said. "Ol' woman wuz ol' an now she gone. Ah be aburyin' her tonight." There was a quickly-stifled murmur from the people. No one spoke, and Lowe Junior continued more softly.

"'Tain't thet whut yo' say ain't got right to hit, Sta' Beulah, 'cause hit do. But hits no law say thet effen yo' buryin' t' do, hit cain't be done in the night."

"Yas, Brothah Culvah, effen yo' *got* t' do hit. Doan seem like t' me hits no hurry . . ." Beulah said.

"Yas'm, hit is a hurry. See, ah feel like ah should take care o' this thang personal. Ol' woman raise me from when ah wuz young, ah wants t' take care o' the buryin' personal."

"Whut's wrong with t'morrow? Yo' answer me thet."

"Be no tellin' jes' where ah'll be t'morrow," Lowe Junior said, lifting one end of the coffin and asking Ben Haskell to help with the other end. They took it into the shack to receive the body.

"Hey, Lowe, yo' sho nuff fixin' t' leave?" Ben could not keep the excitement out of his voice.

"Thass right." Lowe Junior's first knowledge of his decision had come when he heard himself telling Beulah, a moment before.

"Yo' mean yo' ain't even gon' stay t' make yo' crop?"

"Any one o' yo' all wants t' work hit is welcome t' my share. Ah'll sign a paper so Mist' Peterson an Mist' Odum'll know." Temptation and fear struggled in Ben's eyes, and finally he said only, "Ah'll tell d' other'ns . . . but supposin' no one wants t' take hit?"

"Yo' mean 'bout Mist' Peterson . . . well, he got mo' cotton. Fack is, he got 'bout all theah is."

"Lawd's truth," Ben agreed, and went quickly to share the news with the men in the yard. There the women were grouped around Sister Beulah who was threatening to go home. After what she judged to be sufficient entreaty to mollify her hurt dignity, she agreed to remain and conduct the burial, but only because "hits mah bounden duty to see to hit thet the pore daid woman gits a propah Christian service." She led the women into the shack to put the old lady into the coffin.

After everyone had taken a last look at the corpse, Ben Haskell nailed the lid on and the coffin was brought out and placed on the boxes. During the singing of "Leaning on the Everlasting Arms," two of the women began to cry. Lowe Junior stood a short distance off under the shadow of the pecan tree and looked out over the darkness. He took no part in the singing until the lines of "Amazing Grace,"

Ah wunst wuz lost but now ah'm Found,
Wuz blind but now ah See.

In a loud but totally uninflected voice, he repeated "Wuz blind but now ah See."

This unexpected voice, coming as it were from behind her, distracted Sister Beulah who had begun to "line out" the succeeding lines for the benefit of any backsliders who might have forgotten them. She stopped, turned, and glared at Lowe Junior, then continued in the joyful and triumphant voice of one whose seat in the Kingdom is secure beyond all challenge.

"*'Twuz Grace thet taught mah heart t' feah,*" she exulted; "*An' Grace mah feah relieved.*" Her face was illuminated, radiant with the security of grace.

When the coffin was being lowered and was a quarter of the way down, the rope under the head slipped, and it thudded into the hole, almost upright. The people stood in momentary shocked silence. Sister Beulah at the head of the grave raised her massive white-sleeved arms to the sky as though appealing for divine vindication of this sacrilege, the result of Lowe Junior's stubbornness. Lowe Junior quickly lay flat on the edge of the grave, and shoved the high end of the coffin with all his strength. He grunted with the effort and the box slid into place with a heavy thump, followed by the rattle of dirt and pebbles from the sides.

At that moment the sky lightened. They all looked up and saw the risen moon peering from behind a wall of dark clouds that had not been there when the sun set.

"Glorah, Glorah!" a man shouted hoarsely, and the ritual resumed. Sister Beulah had thought to preach her famous "Dead Bones Arisin" sermon, capped with a few well-chosen words on the certain doom of impious children, but recent events had lessened her zeal. Almost perfunctorily she recounted the joys and glories of Salvation and the rewards awaiting the departed sister. Then they piled dirt on the coffin, patted down the pile, and departed.

Lowe Junior sat on the steps. Barely acknowledging the final murmured consolations, he watched the neighbors leave. He realized that he was not alone when the old man approached the stoop.

"Ah heah yo' is leavin', Brothah Culvah. Done any thankin' on wheah yo' goin' an' whut yo' gonna be doin'?"

Lowe Junior did not answer. He in no way acknowledged the old man's presence.

"Thass awright, yo' doan have t' answer 'cause ah knows—yo' ain't! Jes' like ah wuz when ah wuz 'bout yo' age. An ah lef' too, din' know wheah ah wuz agoin' nor whut ah wuz lookin' fo'. Effen yo' doan know whut yo' seekin', Brothah Culvah, yo' cain' know when yo' fin' hit."

Now Lowe Junior was looking at the man; he seemed interested in what he was saying. It was the first interest he had shown in anyone else that evening.

"See, Brothah Culvah, ah traveled aroun' some when
ah wuz yowr age, an heah ah is now. Ah never foun' no
bettah place nowheahs." He shook his head. "Fo' usses,
theah wuzn't none, leastways not thet ah could fin'."

"But at leas' yo' looked," Lowe Junior said.

"Thass why ah'm asayin' t' yo' whut ah is. 'Cause ah
did. Brothah Culvah, yo' a good worker, yo' knows farmin' an cotton, but whut else do yo' know? Ah disbelieves
thet yo' even bin so far as Memphis."

"Well," Lowe Junior said, "t'morrow thet won' be true.
But ah 'preciates yo' kin'ness."

The old man hobbled into the darkness, shrouded in
his own knowledge.

Lowe Junior sat on the steps and watched him leave,
until finally he was alone. He went to the tree, blew the
lamp out, and sat in the darkness. . . . When the sun came
up next morning he had not moved. The astringent
pitchpine smell still hovered in the still air. Lowe Junior
saw that the morning sky was covered by a heavy metal-
lic-grey cloud that had come swirling up from the Gulf
in the dark. He entered the shack and looked about him
for something to take. In the old woman's room he found
nothing. He returned, picked up his hoe, turned around
in the small room, saw nothing else that he wanted, and
started to leave. On the steps he changed his mind and
re-entered the house. In the old woman's room he took
the picture of the Sacred Heart from the frame. Then
from a small wooden box he took a Bible which he held
by the covers and shook. Three crumpled bills fluttered
to the floor. He gave the book a final shake, tossed it into
the box, then picked up the bills and carefully wrapped
them in the picture. He placed the package in the long

deep side-pocket of his overalls. He picked up his hoe from the steps and started out. At the dirt road he turned, not towards the highway, but east towards his section. Soon he could see the top of the oak in the thin dawning light.

"Sho nevah put no stock in all thet talk 'bout thet tree," he mused. "Burned like thet on the sides an so green t' the top, hit allus did put me in min' o' Moses an the burnin' bush. But ah wager a daid houn', ain't no Nigger agoin' t' work thisyer lan' now."

He stood for awhile looking at the tree, at the lean runted plants. "Sho do feels like ah knows yo' evrah one, evrah row an clump o' grass like hit wuz the face o' mah own han' or mah own name."

He strode up to the tree, set his feet, and swung the hoe against the trunk with all the strength of his back. The hickory handle snapped with a crack like a rifle in the early morning. The blade went whirring into the cotton-rows. He felt the shock of the blow sting the palm of his hands, and shivver up into his shoulders. He stepped away from the tree and hurled the broken handle as far as he could into the field.

"Theah," he grunted, "yo' got the las' o' me thet yo' is gonna git—the natural las'."

He started back towards the highway at a dead run. There were tears in his eyes and his breath was gusty. He tired and slowed to a walk. He saw the first raindrops hitting heavy into the thick dust of the road, raising sudden explosions of dust and craters of dampness where they struck. Before he reached the cabin, torrents of water were lashing the face of the Delta. When he reached the highway, he turned once to look at the mean little house, gray and forlorn in the storm. He saw a pool already spreading around the roots of the pecan tree.

The dry earth gave off an acrid smell as the water dampened it. "Be nuff now fo' evrah one, white an black," Lowe Junior thought and laughed. "Sho doan mattah now effen they takes ovah mah fiel'. Hit be all washed out, evrah natural one."

The rain swept down with increased violence. He was completely drenched, streamlets ran down his face, washing away the dust. "Ah nevah seed the like. Sho now, be hongry folk heah this year. Even white folk be hongry in the Delta this winter." He walked steadily down the highway stretching into the distance.

Junius Edwards

Mother dear and daddy

Junius Edwards was born in Alexandria, Louisiana, and was graduated from the University of Oslo, Norway. One of his earliest short stories won the Writer's Digest Award in 1958; he was awarded a Eugene Saxton Fellowship in 1959. His novel, *If We Must Die,* was published in 1963. Edwards is now the owner and director of a successful advertising agency in New York City.

In "Mother Dear and Daddy," five recently orphaned children discover pain and overcome it with the strength of their love for one another.

They came in the night while we slept. We knew they were coming, but not when, and we expected to see them when they did. We never thought that they would come at night. When we got up, well, when John, my brother, got up (he was always getting up early), when he got up, he looked out of the window and ran and jumped back in bed and shook me and called my name.

"Jim, Jim, they here. They here already. Wake up, Jim. They—"

"Hey, quit shaking me. I been woke long time."

"They here," he ran to the window. "Come on look."

He didn't have to tell me "come on look" because I

was at the window when he got there, almost, anyway. They had come all right; we could see the cars parked in the yard, like big cats crouching, backs hunched, ready to attack.

"I'll go tell Mary, then," John said, and bolted out of the room as fast as you could blow out a coal oil lamp.

While he was out telling our three sisters, I stood there at the window and counted the cars. There were five in all, besides our car, and they were all black and shiny as my plate whenever I got through eating red beans and rice. Our car sat over there by itself, dusty and dirty as one of those bums that come by all the time wanting a meal.

I stood there, leaning on the windowsill, with my right foot on top of my left foot, scratching my left foot with my toes, and looking at our car. I could feel my eyes burning, burning, and the tears coming and washing the burns, and me sucking my tongue because of the burning and trying not to make a sound. My body went cold and inside it I could feel something surging up; not like being sick, this surging came up my whole body, my arms too, and ended with my eyes burning. I fought to hold it back, keep it buried. Even when I was alone, I always fought it, always won and kept it down, even at times when it was sudden and fast and got to my eyes and burned like hot needles behind my eyelids, hot needles with legs running around trying to get past my eyelids and spill out on my cheeks, even then I kept it down.

I had fought it for two weeks and I was good at it and getting better. Maybe I was good at it because of that first day. I had not fought it then. I had let it come, right in front of Aunt Mabel, I let it come, not trying to stop it, control it; I let it come.

"What we going to do?" I asked Aunt Mabel, after it had come, had shaken me and left me as empty as an unfilled grave. "What we going to do, Aunt Mabel?"

"Lord knows, son. Lord knows," Aunt Mabel said, sitting in her rocker, moving, slow, back and forth, looking down at me, on my knees, my arms resting on her huge right thigh and my head turned up to her, watching that round face, her lips tight now, her head shaking side to side, and her eyes clouded, and me not understanding her answer, but thinking I should and not daring to ask again and feeling the question pounding my brain: What we going to do? What we going to do?

"The Lord giveth and the Lord taketh away."

But, what we going to do? I could not understand Aunt Mabel. I did not know what her mumbling about The Lord had to do with this. All I knew was she had just told me Mother Dear and Daddy were dead. Mother Dear and Daddy were dead. Mother Dear and Daddy would not come back. Mother Dear and Daddy wouldn't take us home again. What we going to do?

"I want to go home. I want to go home," I screamed and got to my feet and ran to the door, realizing it was Aunt Mabel calling my name. I ran out to the yard where John and our sisters played, and right past them. I did not feel my feet move; I did not feel I owned a body. I wanted to get home. And hearing Aunt Mabel call my name, seeing houses, cars, people, trees, like one big thing made of windows, walls, wheels, heads, branches, arms and legs and behind that one big thing, our house, with our car out front, and our yard and our tree, and then the big thing was gone and I was at our house, running up the steps across the porch, as fast as I could, straight to the screened door, wham! and I lay on my back on the porch looking up at the screen, at the imprints made in it by my head and hands and my right knee. I got right up and started banging on the door, trying to twist the knob.

"Mother Dear! Daddy! Mother Dear! Daddy!" I called as loud as I could and kept banging on the door. Then, I ran to the back door and called again and banged and kicked the door. They did not come.

They would not come.

"Mother Dear! Daddy! It's me. Let me in. Open the door!"

They would not come.

I ran to the front, out to the street and turned and looked up to their room and saw the shades were drawn just as they were drawn when Mother Dear and Daddy took us over to Aunt Mabel's house to stay for the weekend while they went away fishing with cousin Bob.

I cupped my hands up to my mouth.

"Mother Dear. Daddy. Mother Dear! Daddy!"

I called, and called again and all the while I kept my eyes glued on that window, waiting. Any moment now, any second now, now, *now*, waited to see that white shade zoom up and then the window, and then Mother Dear and Daddy, both together, lean out, smiling, laughing, waving, calling my name, now, now, *now*.

They did not come.

They would not come. The shade stood still, stayed still, with the sun shining on it through the window pane; stayed still, as if the sun were a huge nail shooting through the pane and holding it down. It did not go up. It would not go up.

They would not come.

I knew it. Suddenly, just like that, snap, I knew they would not come; could not come. The shades would stay still. I knew they would not come. I lowered my hands, my eyes darting from shaded window to shaded window, around the yard, under the house, searching, for what? I did not know, and then there was the car. My eyes were glued to the car, and I started over to it, slowly at first and then I ran and I stopped short and pressed my head up against the glass in the front door beside the steering wheel. The glass was hot on my nose and lips and forehead, and burned them, but I did not care, I pressed harder, as if by doing so I could push right through the glass, not breaking it, but melting through it. Then, I felt as though I *was* inside, in my favorite spot up front with Daddy, and in back were Mother Dear and John and our sisters; Daddy whistling and the trees going by and the farms and green, green, green, and other cars and Daddy starting to sing and all of us joining him singing "Choo-choo Train to Town," even Jo Ann and Willie Mae, who had not learned the words yet, singing, singing, and ending laughing and feeling Daddy's hand on my head.

"Jim." I turned from the window, and it was Aunt Mabel's hand on my head.

"Come on, son." She took my right hand and led me up the street as if I were a baby just starting to walk.

"What we going to do, Aunt Mabel?"

"You got to be brave, Jim. You the oldest. You got to look out for your brother and sisters."

I decided then that I would not let my brother and sisters see me cry, ever. I was twelve years old and the oldest and I had to take care of them.

"When can we go back home, Aunt Mabel?"

"I guess we ought to move over to your house while we wait for the family to get here," Aunt Mabel said. "It's bigger than mine and your clothes there."

I looked up at Aunt Mabel. I had not expected her to move back with us. I wanted only we children to move back home.

When we got back to Aunt Mabel's house I told John about the automobile accident and that Mother Dear and Daddy were dead. John was only eight, but he understood and he cried and I understood just how he felt, so I left him alone.

The next day we moved back to our house. Aunt Mabel, too. Every time one of our sisters would ask for Mother Dear and Daddy we always said they were gone away. They were too young to understand about death.

Aunt Mabel told me that our Uncles and Aunts and Grandparents were coming. I didn't know any of them. I remembered Christmas presents from them and Mother Dear and Daddy talking about them, but I had never seen them.

"They're good folks," Aunt Mabel said, "and it won't make no difference which one you all go to live with."

"But, Aunt Mabel. We going to stay home."

"You can't, son. You all too young to stay here by yourself and I can't take care of you."

"I can take care of us, Aunt Mabel. I'm the oldest. I can take care of us."

Aunt Mabel smiled. "Bet you could, too. But you all need somebody to be a Mama and a Papa to you. You all got to go live with one of your Aunts and Uncles."

I knew right away that Aunt Mabel was right. I told John about it and we started trying to guess where we would go. The family was scattered all over, mostly in big cities like New York, Philadelphia, and Boston. Our Grandfather on Daddy's side was in Texas. John and I couldn't decide what we liked best: Texas and horses or big cities and buildings. We talked about it every day while we waited for them to come, and now they were here.

I left the window and started to get dressed. John ran back into the room.

"Them won't wake up."

"They can sleep, then," I said. "Let's go see where the cars came from."

We got dressed and ran out to the yard and looked at the license plates. There were two from New York, two from Pennsylvania and one from Massachusetts.

"None of them from Texas," I said.

"Which one you like best?" asked John.

"That one," I said, pointing to the one from Massachusetts. I liked it because it was the biggest one. The five of us could get in it without any trouble at all.

We examined each car carefully for an hour and then Aunt Mabel called us and told us to come in the house.

"They all here," she said, "all that's coming, I guess. Now, you all be good so they'll like you."

I followed Aunt Mabel into the living room. I could feel John right behind me, up close, and I could hear his breathing.

"Here the boys," Aunt Mabel announced, and walked across the room and sat down.

John and I stopped at the door. Our sisters were lined up, side by side, in the middle of the room, smiling. I had heard voices before we came into the room, but now

there was silence and all eyes were on us. They sat in a
half circle in straight-back chairs, near the walls around
the room. I looked at them. I stared at each face. Aunt
Mabel and our sisters were the only smiling faces I saw.
I didn't know about John, but right at that moment, I
was scared. I wanted to turn and run away as fast as I
could. I felt as if I had committed the worst crime and
those faces hated me for it. Besides Aunt Mabel, there
were five men and five women, all dressed in black.
Each man had a black line above his upper lip. The two
men who were fat had thick black lines and other three
had thinner ones. I didn't like the lines. Daddy never
wore one and I always thought his face was cleaner and
friendlier and happier than other men I had seen who
wore them.

I noticed the features of these people right away.
They were all like Mother Dear, Aunt Mabel and our
sisters, and they were pink rose. I knew they were
Mother Dear's relatives. Daddy didn't have any brothers
or sisters and he used to tell John and me whenever
we got into a fight with each other that we should be
kind to each other because we were brothers and it was
good to have a brother and that he wished he had had
brothers and sisters. Mother Dear had plenty of brothers
and sisters. She had three brothers, and I knew them
right away as the three who weren't fat, and three sisters, Aunt Mabel, of course, and the two women who sat
beside the fat men.

I stood there looking, staring at those faces that looked
as if they had just taken straight castor oil. I looked at
John, now standing at my right. He stood there with his
mouth hanging open and his eyes straight ahead. I

could tell he was scared and as soon as I knew he was
scared, I wasn't scared any more and I wanted to tell
him not to be scared because I wasn't going to let anything happen to him. Just when I was about to tell him,
Aunt Mabel broke the silence.

"Come on over here next to your sisters," she said.

We shuffled over to where our sisters were and stood
there like slaves on auction.

"They good children," Aunt Mabel said. "No trouble
at all."

The others still kept quiet, except for whispers among
themselves.

"Say your names, boys," Aunt Mabel said.

"James," I said.

"John," said John.

"We call James, Jim," Aunt Mabel said, and smiled
at me.

I looked at her. It was all right for her to call me Jim.
Mother Dear and Daddy called me Jim. I looked back at
those faces. I didn't want *them* to call me Jim.

"Well," Aunt Mabel said to them, "You all going to
tell the boys your names?"

They introduced themselves to us, not smiling, not
changing those castor oil expressions. Apparently they
had already introduced themselves to our sisters.

"Mabel," one of the fat men said, "why don't you get
these kids out of here so we can talk."

"Jim, you and the children go in the dining room,"
Aunt Mabel said, and when we were going, she added,
"And close the door."

We went into the dining room and I closed the door.
Our sisters sat down in the middle of the floor and

played. John stood over them, watching, but when he saw me with my ear to the door, he came over and joined me. We faced each other with our heads pressed up against the door and we listened. The only voice I could recognize was Aunt Mabel's.

"Carol and I have thought this thing over and we can see our way clear to take the girls," one of the men said.

"Now, wait a minute, Sam," another man said. "We thought we'd take *one* of the girls, at least."

Then, for a minute it sounded as if they were all trying to get a word in. They talked all at the same time, even yelled. It sounded as if everyone wanted a girl.

"Lord have mercy. You mean you going to split them up? You mean they won't be together?"

"Five kids? Frankly, we can't afford two, but we'd be willing to take the three girls."

There was another minute of all of them trying to speak at the same time, at the top of their voices, each one wanting a girl.

"Why don't you all talk like people? I don't like to see them split up, but I guess five is too many for anybody, specilly when they not your own."

"Then you understand that they'll have to be separated? There's no other way, and since we already have a son, we thought we would take one of the girls."

"Well," Aunt Mabel said, "look like to me all you all want a girl. I didn't hear nobody say nothing about the boys yet."

There was silence. John and I pressed harder against the door. John's mouth was open, his bottom lip hanging, and he was staring at me hard. I could tell he was scared and I must have looked scared to him so I closed my own mouth and tried to swallow. There was nothing to swallow and I had to open my mouth again and take a deep breath.

"Come to think of it, you all didn't say one word to them boys," Aunt Mabel said. "Why don't you all want boys?"

"We have a boy."

"We do, too."

"Girls are easier."

"Boys are impossible."

"Lord have mercy."

"Listen, Mabel, you don't understand the situation."

"Don't get on your high horse with me. Talk plain."

"All right, Mabel. The fact is, the boys are—well—they're too, well, too much like the father."

"What?"

"You heard me. I know that's why *we* don't want one, and it's probably why the others don't want one and it's no use avoiding it."

"Is that right? Is that why you all don't want one, too?" Aunt Mabel asked.

There was silence.

"Lord have mercy. I never heard such a thing in all my life. Your own sister's children, too."

"You don't understand, Mabel."

"No, I don't. Lord knows I don't. What you all doing up there? Passing? Huh? That what you doing? No. No. You couldn't be doing that. Even if you wanted to, you couldn't be doing that. You not that light that you can pass, none of you all. Lord have mercy. They too black for you. Your own sister's children."

John looked down at his hands, at the back of his hands and then at me and down at our sisters and at his hands again.

"I never thought I'd live to see the day my own flesh and blood would talk like that, and all the trouble in the world. My own sisters and brothers," Aunt Mabel said.

"Mabel, you've been here in this town all your life. This town isn't the world. You don't know how it is."

John rubbed the back of his hand on his pants and looked at it again.

I kept listening.

"It's hard enough like it is without having these boys, having to always explain about them. You can see that, Mabel. Look at us, how light we are. We'd always have to explain to everyone they're our dead sister's boys and people who we don't explain to will jump to all kinds of conclusions. Socially, we'd be out, too. No, Mabel. That's just the way it is and we can't do a thing about it. I, for one, have certain standards I want to live up to and having these boys won't help."

"I never thought it. I never thought it."

"That's the way it is, Mabel. Those boys will do none of us any good."

John went over to where our sisters played and stood over them, examining them.

Aunt Mabel said: "So that's how come you didn't want her to get married. That's how come you tried to get her away from here."

John kneeled down and touched each one of our sisters. He looked at them and at his hand, at them and at his hand, and then to me. Then, his eyes became shiny and he started batting his eyes and the sides of his face grew, his cheeks puffed way out, his mouth closed tight. He fought it all he could and I knew it was useless, he would not succeed. I could feel the same thing happening to me, but I held it back and concentrated on him, watched his swelling face until it exploded and thinking he might yell out, I rushed to him and got down on my knees and held him, held him close, just as Daddy would have, with my left arm around his back and my right hand behind his head, holding his head to my chest and felt his body shaking like a balloon when you let out the air and I listened to him groan like a whipped dog. I didn't say one word to him. I couldn't. I let him cry and I held him and watched our sisters and they suddenly realized he was crying and they came to us and helped me hold him and tried to get him to tell why he cried and when he would not tell they asked me and when I would not tell they stood there holding both of us until John got control of himself. He sat back on his heels and sobbed and the girls stepped back and watched him. I stood up and watched all of them. The girls stood there and watched him and waited, their faces alert, ready to run to him and help him. It was as if they knew, now, this was not a physical wound that made him cry, not a twisted arm, a stubbed toe, or a beating, and certainly not a cry that would make them laugh and yell "cry baby" at him. It was as if they knew it was a wound they had never had and that it was deeper than skin.

I heard the voices in the living room, louder now, and wilder, so I started back to my place at the door, but before I got there, John lost control again. We got to him at the same time and tried to hold him, but this time he pushed us away, fought us off, and got to his feet and ran into the living room. I got to my feet as fast as I could and ran after him into the living room. He was screaming now and when I ran into the living room, I stopped short at what I saw, John had run in and jumped in the lap of the first man he came to and he was there on his knees in the man's lap screaming and pounding the man's chest and face. The man pushed him off and John fell to the floor on his back and got right up and jumped in the man's lap again, still screaming, and pounded the man's chest and face with both his little fists.

"John, John, John!" I yelled, and ran to him and pulled him out of the man's lap, just in time, too, because the man swung at him back handed, but I had John down and the man missed. John, still screaming, kicking, struggled with me, trying to get away from me so he could get back to the man.

"John, John!" I yelled, shaking him, trying to make him hear me. "John, John!" but I could see he wasn't listening to me even though he was looking straight at me as I stood in front of him holding both of his arms and shouting his name. He only screamed.

Suddenly, I started walking backwards from him, holding his arms still, pulling him along with me until we were in the center of the room and then I smiled at him. "Come on, John, come on, John," I said, and laughed, laughed hard, looking into his eyes, I kept it up, laughed loud and harder still and felt my body shake from it. Then I saw John's face change, first a smile, then he broke into a laugh, too. I stared into his eyes and we laughed. We laughed. We laughed. We laughed. We threw our heads back and we laughed. We held each other's hands and danced round and round and laughed. Our sisters came and joined our dance. We formed a circle, all of us laughing, laughing, and we danced round and round. We were the only people in the world. We danced round and round and laughed and laughed.

"Hey," I said, "Choo-Choo Train, Choo-Choo Train" and they joined me:

> *"Choo-choo train, choo-choo train*
> *We going to take that choo-choo train*
> *Choo-choo train to town*
> *Choo-choo train*
> *Choo-choo train"*

Round and round "Choo-choo train" louder and louder I sang, "CHOO-CHOO TRAIN, CHOO-CHOO TRAIN, CHOO-CHOO TRAIN TO TEXAS" round and round "CHOO-CHOO TRAIN" until I realized what I had said and I screamed happily and said it again and again until they caught on and said it, too. We went faster and faster and said it louder and louder sounding like a Choo-choo Train: TEXAS, TEXAS, TEXAS, TEXAS, TEXAS . . .

Cyrus Colter

Black for dinner

In many ways, Cyrus Colter reminds me of his nineteenth-century predecessor, Charles Chesnutt. He has chosen, like Chesnutt, to delineate sympathetically the lives and problems of a minority within a minority. To Chesnutt, speaking in turn-of-the-century terms, these were "the problems of people with mixed blood which, while in the main the same as those of the true Negro, are in some instances and in some respects much more complex and difficult of treatment, in fiction as in life." In Colter's time, to treat the Black bourgeoisie with honesty and compassion is equally difficult and quite rare.

Colter shares a profession with Chesnutt—the law—and an area—the Midwest: Colter in Chicago, Chesnutt in Cleveland. For Colter, as it was for Chesnutt, writing is an avocation. He did not begin to write his stories until he was fifty years old. The writer in him was born much earlier, and one hopes he adds to his collection of short stories, *The Beach Umbrella*, and his novel, *The Rivers of Eros*, the writings of many years to come.

It was ten o'clock on Wednesday morning, and Anita sat alone at the table in her polished copper kitchen, sipping coffee. She was a pert little brown-skinned woman, short and very plump, almost dumpy, and wore sparkling rimless glasses. All her life she had been a vacillator. Despite almost thirty years as a well-off housewife, she abhorred making decisions and was never quite sure of them when made, but would stew and fret and finally end up asking her husband, Dave, what she should do. But Dave Hill, a wise, tolerant man, never seemed to mind.

For instance, two days hence—on Friday—she was to have in ten people for sit-down dinner; and the responsibilities involved were looming larger by the hour. She had invited Kate Horton, the undoubted social queen of the posh Hyde Park-Kenwood Negro community; and was then surprised, a little awed even, when Kate accepted. It meant effort, she now realized; for everything had to be just so; and Alice Smiley, another guest, and Kate's close friend, was just as fastidious as Kate. Neither had been to Anita's in over two years—not since the downstairs of her big house had been re-done, complete with sumptuous draperies and a new sofa. So she knew everything—furnishings, food, wines—would undergo, albeit with gracious smiles, a searching examination. Yet she felt inert, immobile—unable to plan beyond the menu. Bemused, she lit a cigarette, and stared off into space.

The rib roast had been ordered—there would be Yorkshire pudding to go with it, and Burgundy. And Mrs. Adams had been engaged to do everything—this was no job for Thelma, the regular cook. Thelma could help with the serving. Also, the linen, china and silver must be put out and made ready—tomorrow would be time enough for polishing the silver. She knew she didn't have the silver Kate Horton had, but what she did have was just as fine —twelve place settings: the knife, fork, spoon, salad fork, dessert spoon, and butter spreader. Kate of course had everything—plain and pierced serving spoons, gravy ladles, jelly servers, lemon forks, nut spoons, olive forks, cheese knives, cake servers, relish spoons, and varied other silver instruments Anita could not presently call to mind. And she remembered Kate's china was just as elaborate.

She wished *so* Dave were there. She needed him to lean against, to consult. He had been in New York on business now for two days, and would return that afternoon. But really he couldn't help her, she knew. Planning dinners and such were the remotest things from his world. His life was real estate. But she could at least think out loud to him if he were there—he always listened. She sat for awhile, then absently mashed out her cigarette, and went up the hall toward the living room.

She was proudest of the front part of her house—especially since the refurbishing. The parlor was large, with great expanses of red oriental rugs stretching back under dark, burnished furniture. A Chinese cabinet, pale blue, and beautifully filigreed, stood near the front of the hall-way and contained displays of her mother's Meissen figures—red-coated porcelain soldiers, brown and green shepherds, curtsying ladies of the court, and a flesh-pink, indolent Cupid. On the one unbroken wall of the parlor hung two large oils—a peasant girl, and an Italian landscape—and rouge damask draperies swept back from the windows.

She touched a finger down on an end table for dust, but knew Thelma dusted every day; then she bent over to knead the down-filled cushions on the new sofa, and put-tered briefly with the draperies. But what she longed to do was go upstairs, and take out her new dress again—her new black silk dress. Once already that morning she had taken it from her bedroom closet to inspect it with a mute delight. The very day Kate Horton and Alice Smiley said they could come, she had gone out to Saks and bought it; and it was the only dress she could ever re-member liking from the very first moment the saleslady brought it out, her own plumpness notwithstanding—lately she preferred darker colors that played down her pudgy shape. She felt the dress did this, and was chic and elegant besides—with a softly-full skirt, cut on a bias, *décolletage* tied in black silk. Kate and Alice would ap-prove, she was certain, for they—and the others too, for that matter—recognized fine clothes at a glance. Dave didn't know about the dress as yet, she reflected; it was delivered only yesterday; and it *was* expensive. He would only shrug, though, and smile.

She also remembered now she must have him check his liquor supply. She had already ordered the Burgundy, and a case of very good champagne—she had felt she needed his special permission for the champagne; but you could not serve *these* people a shoddy champagne. As he left for New York, Dave had smiled and agreed—he could be so casual when he was amused at her. He seemed tired these days, though; yet he never complained. Ah, and he must be warned against making any unfunny cracks about Alice's French poodles, for instance—or about Doug Horton's big boat. Anita smiled; and then started up the carpeted stairs—to see her dress again.

* * * *

That afternoon, about four o'clock, Dave came home, letting himself in at the front door. For a man in his mid-fifties, he looked youngish; brown, thick-set, of medium height, he wore a neat gabardine topcoat over his gray suit. But merely carrying his luggage in from the cab seemed to have exhausted him, for he was breathing hard.

Thelma, the husky young cook, smiled as she hurried up the hall to greet him. "Hi, Mister Dave!"

"Hi, child." He looked around wearily. "Where's everybody?"

"Mrs. Hill's upstairs. Here, let me have your bag. You look beat." Thelma took the bag and started up the stairs, as Dave removed his topcoat and hat and hung them in the stairs closet. Soon he too started upstairs.

When he turned at the landing and looked up, Anita was standing at the top with a big smile for him. "Hi, Honey!" she said.

"Hi, Peachie."

"How *was* little old New York?—And the flight?"

"Okay." He kissed her. "The flight was a little bumpy, in spots—coming back."

"Oh, I'd have been scared to death!"

He was impassive as they entered her bedroom.

"What've you been doing with yourself?" He held his smile on her.

"Now, what do you think!" she laughed.

"How *is* the party shaping up?"

She turned to sit down again at her dressing table. "...Okay—I guess." She was tentative. Then, as he stood behind her, she watched him in the mirror. "You're tired," she said.

"Oh, traveling always fags you out some." He walked across the hall to his own room now, and began opening his luggage. Soon he returned and handed her a small wrapped gift; and then went back to his room.

"Oh, my! Thank you! Say, this isn't a peace offering, is it?" she laughed to him across the hall. "Have you been a good boy?" She stretched over for the big pair of scissors on her writing desk, cut the thin gold twine from the package, and took out a small strand of cultured pearls. "Oh, pearls!" she cried.

"Cultured pearls," he said.

"Oh, they're lovely just the same! Lovely!" She held the necklace to her throat before the mirror. "I can wear these with my new black dress!"

Across the hall he was silent.

Thelma appeared at his bedroom door now, with two bourbons and water on a silver tray. "My friend," Dave smiled to her, "you've been reading my mind, you have. If you'll just tote that across the hall there, I'll be right with you."

When he returned to Anita, he was glum, preoccupied.

He lifted his drink off the tray and sank in her big chair. "Why don't you wear a gay dress?" he said, ". . . green, or white, or something—red, even. We'll have the champagne—and shoot 'em up a little." He grinned at her. "You've got the champagne crowd coming, haven't you?"

"Oh, now, honey!—I've got a *new* dress. It's quiet—real elegant. I couldn't promise how I'd look in some loud color, with *my* derrière."

"Your what?"

Anita laughed and adjusted her sparkling glasses. "Oh, forget it, please—we'll talk about it." They were silent, as she grew pensive—then irritable. "You promised we were going down to the Virgin Islands after Christmas," she said. "But you haven't mentioned it lately at all. Why? You need a vacation—I know that. I'm going to take the bull by the horns, Mister, and make the arrangements, myself."

He inspected his drink and said nothing. "Aw, hell, Peachie," he finally said, "Let's talk about that later, too. You'd better be thinking now about feeding all those swells you've got coming in here." He grinned at her again as he stood up to leave the room, holding his drink high as if to give a toast. "Whatta you say, kiddo?—let's shoot 'em up Friday night. And wear something *gay*, will you?"

* * * *

Friday evening arrived cold and rainy in early darkness. From outer Lake Michigan a wet November wind drove the slanting rain inland, dousing streets, parked cars, and the huge, swirling trees around Anita's big house, which from basement to attic was a schooner of blazing lights wallowing in the gale; and, inside, a wild fire leapt up the blackened cave of the fireplace, casting great, weird, frolicking shadows up against the paintings on the far wall.

Mrs. Adams, the cateress, and her staff had arrived and were in full charge. There were two white-coated bar boys—one to mix, and one to serve; a sensual-looking brown-skinned waitress, whom Thelma would assist; and Mrs. Adams, herself—fat, but very efficient. Mrs. Adams at the moment was in the kitchen collecting the oven drippings from the standing rib roast for making the Yorkshire pudding. She checked the clock; it was only six, and things were well along already. The guests weren't due until seven—which, Mrs. Adams knew, meant seven-thirty—so she hummed while she worked.

Dave had left his office at four o'clock and come home early to take a rest before the dinner. He fixed a drink and took it with him upstairs to his bedroom. He was somehow eager, keyed up, over the dinner. It was Anita's party, and he was doting, proud—the best people were coming. It was a good chore for her; might do something for her anemic self-confidence. He sat down, loosened his tie, and sipped his drink. He was convinced it was the *people* that made a party. You could have the finest house, foods, wines and all that, and then waste them on a bunch of boors—like casting pearls. But it wasn't that way tonight.

He undressed, put on a robe, and lay across the bed awhile. Later he took a slow tub bath, and rubbed himself vigorously. He stepped on the bathroom scales—175; weight about okay; down to where Cartwright said it had *better* be. Cartwright loved to warn you; he was an indelicate bastard for a heart man—most doctors were not. A man ought to be left alone to take what's coming to him in his own way, if he's got to take it. Cartwright had deprived him of cigarettes, and to what purpose? But so far, Anita had been kept in the dark about the whole matter—that was the important thing. He gave himself a lazy, methodical shave, and by six-thirty he was all dressed—in a trim grey suit and striped maroon tie; and then went downstairs to watch the preparations.

Upstairs, Anita's bedroom door was closed. She had wanted a nap, but her excitement was like caffeine. Bathed and warm, in mules and a silk robe, she lolled on her chaise longue, listening to the cold rain outside pelt the window panes. It seemed to her she had supervised a thousand details, and still she combed her brain for some disastrous oversight. And the dress. It had trapped her thoughts for two whole days now, holding her in a tumult of indecision; and Dave could not help in this. In fact, he had caused it all. She felt wronged—the dress was brand new, and she liked it *so*; had wanted to look her tasteful best, to wear something simple, expensive, secure. Red!— He was out of his mind. Nothing could be so frustrating as a man who didn't understand that what a woman wore sometimes depended on how she felt. But he had asked specially, which was unusual for him. Telling her what to wear!—he'd never done it before. It was sweet of him though, maybe; you never really knew, he was such a riddle sometimes. Yet so gentle always—a strange, tender man. The whole twenty-nine years of their marriage had been like this—wonderful years. She had just trusted him, and things always came out okay.

It was the same way before they were married—when

they were college students at Howard, in Washington. He was poor and required two jobs on the side; but his grades were always good, far better than hers, despite all the free time she had to study—her father, a Richmond physician, underwrote her education completely. She knew she had not been a good student; hadn't been able to study, couldn't concentrate, and would sit for hours gazing out the University library window daydreaming. Sometimes Dave would help her with her math, but on examinations she felt abandoned. And when he graduated a year and a half ahead of her, she despaired of ever finishing—and could only pray that he would ask her to marry him. That was all she wanted from life—she shut out thought of her future without it. Married to him, she would be rid of all her plaguing anxieties. Wherever they lived, whatever their life, richer or poorer, she would be set—always.

Her father too had liked Dave, from the beginning—but was often obliged to reassure her mother. "The boy is solid," he would say, "Solid." Anita knew how right he was, and still held the tenderest memories of him for helping her land Dave. Above everything her father ever did for her, this was the greatest by far; and when she finally graduated and married, he often visited them in Chicago. To her extravagant delight the two men became cronies. By then, Dave, already with a job in a Southside real estate firm, was scheming to save the money to establish his own business. It was some eight years later, when his business was finally going good, that she had been able to make a thirty thousand dollar contribution to it—at her father's death—and thus satisfy a burning urge to do something really outstanding for their marriage. For this urge had become acute the year before that, when their one child, Timmie, four years old, had died of polio, plunging young Dave into months of a desperate, silent grief that wrenched her heart.

But soon after, things began going better for them—and Dave made money. They traveled now, and some of her finest memories were linked to trips to California, Canada, the Caribbean, and once to South America. This was before they went to Europe, where now they had been three times. Dave loved Italy; and adored Florence—which they had just revisited the past spring. She had never known his moods so bright, his talk so free, as when they tramped the streets of Florence, or he badgered her about her walking shoes, and claimed her feet were flat. He loved to stand in the cloister of *Santa Croce*—of the year 1294 A.D.—and merely touch the crumbling bricks and mortar with his finger tips. And sometimes, with a drink in their hotel room before dinner, he would grow expansive, philosophical, a little wistful; she especially remembered one early evening, after their return from a trek up to the heights of the little church of *San Miniato*.

"The finest view of Florence is from *San Miniato*," he said, sprawled in a big chair in his robe. "You get the oddest feeling up there—looking down across the river onto the cathedral, and that big old dome of Brunelleschi's, and the bell tower. It's a tremendous sight. These church builders were artists—and were probably self-important as hell; they knew when they were putting up these stone piles their names would live for centuries. I guess everybody wishes for something like that, in one way or another—to be remembered; but only a few make it. Most of us are so damned mediocre and insignificant we're forgotten as soon as we're gone." He reflected—". . . Maybe it's not the going so much, as the forgetting."

Anita recalled how she felt, listening to him; it was a feeling of awe, of gratitude to be married to him. That's what she loved so about their trips—he talked more; and although sometimes pensive, he seemed freer. She felt it was the change of scene, of routine, and dreamed now only of their next trip—to the Virgin Islands.

Ah, but the dress again—what of the dress? She lay on the chaise longue as her mind probed and strained and her eyes roved the ceiling. Maybe he'd understand—if she took the time to explain. A "dressy" dress just wouldn't do; besides, she'd bought the dress especially for tonight. Perhaps he didn't really care that much—for months he'd heard her mourn her figure. Yet he knew this when he asked her to wear something "gay"—and still had asked her. She began to weaken now, feeling she should do his bidding, with no questions—he asked so few things of her. Then she thought of Kate and Alice; she wanted *so* to show them she too knew the meaning of good taste. Did it really mean so much to him—*that* much? . . . She could ask him. Yet if she asked him, and he persisted, she couldn't refuse. But if she took a chance and didn't ask him, she might be surprised to find he'd forgotten all about it. She sat up and stared at the wall awhile. Finally she got up, went to the closet, and resolutely took out the black dress.

* * * * *

At seven o'clock sharp the household was ready. The bar boys idled in the pantry, with their highball and cocktail glasses in neat rows and the liquor bottles capped with shining little spouts—as Thelma and the hippy waitress, both in white uniforms, broke the pantry tedium with their hushed, eye-flashing frivolity. Up front, the blaze in the fireplace spread a roseate warmth over the whole parlor and dining area adjoining, and the paintings on the wall, the gilt mirrors bracketing the fireplace, the furniture, the rich draperies and oriental rugs, all fused to create the gracious, elegant atmosphere of the house.

Anita was still upstairs. But Dave was in the kitchen now in folksy talk with Mrs. Adams. He opened the refrigerator, pulled out a horizontal bottle of champagne, and patiently worked the cork out under a covering napkin; then poured them both chilled sparkling glassfuls before, laughing and touching glasses, they drank to the evening's success. Then he paused in thought, and said his wife was probably tired and might like a glass. "Of course," Mrs. Adams said, and went into the pantry for another champagne glass.

When she returned, he was sitting at the kitchen table, limp and perspiring, an ashy-brown color in his face.

"What's the matter, Mr. Hill!"

". . . I guess I had a little sinking spell," he said with heavy breathing.

"What do you think's the matter?" She stood over him.

"I'll be okay in a minute." He looked shaken. "You needn't say anything to my wife—it's nothing. I'll just sit here for a little bit and—" He stared at the door. There stood smiling Anita—wearing her pearls, and her chic black dress.

She saw the champagne. "Oh! You two have jumped the gun!" she laughed gayly.

He only stared at her.

"We sure have!" nervously laughed Mrs. Adams.

Then Anita looked at Dave—and she knew she had guessed wrong. He had not forgotten. Her briefly buoyant spirits sank. But why his shocked expression? She felt it was all her fault. A rising frustration, and anger at herself, welled up inside her. Yet *he* was acting stubborn too, and a little unfair, she thought—about a dress. Still, she experienced a wretched contrition, and longed to run upstairs and change. But it was too late now; there was not time. A dull, preoccupying anguish settled on her for the evening.

Thelma entered the kitchen now, carrying a tray of glasses.

"Thelma, honey," Anita sighed, "when the guests arrive, will you answer the door, and handle the wraps?"

"Sure," Thelma smiled.

Dave sat at the table stony and detached. Soon he got up and went upstairs.

It was twenty-five minutes after seven when the door chimes at last sounded. Thelma jumped. Then recovering, she smoothed her uniform and hurried into the foyer to the front door—followed by Anita. The door opened on Hortense and "Sully" Weaver, smiling and stamping their wet shoes on the mat outside. Hortense, a highly-styled, light brown-skinned woman, stepped in and grasped both of Anita's hands in her own. "Anita, hon!" she purred. "How *are* you, darling?" Sully, dark-brown with gleaming white teeth, a probate lawyer, entered and bent forward chivalrously to kiss Anita on the cheek. "Hi, sugar!" he said. Dave appeared in the foyer now, his face drawn but smiling, and joined in the welcome. After Thelma took the wraps, the guests were ushered into the parlor.

"Oh, the fire, Sully!" Hortense cried, approaching the fireplace and rubbing her hands together. "It's wonderful!—and on a night like this!" They all sat down, and a bar boy entered with a tray of canapes and, as he passed them around, took orders for drinks.

Anita cut in. "Maybe Mrs. Weaver would like champagne," she said to the boy.

"Oh, I would!" cried Hortense. "May I?"

Sully had the same. "You can't go wrong with that," he laughed, "—until the next morning, that is."

"Make it three," Dave laughed to the bar boy.

As the boy left, the chimes sounded again. Anita stood up before she thought; but then gave Thelma time to reach the door, before following. It was Vashti and Walter Cooper. Vashti was a Wellesley graduate and a very proper person. Tall and olive-skinned, she resembled an East Indian—she had in fact traveled widely in the Orient. "Oh, Anita, how well you look" she said, smiling as she entered. Walter, a savings-and-loan association president, was shorter than his wife, and stood back smiling whimsically through black horn-rimmed glasses. "Nice weather," he laughed to Dave at the first pause in the women's talk, "—*lovely* weather." After their wraps were handed over to Thelma, the new guests were escorted into the parlor with the others, where eager friendly greetings went all around. Vashti sat with Hortense on the French love seat and agreed to champagne, but Walter said if they didn't mind he'd stick to Scotch. Hortense immediately remarked about the silver Chinese bracelet Vashti wore, launching Vashti on a rather tedious, but charming, explanation of the dragon figures the silversmith had so intricately worked. The three husbands huddled with drinks in hand, as Dave, in a feat of geniality, appeared to feel well again.

The young Bishops—Kitty and Roger—were the next to arrive. They came in laughing hilariously about what they referred to as the new escalation clause in their baby sitter's contract. Roger was an English instructor at the University of Chicago, and Kitty, of an excellent Atlanta family, had studied at the Sorbonne. They had three fine children and not the means to entertain on any elaborate scale, but nonetheless moved easily among the Southside's most cultivated people. Kitty was brown and beautiful, a girl with laughing eyes, who, despite her children, had retained her lithe, angular figure. She enjoyed the innocent conversation and flattery of older men—and all wives watched her. Roger, tall and athletic-looking, looked more like a football coach than a university instructor—his field was modern literature, and his avocation chess. The pair sparked any party they attended and, not withstanding Kitty's dangerous beauty, they were on the favored list of every hostess.

Ten minutes later, over the mild noise of talk, the door chimes sounded again. Anita, though seized with jitters, did not move this time, and arose only when she saw Thelma enter the foyer. The remainder of the guests had arrived—the Hortons and the Smileys had come together. Kate and Alice swept in—both were bare-headed and swaddled in mink—followed by burly Douglas Horton and "Fritz" Smiley. Dave, too, was at the door now.

"Oh, Anita," Kate said, "how splendid to see you." She embraced Anita and then held her off at arms' length to look at her. "How are you?"

"Oh, I'm fine, Kate!—just fine!" Anita cried happily.

Then Alice Smiley, whom Anita thought looked thinner than ever, embraced her. "How are you, Sweetie?" she said.

"Wonderful, Alice! We're *so* glad you could come!"

As he got out of his overcoat, Doug Horton seemed slightly drunk. He was a light tawny brown; square, beefy, and graying at the temples; and when he smiled exhibited large prominent teeth. He came from one of the most distinguished Negro families in the country, had inherited wealth, and made money in his own right, as a community banker and publisher. But now at fifty-five, he spent more time in travel, and in sumptuous living, than at work. He was known to like women, and whenever he put his cunning eyes on Kitty Bishop an animal turbulence was triggered inside him that persisted for days. He smelled of liquor now as he smiled and quickly shook Dave's hand. Then he made a stiff, smiling bow to Anita, and passed on into the parlor.

Fritz Smiley was a surgeon—and contributed to the medical journals. Like his wife, Alice, he was very light-skinned and thin, almost cadaverous; and though he gave Alice all the money she wanted, he was cold and steel-nerved, rarely showing her affection. But he was cordial to Dave now, as they shook hands.

"How're things?" He studied Dave with a friendly, guarded look.

"Okay," Dave said, "and you?—how do you keep your weight like that?"

"I don't get time to eat," Fritz twinkled. They moved into the parlor.

After Thelma walked away with her arms piled high

with wraps, Kate, Alice, and Anita stood talking briefly in the foyer. "Your house is *so* attractive," Alice, looking about her, said to Anita. "Your draperies are beautiful."

Kate stood preoccupied and, glancing toward the parlor, seemed intent on keeping an eye on her husband. She was totally patrician—a beautifully-proportioned woman of fifty, with erect carriage and soft brown skin; although recently, delicate crow's-feet had appeared at the corners of her eyes. Her features were chiseled and severe, almost satanic—relieved only by a pleasant mouth, and eyes that could dance when amused. She was born and grew up in Chicago, was a graduate of the University of Chicago, and spoke careful, immaculate English. An enthusiast of the serious theatre, she occasionally gave play-reading parties that were brilliant and sought-after. With wealth, culture, and a fading beauty, she was the community's supreme hostess and social figure.

Anita soon noticed Kate's absorption, and deftly guided them toward the parlor. Kate looked at her now. "I like your dress, Anita," she smiled.

The company was at last complete—as the bar boys, in their white jackets, scurried back and forth with drinks. Doug Horton, seated alone, brusquely declined champagne, requesting a dry, "very dry," martini. He then scrutinized a plate of canapes on the coffee table and, after serious study, selected a caviar. He put the morsel to his mouth, skinned off the paste with his top teeth, and dropped the denuded bit of toast in an ash tray. When the martini came, he speared out the anchovy olive and chewed it reflectively; then, lifting the small crystal beaker, coolly drained it off and set it on the coffee table.

He looked across the room now at young Kitty Bishop—she was talking rapidly to Dave and Hortense Weaver—and sighed.

Kitty was telling about her children. ". . . and Gregory caught the poor little kid!—I say 'little', but he was as big as Gregory—and at that point *I* stepped in." Hortense threw her head back and laughed. Dave, now sitting with them, smiled and listened. He thought Kitty more beautiful than he had ever seen her. And the way she talked with her hands!—so self-assured and high-spirited. He felt he'd missed out on women—that is, really alluring women. His nose had been to the grindstone—all the way. He'd played it safe, with Anita. No complications. It was a bit late now, wasn't it, to be overwhelmed, a little sad even, about a beautiful, vibrant girl? She was actually the age to be his daughter. He gave himself a wry smile—yes, a trifle late, old man; but Roger Bishop was plain lucky.

Across the room, Anita took her first glass of champagne from the moving tray. She looked at Dave repeatedly, glad to see his mood improved—even if he persisted in ignoring her. Finally she went over and sat down beside lone Doug Horton.

"I know you hated to put your boat up for the winter," she said brightly.

". . . Oh, sort of,"—Doug was friendly enough—"but the crew got bored, along there toward the last. So it was just as well."

"Oh, Doug, you don't have a drink!" Anita said.

He grinned. "I just finished that martini there." He pointed his big manicured hand at the empty glass.

"Well, you must have another." She looked around for the bar boy.

Doug chuckled. "Katie's watching," he said. "She claims too many drinks before dinner deaden the taste buds."

Anita's laugh was high and forced. Her gloom had not lifted. She was watching Dave—to catch his eye and smile. But he would not look at her. Soon she was miserable. She couldn't understand him! How silly he could be—and about a dress! 'Silly' wasn't the word for it—it was cruel. He had talked to everyone but her. Her hurt and anger mounted—only to be dissolved in moments by her love.

* * * * *

At eight-thirty Thelma entered and whispered to Anita —it was time to move the guests into the dining room. Anita stood up now, smiling, and announced dinner.

The large dining area, adjacent, featured a glittering crystal chandelier suspended directly over the center of the table. A long mahogany sideboard, highly polished and topped with pink marble, extended along one wall, and the window wall next to it was hung with heavy silk draperies of Prussian blue. A hidden wall-speaker leading from Dave's hi-fi set in the rear poured soft tunes from the Broadway musicals into the room. And the entire staff, including Mrs. Adams, had stationed themselves to greet the guests—now led in by Anita, who pointed out the various place cards for seating. Dave sat at the head of the table, with Kate Horton at his right, while Anita, down at the other end, had Doug Horton on her right. Doug had entered the dining room carrying his fourth empty martini glass, and passed it curtly to a bar boy before pulling out Kitty Bishop's chair, next to his. He seated her with a Mephistophelian dead pan, but Kitty seemed very pleased.

As all were seated they found their curry consommé and hot crackers before them. Dave, presiding, though often smiling, seemed tense and formal. He had drunk champagne freely, but it had done him little good. Kate, at his right elbow, pretending exhilaration, hid her pique at Kitty Bishop's placement and bent toward Dave to praise the soup. Then smiling mischievously, she turned to Roger Bishop, on her right, to tell him she knew a twelve-year-old boy at Parkway settlement house (Kate was active in many charities) who, she suspected, could give him a very interesting session at the chessboard. Roger, sipping his soup, laughed and said he didn't doubt it for a second, as chess was largely, as most things in life, a matter of endowment. Alice Smiley, at Dave's left, laughed, and admonished Roger for conceding so readily.

Down at the other end of the long table Anita strove for brilliance, gaiety. With Doug Horton on her right and Fritz Smiley, who used his wit as he used his scalpel, on her left, she felt the need for alertness. But she soon recognized Doug's attention was for Kitty.

"Was this seating by lottery?" Doug, grinning, leaned to young Kitty to ask, "—or by design? I never won *any*-thing by chance."

"The hostess decides on seating," Kitty laughed, "—as if you didn't know!"

"Well then, Anita's a friend of *mine*," he stage-whispered—as Kate's quick eye came down the table.

Anita had turned to Fritz Smiley to enquire about the Virgin Islands, and said she knew he and Alice had been there twice—or was it three times? Fritz said it was twice, and that he liked it very much, but was afraid Alice hadn't particularly, as he had spent a lot of time on the golf course. "Oh, you men!" cried Anita. "But Dave and I are going—right after the holidays."

"Is that right?" Fritz said, and then sipped his soup in silence. She'd go only if she was damned lucky, he thought—if what Cartwright had told him at the hospital was correct: that a man with Dave's clogged aorta was a walking miracle. And Cartwright was a hell of a cardiologist. Almost any day or night now, he had said—touch and go. Anita wouldn't exactly have to worry about her next meal, though, Fritz thought—Dave was in good shape, that way.

Hortense Weaver had had her share of champagne and was now in shrill voice as she talked across the table at Vashti Cooper, who never drank much and was amused at Hortense. Vashti leaned against Sully, Hortense's husband, at her left, and whispered something about Hortense's eyes. Sully laughed and assured her *he* could drive home. Hortense heard and was petulant. "Yes, for once!" she cried, "—just once! D'you think you can, Sully dear—just this once?"

Now came the main course: roast beef, with individual Yorkshire puddings, French string beans, acorn squash, and endive salad. The Burgundy was poured into glinting crystal goblets.

Doug Horton, to his surprise, was enjoying himself more than anyone. He fingered his second goblet of Burgundy and turned from Kitty long enough to smile at Anita. "Anita, my dear," he said dreamily, "you've really slain the fatted calf tonight. The beef—it's superb, superb. *Every*thing's superb." Then he turned again to Kitty, who was laughing at him.

Anita was happy momentarily. But then a shadow would cross her heart. She could not understand her feeling, and was too busy to wonder at it, to probe it. She only knew it was there. Then impulsively with a wistful smile she stared straight down the table at Dave. But if he saw her he gave no sign.

The hubbub of talk and laughter had increased. Once even Dave had let out a sort of whoop, at one of Roger Bishop's clever remarks. At the other end of the table Fritz Smiley sat and watched his friend, Doug, across from him. How in creation, he wondered, could he swill all that alcohol? those lethal martinis—and the food! Fritz gazed now at Kitty. She *was* beautiful—no doubt about it; very. But old Doug would never get her—she was too slick . . . much too slick for *Doug*. She was something special. He suspected *her* case required cold calculation—not liquor. Briefly Fritz imagined himself her vanquisher and experienced vague egoistic gusto.

The main course required more than an hour. Finally the table was cleared for dessert: pears, with Bel Paese cheese, coffee, and yellow chartreuse.

Dave had begun to look tired. He smiled mechanically as he spooned his dessert. Engaging Kate Horton and Alice Smiley in conversation for over two hours was no joke, and he was glad to see the dinner's end approach. Down his whole left arm, through the fingers, a dull ache distracted him from the talk around him. But his darkest secret was the cowing fear.

* * * * *

By one o'clock the house was empty of guests and servants, the ground floor dark. Wearily, Dave had gone upstairs to his room, taken another bath, this time a shower,
and donned fresh pajamas. The wind had risen still
higher during the night, and slammed about the upper
stories of the house. He opened a little cabinet, poured
a tiny brandy and, holding the glass, sat down on the
bed. When he looked up, Anita, now in her robe, stood
in the door with a flippant smile.

"How'd do you like the party?" she said.

"Fine—good party." He was grave.

Still she smiled. "Do you realize, Mister, you didn't
speak to me *once,* the whole evening?—and acted like you
couldn't bear the sight of me?"

He took a sip of the brandy and set the glass down.
"No, I wasn't aware," he coolly lied.

Then she came over and sat down on the bed beside
him. "What's the matter, honey?" she said. "Have I done
something wrong? Tell me, if I have. *Tell* me. But don't
keep acting like this."

He sat in silence. Finally he looked at her. "you
haven't done anything wrong," he said coldly. Then he
stood.

Suddenly she jumped up and ran from the room. And
returned immediately—clutching the black dress in her
left hand, and the big pair of scissors in her right.

He stood horrified.

She began cutting savagely, and cut the dress from the
neck straight down through the bottom hem. Then she
cut it in two along the waist. Laughing and crying now,
she dropped the fabric to the floor, pitched the scissors
onto the bed, and threw her arms around his neck.

"I'll never wear black again, honey!" she cried. "I

promise! I promise! *Never!* No matter where we go, or what we do, I'll never wear it! Do you believe that? Do you believe me?"

He held her in his arms with terror in his heart. "Of course, I believe you," he soothed, "of course . . . of course . . ."

Alice Walker

To hell with dying

"For me, black women are the most fascinating creations in the world," Alice Walker has said. "Next to them, I place the old people—male and female—who persist in their beauty in spite of everything. How do they do this, knowing what they do? Having lived what they have lived? It is a mystery, and so it lures me into their lives. My grandfather, at eighty-five, never been out of Georgia, looks at me with the glad eyes of a three-year-old. The pressures on his life have been unspeakable."

In "To Hell with Dying," Ms. Walker illuminates the connections between one of those old people and a young girl, between the dreams he knew he must deny and the dream he had that the young survivors around him should find realization. Certainly it would gladden the eyes of a man like Mr. Sweet of "To Hell with Dying" to know that Ms. Walker, born in Eatonton, Georgia, had gone to Spelman College and Sarah Lawrence College and that she had grown up to win awards for her skill in recounting the lives of her people in remarkable poetry (*Once, Revolutionary Petunias & Other Poems*) and in short stories (*In Love & Trouble*) and in a distinguished novel (*The Third Life of Grange Copeland*).

"To hell with dying," my father would say, *"these children want Mr. Sweet!"*

Mr. Sweet was a diabetic and an alcoholic and a guitar player and lived down the road from us on a neglected cotton farm. My older brothers and sisters got the most benefit from Mr. Sweet, for when they were growing up he had quite a few years ahead of him and so was capable of being called back from the brink of death any number of times—whenever the voice of my father reached him as he lay expiring. . . . "To hell with dying, man," my father would say, pushing the wife away from the bedside (in tears although she knew the death was not necessarily the last one unless Mr. Sweet really wanted it to be), "the children want Mr. Sweet!" And they did want him, for at a signal from Father they would come crowding around the bed and throw themselves on the covers and whoever was the smallest at the time would kiss him all over his wrinkled brown face and begin to tickle him so he would laugh all down in his stomach, and his moustache which was long and sort of straggly, would shake like Spanish moss and was also that color.

Mr. Sweet had been ambitious as a boy, wanted to be a doctor or lawyer or sailor, only to find that black men fare better if they are not. Since he could be none of those things he turned to fishing as his only earnest career and playing the guitar as his only claim to doing anything extraordinarily well. His son, the only one that he and his wife, Miss Mary, had, was shiftless as the day is long and spent money as if he were trying to see the bottom of the mint, which Mr. Sweet would tell him was the clean brown palm of his hand. Miss Mary loved her "baby," however, and worked hard to get him the "li'l necessaries" of life, which turned out mostly to be women.

Mr. Sweet was a tall, thinnish man with thick kinky hair going dead white. He was dark brown, his eyes were very squinty and sort of bluish, and he chewed Brown Mule tobacco. He was constantly on the verge of being blind drunk, for he brewed his own liquor and was not in the least a stingy sort of man, and was always very melancholy and sad, though frequently when he was "feelin' good" he'd dance around the yard with us, usually keeling over just as my mother came to see what the commotion was.

Toward all of us children he was very kind, and had the grace to be shy with us, which is unusual in grown-ups. He had great respect for my mother for she never held his drunkenness against him and would let us play with him even when he was about to fall in the fireplace from drink. Although Mr. Sweet would sometimes lose complete or nearly complete control of his head and neck so that he would loll in his chair, his mind remained strangely acute and his speech not too affected. His ability to be drunk and sober at the same time made him an ideal playmate, for he was as weak as we were and we could usually best him in wrestling, all the while keeping a fairly coherent conversation going.

We never felt anything of Mr. Sweet's age when we played with him. We loved his wrinkles and would draw some on our brows to be like him, and his white hair was my special treasure and he knew it and would never come to visit us just after he had had his hair cut off at the barbershop. Once he came to our house for something, probably to see my father about fertilizer for his crops, for although he never paid the slightest attention to his crops he liked to know what things would be best to use on them if he ever did. Anyhow, he had not come with his hair since he had just had it shaved off at the barbershop. He wore a huge straw hat to keep off the sun and also to keep his head away from me. But as soon as I saw him I ran up and demanded that he take me up and kiss me, with his funny beard which smelled so strongly of tobacco. Looking forward to burying my small fingers into his woolly hair I threw away his hat only to find he had done something to his hair, that it was no longer there! I let out a squall which made my mother think that Mr. Sweet had finally dropped me in the well or something and from that day I've been wary of men in hats. However, not long after, Mr. Sweet showed up with his hair grown out and just as white and kinky and impenetrable as it ever was.

Mr. Sweet used to call me his princess, and I believed it. He made me feel pretty at five and six, and simply outrageously devastating at the blazing age of eight and a half. When he came to our house with his guitar the whole family would stop whatever they were doing to sit around him and listen to him play. He liked to play "Sweet Georgia Brown," that was what he called me sometimes, and also he liked to play "Caldonia" and all sorts of sweet, sad, wonderful songs which he sometimes made up. It was from one of these songs that I learned that he had had to marry Miss Mary when he had in fact loved somebody else (now living in Chi-ca-go, or De-stroy, Michigan). He was not sure that Joe Lee, her "baby," was also his baby. Sometimes he would cry and that was an indication that he was about to die again. And so we would all get prepared, for we were sure to be called upon.

I was seven the first time I remember actually participating in one of Mr. Sweet's "revivals"—my parents told me I had participated before, I had been the one chosen to kiss him and tickle him long before I knew the rite of Mr. Sweet's rehabilitation. He had come to our house, it was a few years after his wife's death, and he was very sad, and also, typically, very drunk. He sat on the floor next to me and my older brother, the rest of the children were grown-up and lived elsewhere, and began to play his guitar and cry. I held his woolly head in my arms and wished I could have been old enough to have been the woman he loved so much and that I had not been lost years and years ago.

When he was leaving my mother said to us that we'd better sleep light that night for we'd probably have to go over to Mr. Sweet's before daylight. And we did. For soon after we had gone to bed one of the neighbors knocked on our door and called my father and said that Mr. Sweet was sinking fast and if he wanted to get in a word before the crossover he'd better shake a leg and get over to Mr. Sweet's house. All the neighbors knew to come to our house if something was wrong with Mr. Sweet, but they did not know how we always managed to make him well, or at least stop him from dying, when

he was often so near death. As soon as we heard the cry
we got up, my brother and I and my mother and father,
and put on our clothes. We hurried out of the house and
down the road for we were always afraid that we might
someday be too late and Mr. Sweet would get tired of
dallying.

When we got to the house, a very poor shack really,
we found the front room full of neighbors and relatives
and someone met us at the door and said that it was all
very sad that old Mr. Sweet Little (for Little was his
family name although we mostly ignored it) was about
to kick the bucket. My parents were advised not to take
my brother and me into the "death-room" seeing we
were so young and all, but we were so much more accustomed to the death-room than he that we ignored
him and dashed in without giving his warning a second
thought. I was almost in tears, for these deaths upset
me fearfully, and the thought of how much depended on
me and my brother (who was such a ham most of the
time) made me very nervous.

The doctor was bending over the bed and turned back
to tell us for at least the tenth time in the history of my
family that alas, old Mr. Sweet Little was dying and that
the children had best not see the face of implacable
death (I didn't know what "implacable" was, but whatever it was, Mr. Sweet was not!). My father pushed him
rather abruptly out of the way saying as he always did
and very loudly for he was saying it to Mr. Sweet, "To
hell with dying, man, these children want Mr. Sweet!"
which was my cue to throw myself upon the bed and kiss
Mr. Sweet all around the whiskers and under the eyes

and around the collar of his nightshirt where he smelled so strongly of all sorts of things, mostly liniment.

I was very good at bringing him around, for as soon as I saw that he was struggling to open his eyes I knew he was going to be all right and so could finish my revival sure of success. As soon as his eyes were open he would begin to smile and that way I knew that I had surely won. Once though I got a tremendous scare for he could not open his eyes and later I learned that he had had a stroke and that one side of his face was stiff and hard to get into motion. When he began to smile I could tickle him in earnest for I was sure that nothing would get in the way of his laughter, although once he began to cough so hard that he almost threw me off his stomach, but that was when I was very small, little more than a baby, and my bushy hair had gotten in his nose.

When we were sure he would listen to us we would ask him why he was in bed and when he was coming to see us again and could we play with his guitar which more than likely would be leaning against the bed. His eyes would get all misty and he would sometimes cry out loud, but we never let it embarrass us for he knew that we loved him and that we sometimes cried too for no reason. My parents would leave the room to just the three of us; Mr. Sweet, by that time, would be propped up in bed with a number of pillows behind his head and with me sitting and lying on his shoulder and along his chest. Even when he had trouble breathing he would not ask me to get down. Looking into my eyes he would shake his white head and run a scratchy old finger all around my hairline, which was rather low down nearly

to my eyebrows and for which some people said I looked
like a baby monkey.

My brother was very generous in all this, he let me do
all the revivaling—he had done it for years before I was
born and so was glad to be able to pass it on to someone new. What he would do while I talked to Mr. Sweet
was pretend to play the guitar, in fact pretend that he
was a young version of Mr. Sweet, and it always made
Mr. Sweet glad to think that someone wanted to be like
him—of course we did not know this then, we played the
thing by ear, and whatever he seemed to like, we did.
We were desperately afraid that he was just going to
take off one day and leave us.

It did not occur to us that we were doing anything
special; we had not learned that death was final when it
did come. We thought nothing of triumphing over it so
many times, and in fact became a trifle contemptuous of
people who let themselves be carried away. It did not
occur to us that if our own father had been dying we
could not have stopped it, that Mr. Sweet was the only
person over whom we had power.

When Mr. Sweet was in his eighties I was a young
lady studying away in a university many miles from
home. I saw him whenever I went home, but he was
never on the verge of dying that I could tell and I began
to feel that my anxiety for his health and psychological
well-being was unnecessary. By this time he not only had
a moustache but a long flowing snow-white beard which
I loved and combed and braided for hours. He was still
a very heavy drinker and was like an old Chinese opium-
user, very peaceful, fragile, gentle, and the only jarring

note about him was his old steel guitar which he still played in the old sad, sweet, downhome blues way.

On Mr. Sweet's ninetieth birthday I was finishing my doctorate in Massachusetts and had been making arrangements to go home for several weeks' rest. That morning I got a telegram telling me that Mr. Sweet was dying again and could I please drop everything and come home. Of course I could. My dissertation could wait and my teachers would understand when I explained to them when I got back. I ran to the phone, called the airport, and within four hours I was speeding along the dusty road to Mr. Sweet's.

The house was more dilapidated than when I was last there, barely a shack, but it was overgrown with yellow roses which my family had planted many years ago. The air was heavy and sweet and very peaceful. I felt strange walking through the gate and up the old rickety steps. But the strangeness left me as I caught sight of the long white beard I loved so well flowing down the thin body over the familiar quilt coverlet. Mr. Sweet!

His eyes were closed tight and his hands, crossed over his stomach, were thin and delicate, no longer rough and scratchy. I remembered how always before I had run and jumped up on him just anywhere; now I knew he would not be able to support my weight. I looked around at my parents, and was surprised to see that my father and mother also looked old and frail. My father, his own hair very gray, leaned over the quietly sleeping old man, who, incidentally, smelled still of wine and tobacco, and said as he'd done so many times, "To hell with dying, man! My daughter is home to see Mr. Sweet!" My brother had not been able to come as he was in the war in Asia. I bent down and gently stroked the closed eyes and gradually they began to open. The closed, winestained lips twitched ed a little, then parted in a warm, slightly embarrassed smile. Mr. Sweet could see me and he recognized me and his eyes looked very spry and twinkly for a moment. I put my head down on the pillow next to his and we just looked at each other for a long time. Then he began to trace my peculiar hairline with a thin, smooth finger. I closed my eyes when his finger halted above my ear (he used to rejoice at the dirt in my ears when I was little), his hand stayed cupped around my cheek. When I opened my eyes, sure I had reached him in time, his were closed.

Even at twenty-four how could I believe that I had failed? that Mr. Sweet was really gone? He had never gone before. But when I looked up at my parents I saw that they were holding back tears. They had loved him dearly. He was like a piece of rare and delicate china which was always being saved from breaking and which finally fell. I looked long at the old face, the wrinkled forehead, the red lips, the hands that still reached out to me. Soon I felt my father pushing something cool into my hands. It was Mr. Sweet's guitar. He had asked them months before to give it to me, he had known that even if I came next time he would not be able to respond in the old way. He did not want me to feel that my trip had been for nothing.

The old guitar! I plucked the strings, hummed "Sweet Georgia Brown." The magic of Mr. Sweet lingered still in the cool steel box. Through the window I could catch the fragrant delicate scent of tender yellow roses. The man on the high old-fashioned bed with the quilt coverlet and the flowing white beard had been my first love.

Ann Allen Shockley

The funeral

The funeral is one of the central rituals of the
Black community. Students of African survivals
find in it rituals that preserve customs from the
old country in the new one. Students of history
know that from the attempt to prepare for the
funeral came the oldest Black enterprises in
America. Students of our culture know that the
funeral transmits to the most uprooted urban-
ites the solace of our songs and our sermons
and, at the wake, the solace of our humor and
our food.

Ann Allen Shockley was born in Louisville,
Kentucky, and attended Fisk University and
Western Reserve. She has been Special Collec-
tions Librarian at Fisk University since 1969.
Her writing usually is concerned with professional materials for librarians. Her gift as a
delineator is broader than that; one hopes she
will turn to fiction again.

The death of Melissa's grandmother had been expected. She had been ailing a long time, beset with the
genealogical diseases of the old: arthritis, high blood
pressure, and diabetes advanced by her eighty years,
until these were finally laid to rest by a heart attack.

The funeral was already paid for. *Had* been paid for

years ago through the fifty-cents-a-week policy taken out with the Black Brothers Burial Society. Undertaker C. B. Brown had nothing to worry about along those lines. Neither did the Reverend Thomas Cooke have reason to fret over the funeral services because all that information had been foretold to him time before time and locked in the Zion Methodist Church's metal strongbox.

The occasion had been prepared for well, and all involved rose nobly to meet it. Even the tired decrepit four-room house, whose once white frame was archaically grimy with red dust from the patch of yard surrounding it—where no grass appeared ever to be able to grow—managed to look less worn, less dull, to accommodate the throngs of people stopping by to share the grief. Helpful neighbors and friends came in hushed, sad-eyed groups, bringing plates of fried chicken, potato salad, greens, and homemade pastries to Melissa, too bereaved to bother with the mundane.

There was more food than Melissa could ever eat, since with her grandmother dead, she was left alone. If there were any other relatives, Melissa knew nothing about them, scattered here and yond up north and east and God-knows-where.

There had only been the two of them living in the house. Just the two of them facing each other in the evenings in the small living room with the shades tightly drawn: Granny rocking slowly back and forth in the ancient rocker with its high straight arrow back, and Melissa, absorbing herself in preparing for the next day which would end like the day before.

Granny sewed when the arthritic pain wasn't drawing her hands, brown fingers weaving in and out, no longer swift, only halfway sure. But when the pain was there curling up the gnarled hands that had known work since thoughts could remember—cleaning up the big house for the white folks and making their children spotless— Granny would open the frayed family Bible scrawled with census records, and slowly, very slowly form the biblical words aloud with her lips. Frequently she paused to peer over at Melissa, shakily pointing to a passage she wanted read at her funeral.

Granny talked a lot to Melissa about the funeral. Especially about the clothes she wanted to be buried in— an old black satin with a lace embroidered shawl, and the black square-heel shoes kept shiny under her bed. When talking about the funeral, Granny's skinny flat chest would heave with tiny ripples like a small wind trying to press the sea into waves.

Melissa would listen sometimes, and sometimes she wouldn't. The woman was old and Melissa could smell death around her. Once in a while even see it—a dismal shadow hovering near. There were unjust moments when she wished the shadow would stay so she could make the lamps brighter and turn the tiny boxlike radio up to cheerful sounds. Now she couldn't. Bright lights hurt Granny's cataracts, and the blaring music wasn't the sound of the Lord's.

Now and then some evenings when Granny talked about the funeral, Melissa would stare blankly at her with the hand-knitted robe thrown across her lap winter and summer, focusing her eyes dreamily at the vacant corner behind the rocker where she hoped to put a secondhand television—after it was over.

"That song, Melissa. Don't forget I want Sister Smith to sing *Just a Closer Walk with Thee* right before the preaching. You hear me?" Granny's voice would rise, squeaking in the manner of a worn out reed.

"Sure, Granny, sure."

After various intervals, Melissa would get up and go through the plastic curtain door to the kitchen on the pretense of getting a glass of water. There she would turn on the faucet vigorously while reaching quickly behind the flour can for the pint of Gordon's gin. She would hurriedly gulp down the drink, choking in her haste, then return to the room, smiling a little now, able to endure the talk and the death in the chair whose cushion had long worn down with the weight and the words.

In the chair was where she died: the thin, wasted body crumpled in the rocker, head down, white hair straggling outrageously from its knot, just as if she had nodded to sleep.

Now there was no longer the quietness in the house. The door was left unlocked to admit the endless string of church members and lodge sisters, and even some of the white folks for whom Granny had scrubbed and worked and fussed over.

Granny had insisted on being laid out at the house—no funeral parlor where it was unfriendly and reeking with embalming fluid—but laid out in her satin dress with her hands crossed to show the round tarnished wedding band right in her own living room.

Since that was where she wanted to be, the living room was always the one papered each year to keep down the smoke stain ruins of the potbellied coal stove fired in the winters. The coffin was large for the room and the couch had to be moved into the bedroom to make space. Extra folding chairs were brought in by the undertaker and cardboard fans advertising C. B. Brown's Funeral Home ALWAYS THE FAMILY FIRST were distributed noticeably even though there was no need.

Melissa stayed in the bedroom, letting the visitors feel free to drift in and sign the register while Undertaker Brown stood solemnly at the door, neatly attired in his navy suit, whispering professional instructions. Across from him was stalwart Sister Mary Smith, head of the church's stewardess board, in her stiff white uniform, handling the viewers with equal aplomb.

Watching the people drift in and out, leaving behind the soft rustle of dresses and ragged shuffling of feet moving past the body, Melissa could tell the town remembered and loved Miss Eliza. That was what they all called her—Miss Eliza—young, old, white folks alike. She had been a fixture in the town like the Confederate soldier in front of the court house. A born and bred fixture claimed by time.

Melissa could hear the laments as they filed by:

"Don't she look nat-u-ral?"

"Poor Miss Eliza. God's restin' her now. Put her out of her mis-ery."

And the younger ones, impatiently: "Wonder if'n I'll live to get *that* old?"

An answering giggle. "Not at the rate you goin' now!"

"Please . . ." the smooth articulate voice of the undertaker, "move on by the casket and sign the register. Others are waiting. . . ."

A tray of hot food was brought to Melissa, urged upon her, heedless of her feeble sign of refusal. But finally the aroma of hot bread and chicken pressed close to her nose made her relent.

"We goin' to stay all night for the wake, honey," one of the lodge sisters murmured consolingly. "Now you lay down 'n rest. Don't cry now. The Lord giveth and the Lord taketh away."

"Give her a hot toddy . . ." another voice suggested. "That *always* helps at times like these."

The undertaker thrust his head into the room. "Is Miss Melissa all right?"

"Doin' fine."

Melissa sipped the toddy, feeling a warm glow kindle within her, spreading some life into her tired body.

"Wait! Undertaker Brown . . ." she called, beckoning him back. "Don't forget the expensive hearse tomorrow. The *Cad-il-lac*. Granny always said that that'd be one time she rode in style. Even if it was to her grave."

"Of course . . . of course."

"And all the white folks' messages read *first*."

"Naturally."

Melissa drank longer on the toddy, not minding the burning hot sting this time, talking excitedly now like Granny used to do. "That pretty white spray of carnations from the white folks I work for I want right in *front*."

The undertaker nodded affirmatively, his shining bald head bobbing quickly. "Thy will be done."

A small tuneless wail suddenly rose in the outer room,

coiling in a feverish pitch. "Oh Lord . . . Lordy . . . po' Melissa. Where's the chile?"

A stooped old woman bundled in a threadbare coat groped into the room towards Melissa. "Chile . . . chile . . . I knowed your grandmother ever since we wuz chillen. I'm goin' next. I can feel it in my bones. Death don't never stop at one. It takes more 'n more. . . ."

"Sh-h-h, Miss Reva, don't cry," Melissa consoled, hugging the woman close to her. "You go on home and get a good night's sleep. You to ride with me tomorrow. You an old friend of the family. I ain't got nothing but old friends to ride with me."

Sobbing louder, the woman was aided out. "Oh, Lord, God help us all."

Melissa stretched out on the bed. Someone threw a quilt over her, persuading her to sleep. She heard the women's preparations of turning off the lamp by the bed and quietly closing the door, leaving her alone to rest. A thin shred of light shone vigilantly under the door where Granny was, and watching it, she found it hard to sleep.

The morning of the funeral was cold and gray, hanging heavily with impending rain.

"A good sign," one lodge sister said, looking out the window. "When it rains, they goin' to heaven."

Melissa sighed, fumbling with her black veil, feeling weak and worn from the four-day ordeal of death. The house reeked nauseously, emanating the sweet odors of the myriad sprays. Her arms and legs felt lifeless, debilitated by people and emotions. But inwardly she had the sensation of being alive with excitement and anticipation over the drama orbiting around her.

"Everything is in readiness," Undertaker Brown murmured gently, glancing anxiously at her. "The cars are waiting."

Melissa lowered her head in what she judged to be a proper angle, not too low or too high, but leveled to see her steps and that around her too. Sister Mary Ellen and a nurse supported her on each side as she moved falteringly on her Sunday best heels into the gray foggy mist.

The black Cadillac hearse gleamed brilliantly, and seeing it, Melissa knew how proud Granny would be. She got in the sleek family limousine whose interior was spotless. Undertaker Brown sure kept his cars up nice, she thought. Granny always said that, and Granny ought to know because she never missed a funeral. "Goin' to ever'body's. I got no folks livin' I know of 'cept you. If I go to other peoples', they'll come to mine," Granny used to say.

True to Granny's words, they were there, Melissa noticed as the car came slowly to a stop in front of the church. People were standing on the outside and in the church's doorway. Melissa furtively lifted her veil to survey the scene as the other cars came slowly to a stop behind them in the section reserved.

The sounds of sobs and moans surrounded her, reminding her of those beside her. She took a deep harsh breath, letting herself be half lifted out of the luxuriously plush seat that was better than a sofa.

"Steady . . . steady," the undertaker whispered, stationing her at the head to lead the long line of lodge sisters, friends, and members of the burying order into the church. "The procession is now ready to begin . . ."

The church organist was softly playing the piece Granny wanted, *Nearer My God to Thee*. Melissa sniffled, fumbling for her handkerchief. Arms tightened around her shoulders and gently guided her through the parting crowd to the front pew by the casket.

The Reverend Cooke cleared his throat and stretched his black robed arms wide in twin hawk's wings, engulfing the congregation. "Jesus said, 'I am the resurrection, and the life: he that believeth in Me, though he were dead, yet shall he live; and whosoever liveth and believeth in Me shall never die.' Let us pray. Our Father . . . ."

Melissa's fingers tightly gripped her wet handkerchief, twisting it to dabble at her eyes. Moments later, the loud resounding voice of Sister Smith filled the church with Granny's favorite hymn, *Just a Closer Walk with Thee*, punctuated by foot tapping rhythm and shouts:

"Sing it, Sister, sing it."

"She's gone . . . *gone*."

"Oh, God, have mercy."

Melissa swayed and the nurse pushed a bottle of smelling salts under her nose.

The Reverend rose again, paused, and in deep sonorous tones started his eulogy. "A good and Godly woman was Sister Eliza. Loved by all who knew her. A fine church worker has left us, who God has called to work in His heavenly church above."

"A-men."

The words of the preacher drifted around her in swelling billows that would not stop long enough for her to grasp them. So she sat still, eyes downcast, thoughts locked in nothingness.

In what seemed like a long time, the choir later began to sing softly as the minister called for the president of the Burial Society to read the obituary. The acknowledgement of cards and flowers followed, given by the head of the church's stewardess board.

"They goin' to view the body now," the nurse said softly, looking anxiously at Melissa.

Melissa heard the organist playing *Steal Away* as she half watched the long column of men, women, and children filing past to gaze one last time at Granny. A female voice shrieked hysterically, and Melissa pushed her head slightly forward to see who it was.

And last, the family. Strong capable hands clutched Melissa, and she found herself being shelteringly steeled against a large warm bosom, steadying her to look down upon Granny's sleeping face. The face was peaceful, serene, no longer complaining of the ache in her joints— especially on rainy days like this. This was one rainy day when Granny wouldn't have an ache.

Melissa reached out to touch Granny for the last time, just once more. That's what Granny had asked her to do: reach out and touch her. Melissa's hand moved slowly, hesitantly, and suddenly paused in midair, a breath away from the sunken brown cheek. She *couldn't*. A drowning siege of dizziness covered her, a temporary black cloud passing over to hover for a tiny vacuous second before going beyond.

Then poised as a tense wary bird for sudden flight, one finger extended out from the rounded mold of her hand to gently touch the cheek. And when she did, she knew that she would never forget its unyielding tough chill. Far off, she imagined hearing Granny saying, "Well done, chile, well done."

Laboriously she sat back on the bench, now aware of its hardness, and that her feet ached in the shoes she seldom wore, and the girdle was making ridges around her stomach.

The funeral had been long. Outside, rain pushed harder against the multicolored stained windows, as if to intrude with sound if nothing else. She realized by the beginning restless stirrings many of the women were listening to it and becoming angry because their hair would get wet standing in the graveyard.

There was an indistinct prayer mumbled by the minister, and through the light pressure of the protective hands beside her, she understood that it was all over. The choir rose to sing *Swing Low, Sweet Chariot,* just as Granny wanted.

They had gone. The house was the same once again, quiet, still, but not the same either. She had told them there was no need to stay with her tonight. They were being nice and polite, but the commotion was over. They had to get back to their normal routines of work and everyday living until the next funeral which would come in the manner of a charging white horse to interrupt the dull monotony of their plodding lives. Then again, they would be rejuvenated in baking their pies, caring for the living, and crying for the dead.

It was still raining, an all-night incessant dirge. She was glad everything had been carried out as Granny wished: a big expensive funeral to put her at rest in the family plot. Granny was now covered by a blanket of dirt. Ashes to ashes, dust to dust, just like the preacher said at the grave.

Melissa rose slowly and went to the kitchen, taking

down a fresh bottle of gin. Pouring a drink, she started to down it quickly to keep Granny from calling and asking why she was so long in the kitchen.

Then remembering, she shrugged, picked up the bottle and glass, and went back to the living room. Wearily she sat down in the rocker which seemed still warmed by Granny's long sitting and waiting.

She began to rock slowly back and forth in Granny's rhythm with her head resting against the chair. The blinds were drawn and the room was half shadowed in illusions. She closed her eyes, listening to the measured screaks of the old rocker, a soft sound from the past, and began to wonder what would happen when she was gone someday. For everybody's got to go—someday.

Pearl Crayton

The gold fish monster

Pearl Crayton was born on a plantation in Natchitoches Parish, Louisiana. She has spent most of her life in Alexandria, Louisiana, where she received her early education and where for a brief period she was later editor of the Alexandria *News Leader*. Her earliest published work was a poem which appeared in the *Nashville Anthology of High School Poetry*. She has continued to write poetry, and in 1972 won the North American Mentor Poetry Award; in 1973 she won an Honor Award from the same publication.

"I live in a world of such beautiful stories that I have to write one every now and then," she has said. She has taken one of those beautiful stories in "The Gold Fish Monster" and, with craft and grace, she has turned it into a work of art.

Old man Beauford Winslow liked to ride his fishing boat up and down Little River but he didn't like to fish—he rode for the joy of the ride. He sat in his boat, gliding along the water, his long, bushy hair as white as a cloud, his face as black as a stormy night, and in the twinkling of an eye he was sailing as free as the wind across the heavens. Little River Lane Plantation beyond the banks of the river was beneath him—he saw it from far, far away, for the stars were but a hand's reach from him, the crescent moon but a short row away. From the firmament of the heavens he looked down on his plantation neighbors walking the ruts of life like chained slaves. Generation after generation men had followed mules and plows across those fertile fields, women had hung their boiled washes in the sun, children had played the same games, screamed over the same joys and pains, chickens had cackled and crowed, cows had mooed, horses had neighed, pigs squealed again and again with such a dreadful sameness as could dull the soul of anyone who had not sense enough to reach beyond the ordinary and grasp the mysterious magic of life. Such magic old man Beauford had discovered in the sweet and fiery liquor brewed by the one-eyed Cajun on the hill, and by it he shaped the world and the heavens to his liking. As often as he cared to he threw off the harness of his feeble flesh and became as daring and devilish as a young blade in love, or as sly and tough as John Dillinger, or anything he cared to be. And in his boat he sailed wherever he willed, not only across the heavens of that year of '38, but back into the past to the time of Moses and before, and as far as he cared into the future. And in the heavens he was never called old man or Beauford. Never. There among his ethereal friends he was called by a beautiful, poetic name too secret to be mentioned. And he was honored, respected, loved. And never was he lonesome, for sailing the heavens, he frolicked with all the great departed folk of story, poem, and song who rode the clouds back and forth around the world and made sport at the doings of men. Such a merry time he had that never again would he have set foot on humdrum Little River Lane Plantation had it not been for his dear Louiza, for even among the stars there was nothing better than the potato pies which she baked for him.

On his magic ride he sailed in the fragrant, dew-freshened morn from one tip of the new moon to the other, and it was such a great distance across that he had to stop his boat in the very center and take a few sips from a bottle of the one-eyed Cajun's magic brew. And how grand it was to sit with his legs hanging over the edge of the moon! On he rowed off the tip of the moon to a cloud and knew sheer ecstasy. The cloud was as soft as biddy's down and as fragrant as daffodils, but it kept changing so that it was difficult for him to keep his boat inside it. He had one hectic, exciting ride turning his boat this way and that to keep inside the cloud, and finally he rowed too close to the edge of it and the cloud slipped away, changing and rechanging itself on its sail across the heavens. He shook his fist at the cloud and swore to ride it again one day all the way to Mexico. The challenge aroused in him the spirit of a daredevil, of a dashing, wicked young blade.

"Hey there, old man Beauford! You caught your gold fish yet?" A voice boomed so loud that the sound of it carried all the way to the heavens.

Old man Beauford squinted his eyes, peered down at

the figure standing on the river bank, and recognized Rufus Trotter, his neighbor. "No, not yet! But I'm looking for him to jump into my boat any minute now!"

"I declare, old man Beauford, you're the biggest tale teller in the whole state of Louisiana!" And Rufus went into a fit of laughter.

Old man Beauford rowed behind a thunderhead for he didn't like to be reminded of the gold fish. Every day a couple or more of his neighbors came to the river bank while he was rowing along and teased him about the gold fish and he didn't like it at all! The jeering sound penetrated the thunderhead, spoiling his magic, pulling him down from the sky. Abruptly, his boat hit the water and he was aware of the pull of his oars against the current of the river. And he was painfully aware again that he was a poor, earthbound sharecropper whose neighbors treated him like an outcast. He rowed on down the river to escape the sound of laughter, but it followed him, even after he was out of earshot of it, even after Rufus had stopped laughing, for he had heard the sound so many times over so many years that it was in his head like a gramophone record. It wasn't only his neighbors laughing about his gold fish, it was children along the road clapping their hands, laughing, singing:

"Here comes the Devil and old man B!
"They're both half drunk, can't you see,
"They're going straight to Hell on a singletree!"

It was folk standing everywhere, laughing as he passed by, making circles on the air with one finger pointed toward their heads—the plantation code for screwy, coo-

coo, odd ball, crazy. Every day of his life a song of laughter followed him everywhere he went and it was like a gramophone record in his head. Only the prick of an insult was needed to set it to playing.

If only th' Lawd had let me be born on one o' th' stars all by myself! Folks o' this world just won't let me live my life in peace! Just 'cause I ain't crazy th' way they're crazy, they're always meddlin' at me. This here river is th' only place in this here world where I can be happy 'n they done spoiled that! His whole being shivered with mute mourning and his spirits were too crushed to sail again across the heavens. He rowed to the river bank and pulled his boat out of the water. All his magic daring drained away by self-pity, he walked slowly up the bank to his house, hurt, lonesome, and very, very old.

His dear Louiza was standing akimbo in the doorway when he walked into the yard. "Old man, I see you didn't catch any fish again today, 'n that don't surprise me none 'cause you ain't got no fishin' pole. Ain't nobody ever caught any fish bu' doubt a fishin' pole."

"Old woman, I done told you, I done had a dream what th' Lawd his'self give to me that one o' these days a great big old fish gonna up 'n jump in my boat wit a fifty dollar gold piece in his mouth," old man Beauford defended himself. "'N this here fish, he ain't gonna come close to my boat if he sees I got a fishin' pole! That's what th' Lawd done give me in my dream!"

"Aw, shucks, old man, you been talkin' 'bout that gold fish for nigh onta three months now 'n you ain't caught him yit! You know that ain't nothin' but a tale you done got up to keep me from raisin' sand over you idlin' off yo' time in that old boat!"

Old man Beauford wouldn't let on how truly she had stated the case. "Old woman, if it hadn' been for yo' blabber mouth tellin' everybody on Little River Lane 'bout my dream, I'd a done caught my fish by now! I done told you, th' Lawd's holdin' back my fish 'cause you don't believe, just like He held back th' baby from Abraham on account o' his wife! Now just as soon as you hush yo' fuss, you'll see what'll happen!"

Though he wouldn't say so, old man Beauford regretted having told the gold fish tale. It had grown into a monster that brought ridicule from his neighbors down on his head like rain, and he'd give his right arm to destroy it. He plopped into his rocking chair on the front porch and cudgeled his brain for a way to get rid of the monster. His eyes drifted to the fields beyond his house covered by cotton stalks heavy with bolls, and the thought occurred to him, *If only I had my cotton picked 'n my share o' th' money in my pockets, I could make pretend I'd caught that gold fish 'n flash a few dollars to prove it. Then I'd be shed o' th' monster.* But on second thought, *No, that wouldn' work, not around Louiza's blabber mouth. Th' only way I'll ever git rid o' that durn fish is to catch him.* And immediately he realized that the thought was a flash of genius. He jumped up. "By golly, that's what I'll do! I'll catch him!" and he hopped off the porch and ran to his barn.

For the rest of that day old man Beauford sat in his boat making a fishing net of grass sacks, pausing only for an occasional sip of moonshine. Late in the evening he set his creation in the river and went home. The next morning he pulled the net from the water, took out the largest fish and let the others go free. Then he went rowing up and down the river, but not once did he venture to the heavens for he had work to do on earth. He simply rowed and waited, humming a merry little tune of mischief that flowed from a wellspring in his soul.

Stiff Jackson stood on the river bank and laughed at him, but old man Beauford knew that Stiff had eleven head of children to feed, so he kept on rowing.

Little Jesse Burns stood on the river bank and laughed at him, but old man Beauford knew that Little Jesse was working his fingers to the bone trying to make enough money to go to undertaking school, so he kept on rowing.

Loudora Valley stood on the river bank and laughed at him, but old man Beauford knew that Loudora was a sporting woman who spent every cent she laid hands on for flashy clothes, so he kept on rowing.

Many others came and stood and laughed, but old man Beauford took their ridicule as silently as Joshua's host circling the city of Jericho, for he was absolutely certain that the last laugh would be his. He took a fresh fish from his net each morning and rowed up and down the river, patiently waiting. On the third day he spied two men walking along the river banks towards him and he was overjoyed for he knew that his hour was at hand.

"Hey there, old man Beauford! You caught your gold fish yet?" sang the slow, nasal drawl of Hillary Malencon, overseer of the plantation.

"Hehehehehehehe!" giggled his companion.

"Got him! Oh, by gosh, I got him! Help! Help! He's gettin' away!" Old man Beauford shouted with the full power of his lungs, wrestling with the dead fish and making the biggest commotion.

"Does that fish have the gold piece in his mouth, old man Beauford?" the overseer asked.

"Yeah! He got a fifty dollar gold piece, just like in my dream! I'm most to git it out! If I just had somebody to hold him still! If one o' you gentlemen got a mind to help me, half o' this here fifty dollar gold piece is yo's!"

As soon as the word was spoken there was one big splash into the water and there followed it one big cry of "Help!"

Aware of the overseer's great and burning love for the dollar, old man Beauford knew who it was had jumped. Still he wrestled with his fish. "Ain't that you standin' there, B'rer Trotter? Looks like you gonna have to help Mister Malencon, 'cause looks like he can't swim! I'd help him myself if I didn't have to hold on to this here fish what th' Lawd done give me!"

"I can't swim neither!" B'rer Trotter shouted back. "You'd better jump in there and save him, and pretty quick too, 'cause he's drowning fast as time can roll!"

Old man Beauford pitched the dead fish high enough so that B'rer Trotter would think he'd jumped into the river, then slipped off his shoes and jumped from his boat. He swam straight to the overseer, gave him a whopping good sock on the head to stop his threshing about, and drug him to the bank.

After the two men had knocked the water from the overseer's lungs and stood him on his feet, B'rer Trotter told him of the supreme sacrifice that had been made to save his life. "This here man done done more for you than any other man on Little River Lane done ever done for you, 'cause this here man done throwed away a fish

with a mouth full of gold to save you from drowning!
This here man is your true, sure-enough, honest-to-good-
ness *friend!"*

And immediately old man Beauford took advantage
of the lead. "Aw, shucks, B'rer Trotter, Mister Malencon worth more to this here plantation than all th' gold
in th' world! Why, this here man loves his colored folks,
he really does! Every nineteenth o' June he gives us a
whole goat to barbecue, 'n every Christmas he gives us
a white horse to th' commissary! Ain't no other overseer
no where in this here world as good as this one we got
right here! Why, B'rer Trotter, if I'd let him, Mister Malencon'd give me th' whole fifty dollars what I done
chunked away, but I ain't gonna let him give me no more
than ten dollars for my loss. That's how much I loves
my white folks!"

A forced smile hid the overseer's displeasure over this,
but he knew that he, a white man, dared not be miserly
to that smiling swindler who stood before him, forever
after to be known among the sharecroppers as the man
to whom he owed his life. The burden of the white man's
long, long heritage of chivalry fell a crushing weight
upon him and he said, "Sure I would! Sure I would!"
reaching in his back pocket for his purse. Ten dollars
was all he had in it and old man Beauford got that.

Old man Beauford caught his gold fish again one day
when the preacher stopped on the river bank to laugh
at him, and again when the schoolteacher, Dan Kemp,
stopped by, and each paid well for his rescue. Each man
swore that he'd seen a fish jumping around in old man
Beauford's boat, and Kemp added that he'd even caught
a glimpse of the gold piece in his mouth glittering in

the sunlight. Not a soul who heard their accounts ever let on he didn't believe them, for nobody wanted to imply that an old man as screwy as old man Beauford had outsmarted the three most important men on Little River Lane. And they left old man Beauford and his gold fish alone, for not one of them wanted to be the one to prove that he had.

Afterword

Were it not presumptuous of me, I would have dedicated this collection to Richard Wright, a man I knew only from a brief introduction and from seeing him walk along Paris streets. But the dedication would have been to a man I knew even less than that. It would have gone to a man who years earlier had written in *Black Boy:*

After I had outlived the shocks of childhood, after the habit of reflection had been born in me, I used to mull over the strange absence of real kindness in Negroes, how unstable was our tenderness, how lacking in genuine passion we were, how void of great hope, how timid our joy, how bare our traditions, how hollow our memories, how lacking we were in those intangible sentiments that bind man to man, and how shallow was even our despair. After I had learned other ways of life, I used to brood upon the irony of those who felt that Negroes led so passional an existence! I saw that what had been taken for our emotional strength was our negative confusions, our flights, our fears, our frenzy under pressure.

Whenever I thought of the essential bleakness of Black life in America, I knew that Negroes had never been allowed to catch the full spirit of Western civilization, that they lived somehow in it but not of it. And when I brooded upon the cultural barrenness of Black life, I wondered if clean, positive tenderness, love, honor, loyalty, and the capacity to remember were native with man. I asked myself if these human qualities were not fostered, won, struggled and suffered for, preserved in ritual form from one generation to another.

I would say that here are some stories I wish you could have read to remind you of some experiences which I'm sure you shared. I didn't start with a theme; I began with some stories I treasured and watched them fall into a pattern. The pattern they took was the simple life-cycle one—a journey through many facets of the Black experience as treated by Black writers ranging from childhood and adolescence through maturity, aging and death. In taking us on that trip, the writers carry us to urban and rural settings, to prisons and dinner parties, to poor families and comfortable ones, to small towns and big cities, to farms and factories, to violence and tenderness, to oppression and survival. My hope is to help end any young Black person's brooding upon "the cultural barrenness of black life" and any wondering "if clean, positive tenderness, love, honor, loyalty, and the capacity to remember were native with man."

Quandra Prettyman Stadler
JANUARY 1974